East Wind Rain

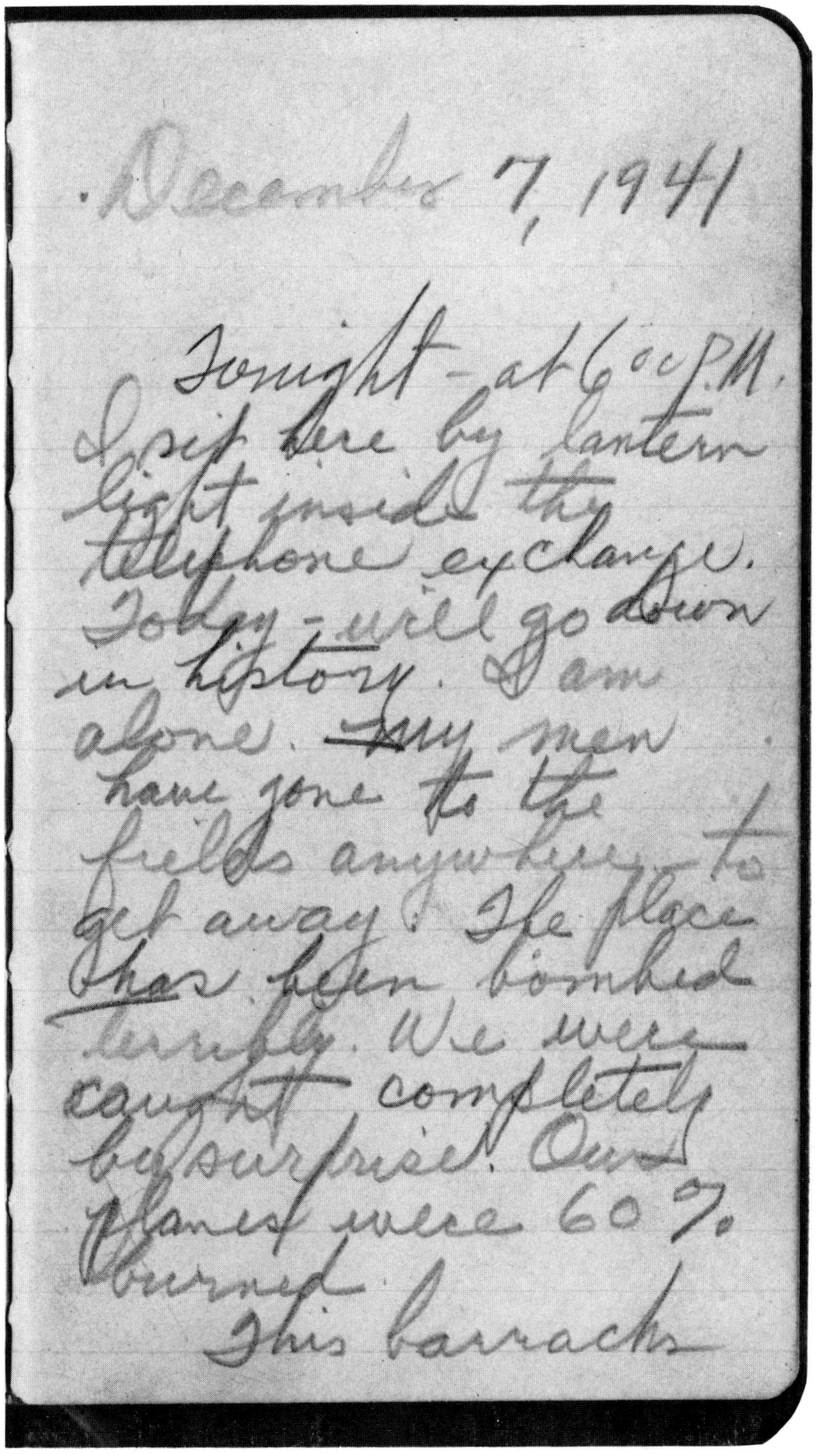
December 7, 1941

Tonight - at 6 oc P.M. I sit here by lantern light inside the telephone exchange. Today - will go down in history. I am alone. my men have gone to the fields anywhere to get away. The place has been bombed terribly. We were caught completely by surprise. Our planes were 60% burned.

This barracks

Battleship Row as depicted by a Japanese artist on a post card issued by the Imperial Japanese Navy Supply Office.

EAST WIND RAIN

A PICTORIAL HISTORY OF THE PEARL HARBOR ATTACK

By Stan Cohen

Pictorial Histories Publishing Company
Missoula, Montana

LIBRARY OF CONGRESS
CATALOG CARD NO. 81-83760

ISBN 0-933126-15-8

First Printing: October 1981
Twentieth Printing: October 1990

First Printing Revised: September 1991
Second Printing Revised: March 1992

Cover artwork by Mel Brown, Austin, Texas
Typography: Arrow Graphics, Missoula, Montana

The book title, "East Wind Rain," was the code phrase used by the Japanese government to notify its diplomatic corps worldwide that it had made the decision to go to war with the United States.

PICTORIAL HISTORIES PUBLISHING COMPANY
713 South Third Street West
Missoula, Montana 59801

Introduction

Individual events can change the course of history. During the moments, minutes or hours in which the outcome of such an event is still uncertain, the world's future can hang in the balance. Certainly American history was in limbo when the 'shot heard round the world' was fired at Lexington, when South Carolinians fired on Fort Sumter, when Presidents Lincoln and Kennedy were shot down and when Black Tuesday heralded the 1929 stock market crash.

The two-hour attack on Pearl Harbor, Hawaii, on Sunday morning, Dec. 7, 1941, ranks among those remarkable moments that changed not only American history but events in the rest of the world. One could say that from the time the Japanese planes left their carriers until the first bomb dropped at 7:55 a.m., the world was in limbo. It is easy to sit back 50 years later and second-guess the actions of those who took part in this momentous event, and to speculate about the "what ifs." What if the Japanese had made a third attack and knocked out the fleet's fuel tanks or shipyard facilities, forcing all U.S. ships back to California? What if intelligence from Washington had resulted in a full-scale military alert in Hawaii before the attack? What if the Japanese fleet had been spotted at sea before December 7, or if radar contacts of the incoming enemy planes had been interpreted and reported effectively?

The events leading up to the December 7 attack will probably always be clouded in controversy. Some historians have suggested that President Roosevelt knew about the attack in advance or virtually provoked an attack in the belief that such a shock would be the only way that the American people could be coaxed into the war against the Axis powers. There is some evidence which points to that hypothesis, but his motivations and intentions remain one of history's secrets. The Pearl Harbor attack is the subject of dozens of books, both pictorial and narrative. I have not tried to uncover anything new, but to present the most comprehensive collection of pictures of the historic event that has yet been done. Recently visiting the sites of military bases that were attacked, I snapped pictures from the vantage points of the photographers who took the spectacular December 7 photos included in this book. It was like stepping back in time, and it was not hard to imagine the sound of exploding bombs and machine gun fire, and to see the sky filled with oily smoke.

If you are old enough to remember Pearl Harbor or were actually there, return now to that Sunday morning and relive those stunning, world-shaking moments. If you are too young to remember, I hope that as this pictorial history unfolds before you, you can better understand what happened and how those few hours changed the course of history.

50th Anniversary Introduction

It has been 10 years since the introduction of this book. Thousands of copies have been sold throughout the world. It has been extremely gratifying to see that one of the most towering events in American history still captures the interest of people.

In the past 10 years, much new material about the attack has surfaced, along with many new photographs. Corrected revisions along with new material abound in this 10th anniversary edition, which is fittingly published on the 50th anniversary of the attack.

Much has happened in the 50 years since Dec. 7, 1941. Our enemies are now our friends, and even one of our friends (the USSR)—which became our enemy—is now friendly again. The world order has changed considerably. While America is undoubtedly the world's military power, Japan has risen to the forefront as an economic force. As a result, Japan has purchased much of Hawaii and owns a considerable stake in business throughout the United States proper.

How history has come full circle in the past five decades.

I hope this expanded and revised *East Wind Rain* will stand as the definitive photo history of the event. Also hopefully this edition will serve as a learning tool for younger generations and a nostalgic trip for the generations old enough to remember.

—Stan Cohen

Acknowledgments

The following people provided assistance in the preparation of the first edition of this book in 1981: R.H. Rothrock and Lt. Cmdr. Art Humphries, Pearl Harbor Naval Base Public Affairs Office; Gary Beito, Arizona Memorial Museum Association; Gary Cummins and staff, Arizona Memorial, National Park Service; Dorothy Fuller, Naval Base Library; Kaye Jordan, Wing Historian, Hickam AFB; Maj. Dan Arnold, Wheeler AFB; Sgt. Jack Lowney and Capt. Glenn Exum, PAO, Schofield Barracks; John Fairbank, PAO, Pearl Harbor Naval Shipyard; John Burlage, PAO, U.S. Pacific Fleet; Dennis Fujii and Staff Sgt. Laura Murphy, PAO, Hickam AFB; Will Kranz, PAO, U.S. Army, Ft. Shafter; Capt. Bill Wood, PAO, Kaneohe MCAS; Lt. Cmdr. Joe Herrell and Warrant Officer Robert Geihl, PAO, Barbers Point NAS; JOC Cindy Adams, PAO, Submarine Base, Pearl Harbor; Tom Fairfull, U.S. Army Museum Hawaii; and Werner Stoy, Camera Hawaii, Honolulu.

This revised edition could not have been completed without the able assistance of Ernest Arroyo and Robert Bracci, who reworked most of the captions, provided many new photos and gave editorial advice; David Aiken, who supplied much new material on the attack's aerial episodes; Paul Bender, who provided the aircraft profiles and original drawings; Ray Emory, a Pearl Harbor survivor, who furnished much new technical data; Mel Brown with his new cover artwork; and Al Makiel, who has supplied information and photos for many years; and to the following members of the Pearl Harbor History Associates: Robert Varrill, Jesse Pond Jr., Gene Camp, John DiVirgillio and William Cleveland.

The Hawaiian connection was essential to the completion of this new volume. In particular, Dan Martinez, chief historian at the Arizona Memorial; Bob Chenoweth, curator at the Memorial; and Burl Burlingame, reporter for the *Honolulu Star-Bulletin*.

In addition, I wish to thank Bob Cressman and Bob Sumrall for providing new photos; John Lambert, Harry Brown and Lee Embree for new aerial activity photos and information; Skip Rains for some new stories; Otto Lang; and Dr. Martin Davis. The staff of the Admiral Nimitz Museum; the Intrepid Sea-Air-Space Museum; and Patriots Point Naval and Maritime Museum provided photographs. Daniel Lenihan of the Submerged Cultural Resources Unit of the National Park Service provided photos and drawings of the sunken *Arizona* and *Utah*.

And finally, much thanks to the Pearl Harbor Survivors Association, and especially Ed Chappell, who have allowed me to attend their national conventions for the past 10 years and interview hundreds of survivors.

Charles Hood of the University of Montana Journalism School edited the original manuscript and Chris Harris proofread the revised copy. Bruce Donnelly produced the maps and Dick Guth and Leslie Over keyboarded the revisions. Arrow Graphics typeset the revised edition.

Photo Credits

Photographs for this book were obtained from many sources. The following abbreviations have been used with negative numbers, where possible:

NA–National Archives
USN–United States Navy Archives
USA–United States Army Archives
USMC–United States Marine Corps Archives
HA–Hawaii State Archives
AMC–Arizona Memorial Collection
EA–Ernest Arroyo Collection
AM–Al Makiel Collection
UH–University of Hawaii Archives

Photos not credited were taken by the author or are from his collection. Other sources are acknowledged.

Contents

This June 14, 1941, issue of *Collier's* Magazine had a long article on the defenses of Pearl Harbor. Six months later the Japanese would make a mockery of "Impregnable Pearl Harbor."

"On the day of Pearl Harbor, America's slowly rising interest in the troubles of Great Britain crystallized instantly into an understanding of dangers confronting America. On that day, Dec. 7, 1941, the words 'Pearl Harbor' took on a meaning of time, formerly they meant only a place. Now we say, 'before Pearl Harbor,' or 'after Pearl Harbor.' America thinks of 'Pearl Harbor' as the day of her great decisions." William R. Furlong

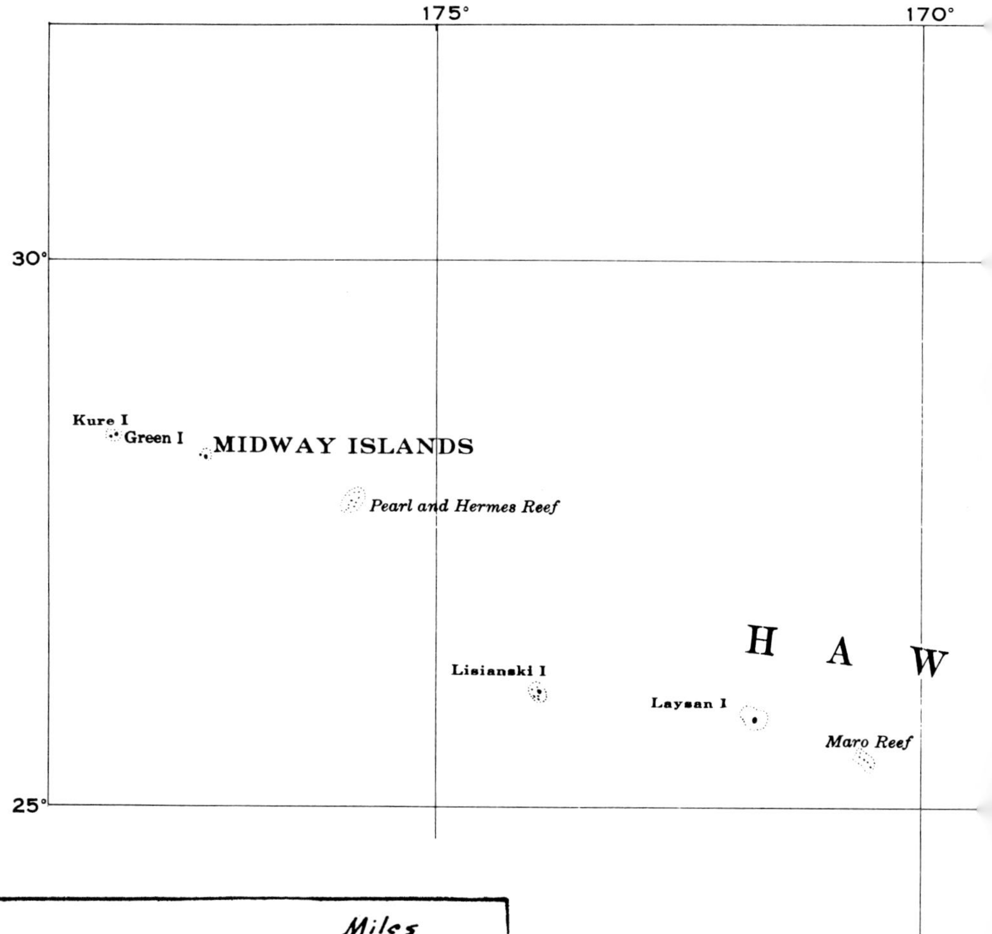

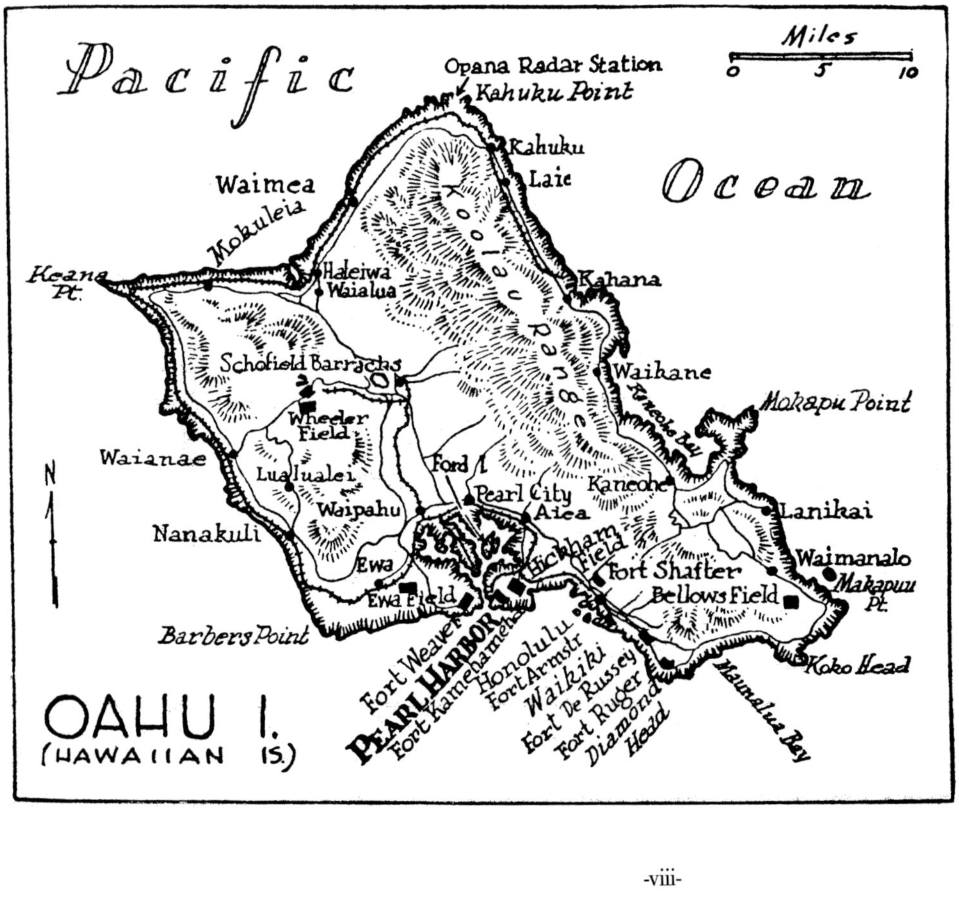

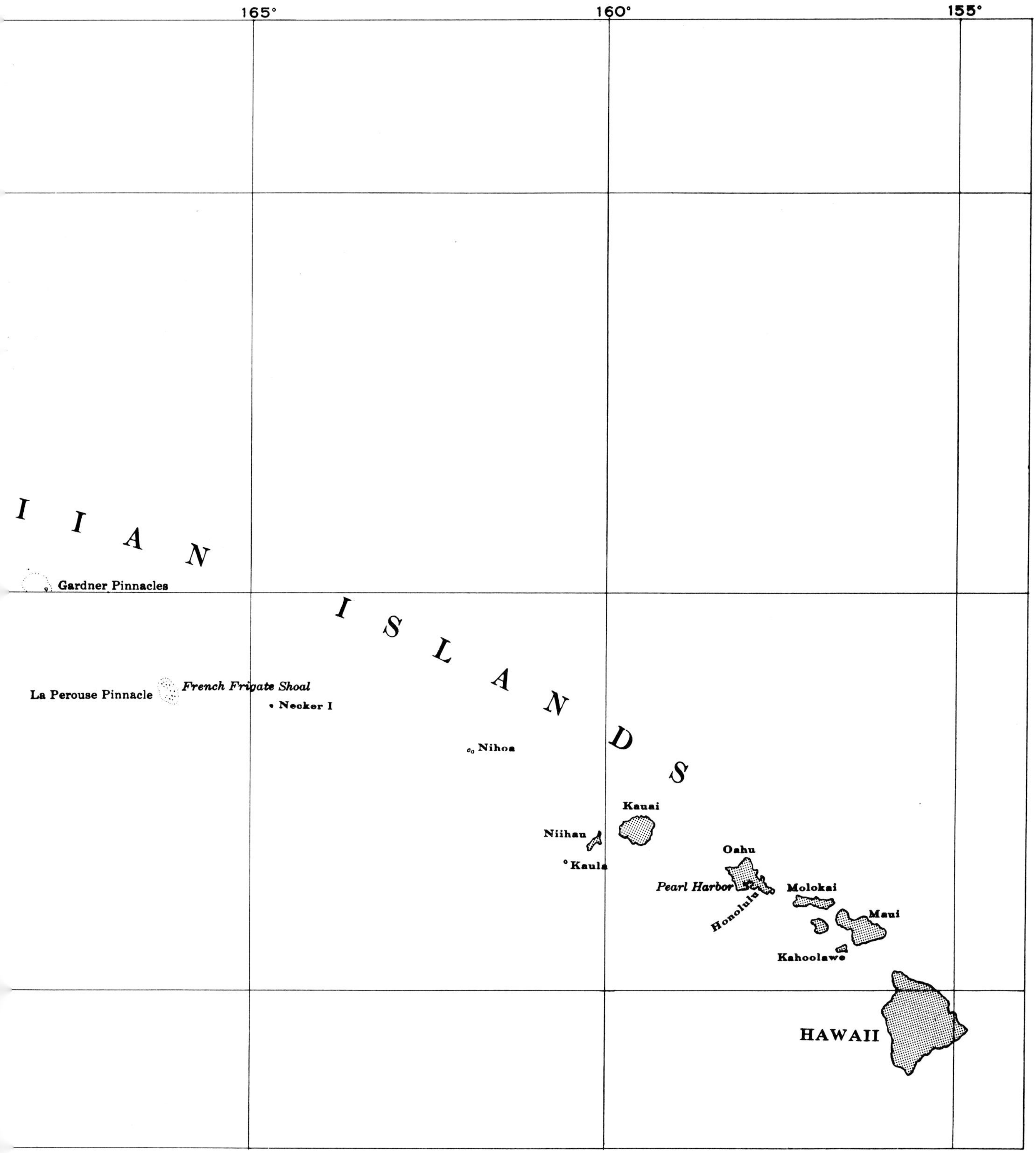
165°
160°
155°
I I A N
I S L A N D S
Gardner Pinnacles
La Perouse Pinnacle
French Frigate Shoal
Necker I
Nihoa
Kauai
Niihau
Kaula
Oahu
Pearl Harbor
Honolulu
Molokai
Maui
Kahoolawe
HAWAII

Remember Pearl Harbor

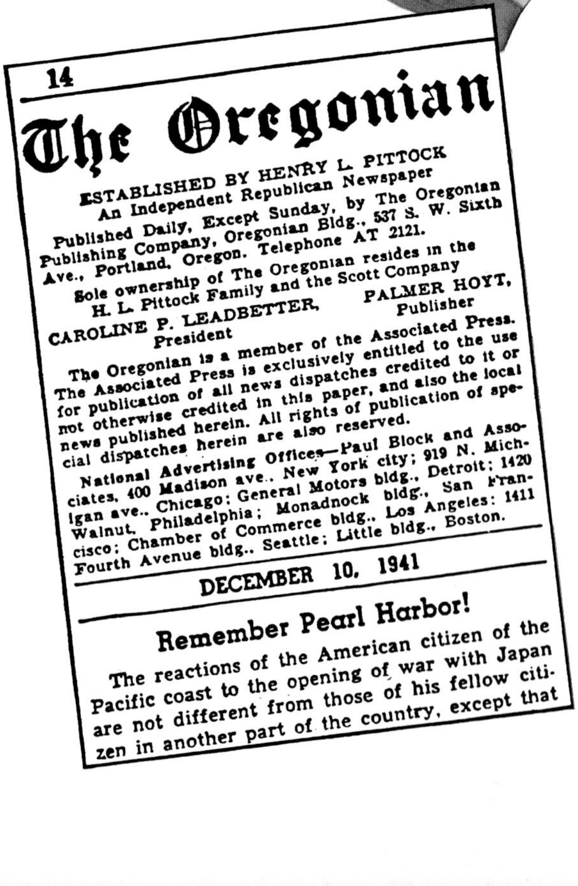

14

The Oregonian

ESTABLISHED BY HENRY L. PITTOCK
An Independent Republican Newspaper

Published Daily, Except Sunday, by The Oregonian Publishing Company, Oregonian Bldg., 537 S. W. Sixth Ave., Portland, Oregon. Telephone AT 2121.

Sole ownership of The Oregonian resides in the H. L. Pittock Family and the Scott Company

CAROLINE P. LEADBETTER, President
PALMER HOYT, Publisher

The Oregonian is a member of the Associated Press. The Associated Press is exclusively entitled to the use for publication of all news dispatches credited to it or not otherwise credited in this paper, and also the local news published herein. All rights of publication of special dispatches herein are also reserved.

National Advertising Offices—Paul Block and Associates, 400 Madison ave., New York city; 919 N. Michigan ave., Chicago; General Motors bldg., Detroit; 1420 Walnut, Philadelphia; Monadnock bldg., San Francisco; Chamber of Commerce bldg., Los Angeles; 1411 Fourth Avenue bldg., Seattle; Little bldg., Boston.

DECEMBER 10, 1941

Remember Pearl Harbor!

The reactions of the American citizen of the Pacific coast to the opening of war with Japan are not different from those of his fellow citizen in another part of the country, except that

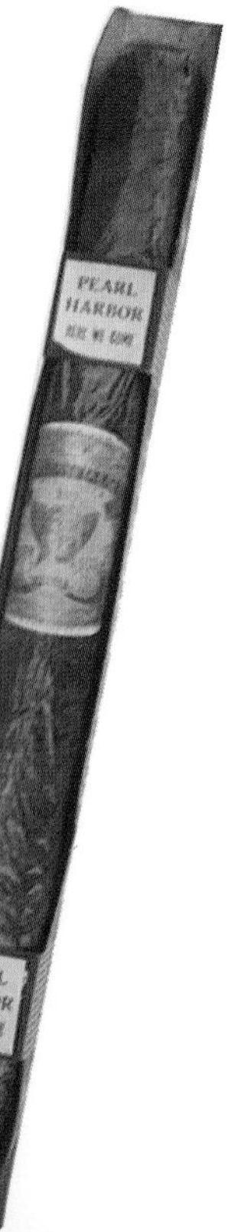

Background

Rising Sun Over the Pacific

The Pacific Fleet sometimes anchored at Lahaina Roads on the west coast of Maui. Just before the attack, the Japanese launched a float plane form the cruiser *Tone*, to make sure the *Anchorage* was empty, thus confirming their intelligence that the fleet was at Pearl Harbor. USN

Japan's aggressive tendencies had shown themselves much earlier, when without warning, she had attacked China in 1895 and the Russians in the Far East in 1904. The victories contributed to the notion among some Japanese that Nippon could – and should – expand her territory and influence to other parts of the Pacific.

With limited land and natural resources and an expanding population, Japan inevitably looked beyond her borders to find solutions to her problems. Under the aegis of the Greater East Asia Co-Prosperity Sphere, she expanded her interests in the Pacific, milking anti-colonialist sentiment by advocating "Asia for the Asians." She was also strengthening her army and navy. In 1931, Japan invaded Manchuria and set up a puppet government. Though she had signed the 1922 Washington Naval Treaty, which limited the size of the British, American and Japanese navies, she renounced the agreement in 1936 and built up her navy until it had reached parity with those of Britain and the U.S.

The United States had historically been committed to maintaining China's independence, and when Japanese troops in Manchuria invaded China proper in July 1937, the seemingly inevitable slide toward an armed conflict between America and Japan began.

In Europe, Germany and Italy were paralleling Japan's aggressiveness. The United States was increasingly torn between conflicting notions: the impulse toward her isolationist traditions, and, on the other hand, the desire to help friendly nations who were being gobbled up by aggressors.

On Nov. 25, 1936, Germany and Japan signed their Anti-Comintern Pact. Italy joined them in 1937. In September 1940, Japan signed a treaty of alliance with Germany and Italy, which assured each country mutual assistance in time of war and set up spheres of influence for each country.

The world finally went to war in September 1939. With the fall of France in 1940, Japan occupied part of French Indo-China and eyed the rich natural resources of Thailand, Malaya and the Dutch East Indies.

As Japan continued to press its militaristic policies, the relations between that country and the United States deteriorated rapidly. In April 1940, the U.S. fleet sailed for maneuvers in the Hawaiian area. A month later, President Roosevelt ordered that the fleet be stationed in Hawaii indefinitely as a deterrent to further Japanese expansion in Asia. In July 1940, Roosevelt invoked the Export Control Act, prohibiting the export of strategic minerals and equipment and the flow of oil, scrap iron and steel to Japan.

When the oil embargo was imposed, Japan had a reserve of more than six million tons, which with strict economy would last three to four years. Without oil, Japan would have to bow to the will of the Allied powers. This she would not do. She needed the oil of Southeast Asia.

By 1939, powerful Japanese officials were dedicated to a policy of war. In October 1941, the conservative members in the Japanese government, including Premier Konoye, were forced to resign. The hawkish army faction gained control, and established Gen. Hideki Tojo as the new premier.

Adm. Harold Stark, chief of naval operations at the time of the attack. USN NH 61815

The United States of the early 1940s also was gearing up for war. In August 1940, the National Guard was mustered into federal service. In September, 50 U.S.-built destroyers were transferred to Great Britain, and in the same month, the first peacetime conscription law was enacted. In March 1941, the Lend-Lease Act was signed into law, making the United States for all intents and purposes a belligerent without having decalred war. All Japanese, German and Italian assets in the United States were frozen in June and July. About the same time, Lend-Lease was extended to Russia in June after she was attacked by Germany. An August 1941 meeting between Roosevelt and Prime Minister Churchill of Great Britain produced the Atlantic Charter, which stated the aims of the two countries regarding a future world order.

On Sept. 3, 1941, the United States asked Japan to accept the following four principles as a basis for any further discussions: (1) respect for the territorial integrity and sovereignty of all nations; (2) noninterference in the internal affairs of other nations; (3) equality of opportunity in trade and economic matters; (4) status quo throughout the Pacific area. In October, the U.S. requested that Japan withdraw from China and Indo-China.

Of course, Japan had no intention of bowing to these American demands. Already planning the surprise attack on Pearl Harbor, she continued to take part in diplomatic negotiations with America.

Special ambassador Saburo Kurusu joined Kichisaburo Nomura, the Japanese ambassador in Washington, to take part in the increasingly strained negotiations with the U.S.

A Japanese inspection party at the 1933 Gymkana (horse and transportation show) at Schofield Barracks.
COURTESY LYMAN WOODMAN

Officers of the Navy's Hawaiian detachment with army officers at Hawaiian Department Headquarters in 1940. Front row from left are Rear Adm. J. H. Newton, Rear Adm. R. E. Ingersoll, Vice Adm. A. Andrews, Maj. Gen. Heron and Rear Adm. R. S. Holmes. Middle row: Lt. Comdr. Bell, Capt. T. S. Wilkinson and an unidentified army officer. Top row: unidentified Army and Navy officers, Lt. Flynn. USN

Cordell Hull, Secretary of State from 1933 to 1944, led the negotiations with the Japanese during the months leading up to the Pearl Harbor attack. NA

Joseph Grew, United States ambassador to Japan, 1932-1941. Interned in Japan after Pearl Harbor, he was exchanged in 1942 for Japanese diplomats. USN

They presented what would become Japan's final set of proposals on Nov. 20, 1941.

Secretary of State Cordell Hull countered on Nov. 26 with proposals that he knew would not be accepted. They called for Japan to withdraw from all the territories she had conquered by military on diplomatic means. While Hull's proposals were being studied in Tokyo, the Japanese fleet was steaming toward Hawaii.

Meanwhile, U.S. cryptographers, with the aid of a remarkable machine, had broken Japan's Purple Code, thus giving American officials access to secret Japanese diplomatic cables. Code-named "Magic," the information obtained from the decoded Japanese dispatches was enormously valuable to the American government. However, the date and place of the planned attack on the U.S. apparently were not transmitted to Washington.

The last days of November and the first week of December 1941 were critical to both sides. On November 30, Tojo rejected the final American proposals, and on December 2 the U.S. intercepted an encoded Japanese message directing all diplomatic and consular posts to destroy codes and ciphers and to burn confidential and secret material. The consulate in Honolulu was ordered to continue to send reports of ship movements at Pearl Harbor, a task it had been performing in secret for some time.

The "winds" messages, announcing its military intentions were broadcast to Japanese diplomats throughout the world. One of these—"East Wind Rain"—was the code phrase for war with the United States.

At 1 p.m. Washington time on December 7, the two Japanese ambassadors in the American capital were to present Secretary Hull a note stating that negotiations were broken off and that a state of war existed between the two nations.

To achieve technical compliance with international rules of war, the message was to be delivered about one half hour before Japanese planes struck Pearl Harbor, but owing to decoding difficulties at the Japanese embassy the note was not delivered until after hostilities had begun. Apparently the two ambassadors had not been informed of the surprise attack plans in advance.

During recent months the United States had been beefing up her military strength in Hawaii, but at the time of the attack American defenses were still far from adequate. In April and May 1941, one quarter of the Pacific Fleet was transferred to the Atlantic to help meet the threat to Lend-Lease shipping posed by German submarines. Between April and December of 1941, the U.S. gave thousands of patrol planes and anti-aircraft guns to allies, even though U.S. commanders in Hawaii were begging for them.

The Army was in charge of Oahu's defenses, but its air

Adm. Husband E. Kimmel, commander-in-chief of the U.S. Pacific Fleet from Feb. 1 to Dec. 17, 1941. He was censured by the Navy as an outgrowth of the Pearl Harbor attack and relieved of command. He applied for retirement and took no further part in the war. He died in 1968. USN

Lt. Gen. Walter C. Short, commanding general of the Army's Hawaiian Department at the time of the attack. Relieved of command on Dec. 17, 1941, he was never brought to trial to face allegations that he did not properly prepare for the possibility of a surprise attack.

force was woefully inadequate. Only six B-17 bombers were in flyable condition; 180 were considered necessary. Many Army fighters were obsolete. The Army had 82 three-inch anti-aircraft guns and needed 98; it had 20 37-millimeter guns and needed 135.

Lt. Gen. Walter Short, commander of the U.S. Army in Hawaii, had been advised of possible sabotage of his planes so he ordered them to be grouped together at Hickam and Wheeler. They would be much easier to guard than if they were scattered around the airfields.

Forty-five thousand men operated Oahu's coastal defense batteries, anti-aircraft guns, radar installations, air bases and other installations.

Five mobile stations employing newly invented radar equipment were in use by December 7, but they were inadequately staffed and the men were not yet fully trained. Gen. Walter Short, commander of the Hawaiian Department, had tried successfully to get permanent stations installed.

Navy aircraft patrolled the seas within a 600-mile radius of Oahu, but on the morning of the attack only three* PBY flying boats were on patrol, and none was north of the island where the Japanese fleet was launching aircraft. The Navy had only 49 patrol planes in flying condition and was further hampered by a shortage of crews and spare parts.

But if American forces were ill-equipped and undermanned, their main deficiency was that they just were not in a proper state of readiness to meet an attack with the resources they had. Partly because the Army and Navy were not under a unified command, coordination and cooperation were minimal. And—despite "war warnings" from Washington issued to the Pacific Fleet as early as November 27—there is evidence that U.S. officials did not give the Hawaii commanders all the available intelligence about a Japanese attack planned for sometime in December, possibly in Hawaii. For example, Joseph Grew, the American ambassador in Tokyo, had been advised by the Peruvian ambassador to Japan of a possible Japanese attack on Hawaii. Grew, however, apparently dismissed the information as another rumor; in any event, he thought he could keep hostilities from breaking out by keeping his ties with the moderates in the Japanese government.

He was, of course, dead wrong.

*There were a total of seven PBYs in the air pre-attack. Three were on patrol of inshore/restricted areas and four were on maneuvers with the U.S. submarine *Gudgeon* near Lanai Island.

The *West Virginia* rounding Hospital Point as she entered the Pearl Harbor naval base on 25 May 1935. The huge 760-foot radio towers, a prominent feature of the base for many years, were dismantled in 1937.
USN NH 77062

This peacetime panorama of Pearl Harbor on 30 Oct. 1941, looking east toward Honolulu, is just six weeks before the attack. Ford Island, East Loch Anchorage and Battleship Row are at left. The navy yard, sub base, supply depot and tank farms are to the left of the huge Hickam Field complex (right center) and the section base. Fort Kamehameha and the Pacific Ocean are extreme right. Note the two destroyers in the main channel passing through the anti-submarine nets that guarded the harbor entrance. NA 80-G-182873

The Submarine Base and fuel oil storage tanks on Oct. 13, 1941. These would have been among the prime targets had the Japanese launched a third strike. The ever-cautious Admiral Nagumo, however, felt that his forces had accomplished their main mission, the destruction of the U.S. Battle Fleet. Leaving all naval support facilities undamaged would prove, in time, to be a fatal mistake by the Japanese. USN

Looking from the end of Drydock One in 1933, several ships are moored alongside the site of the soon-to-be-constructed TenTen Dock. It was so named because its length would be 1,010 feet long. USN

The administration building at the Naval Base, Pearl Harbor. USN

Floating Drydock YFD #2 in place on Oct. 30, 1940. The *Shaw* was in drydock here on Dec. 7. It took 45 days to tow the drydock from New Orleans to Pearl Harbor, a voyage of over 5,000 miles. USN

In Oct. 1940, Adm. James Richardson, right, visited Washington to protest the continued basing of the U.S. Fleet at Pearl Harbor. With him, from left, are Adm. Harry E. Yarnell, Ret. Adm. H. R. Stark and Secretary of the Navy Frank Knox. USN

On Feb. 1, 1941, Adm. James O. Richardson turned over command of the Pacific Fleet to Adm. Husband E. Kimmel. The ceremony took place on the fleet flagship, the *Pennsylvania* at Pearl Harbor. HA

> *I was present at Luke Field during the winter of 1931–32 when the Army and Navy conducted joint maneuvers during which the planes from the two carriers then in Navy inventory made a sneak attack on Pearl Harbor. The umpires ruled that all facilities were put out of commission. Our planes were not at the field and they searched and were credited with sinking one carrier. Several years ago I read an article written by a Japanese naval officer who was a Naval attaché and observer of the maneuvers and later a staff officer of the commander of the Japanese carrier force that attacked Pearl. He stated that the idea and pattern of the attack was largely initiated from his observations during the maneuvers.*
>
> —MAJ. KENNETH HORNER, AUS RET.
> Phoenix, Oregon

Gov. Joseph B. Poindexter, Hawaii's territorial governor from 1934 to 1942. At 3:30 p.m. on Dec. 7, he declared martial law in Hawaii at the urging of the Army commander. HA

URGENT -:- WARNING -:- URGENT

"BLACKOUT ENEMY" Planes will Simulate Attack on Your Island, Thursday Night, May 23rd, 1940, sometime between 8:30 and 9:00 p.m. When warning bells are rung or sirens are sounded, IMMEDIATELY put out all lights, inside and outside. TURN OFF ALL SIGNS. Don't use flashlights, matches, etc.

BLACKOUT COMPLETELY.

While this raid is only make-believe, do your part in this rehearsal for an event we hope will never come.

"OUTBLACK THE LAST BLACKOUT"

燈火管制についての警告

来る五月二十三日(木曜日)の晩八時半より九時までの三十分間假裝敵國の飛行機が貴島を襲撃する、その時には警報としてサイレン又は鐘を鳴らす、同時にすべて内外の燈火を消す事、店のネオン・サイン、飾窓の燈火も消す事、フラッシ・ライト及マッチも使用せぬ事、完全に消燈すべし

この襲撃は元より假裝なるも市民は實際の時と同じ氣持にて共力せられん事を望む、去年の燈火管制より尚一層眞暗にする事

布哇縣燈火管制委員
ホノルル郡委員長 ベン・エフ・ラッシュ
布哇郡委員長 エチ・シ・ウオルタス
馬哇郡委員長 ロバート・イー・ヒュース
加哇郡委員長 ウイリアム・エリス

重要警告

本島定於五月二十三號(即禮拜四晚)。由八點半至九點鐘。舉行防空演習。施行燈火管制。屆時以鳴鐘或響笛爲號。無論內外燈火。及各種電招牌。皆須立刻熄滅。甚至電筒火柴等。均在受管制之列。務使完全黑暗。切切至要。(防空演習時間內。請各盡職責。惟望真正空襲。永不來臨)。

「黑暗比前次更黑暗」

檀山疆省燈火管制委員會啟

NAINGET -:- PAKAUNA -:- NAINGET

"PANAGSIPNGET KABUSOR" NGA AIROPLANOS KASDALA RAOTEN DAYTA ISLA NGA YANMO INTON RABII TI JUEVES, MAYO 23, MANIPOD ORAS TI LAS 8:30 INGANAT LAS 9:00 P.M. INTON MANGNGEGYO DAGITI CAMPANAS NGA AGAWENG KEN PANAGTIMEK DAGITI SILBATOS, IDDEPENYO A DAGOS DAGITI SILAWYO ITI UNEG KEN RWAR. IDDEPENYO AMIN DAGITI MARKA NGA NASILAWAN. SAANKAY NGA AGGAMIT ITI LENTE, GURABIS, KEN DADDUMA PAY NGA UMAPOY. PAGBALINENYO NGA NASIPNGET.

(No man pay daytoy nga iraraot saan nga napaypayso, aramidenyo ti rebbengenyo iti daytoy a panagpadas tapno masagsaganakayo iti aniaman a dumteng, sapay koma to saan met la a mapasamak.)

"NASIPSIPNGET PAY KOMA NGEM ITI DAYDI NAUDI A PANAGSIPNGET"

TERRITORIAL BLACKOUT COMMITTEES:

Ben F. Rush, General Chairman, Honolulu County; H. C. Walters, General Chairman, Hawaii County; Robt. E. Hughes, General Chairman, Maui County; William Ellis, General Chairman, Kauai County.

A flyer announcing a blackout drill in Hawaii. Although the military was caught by surprise on Dec. 7, defense preparations had been going on for more than a year. MILITARY SHOP OF HAWAII

Japanese Plans

The Watchword Was Secrecy

Emperor Hirohito, the supreme ruler of Japan, reviews troops in 1940. The new modern Japan had very close ties with its past. The Emperor was still revered as a god. USN

The Pearl Harbor attack was not an isolated incident, but part of an overall plan for the conquest of Southeast Asia and the promotion of what the Japanese called the Greater East Asia Co-Prosperity Sphere.

To have a free hand in establishing their control over the Dutch East Indies, Malaya, Thailand, the Philippines, Singapore, Hong Kong and the islands of the southern and western Pacific, the Japanese would have to neutralize the United States Pacific Fleet.

As early as 1940, Adm. Isoroku Yamamoto had given some thought to an attack on Pearl Harbor and had requested that Rear Adm. Takajiro Onishi, a naval aviator, investigate the possibilities.

Yamamoto knew America, having served a tour of duty in Washington, and was highly regarded by American officers. He had been vice-minister of the Japanese Navy before being named commander-in-chief of the Combined Fleet in 1941. A firm believer in the value of naval aircraft in modern warfare, he became convinced that a surprise aerial attack on Pearl Harbor was the best way to keep the American fleet from interfering with Japanese plans in Southeast Asia.

Adm. Isoroku Yamamoto, from an official portrait in 1943. He was the architect of the Pearl Harbor attack and commander-in-chief of the Japanese Combined Fleet. He was shot down and killed in the Solomons in April 1943 by American planes. USN

The Japanese had been impressed with the success of the 24-plane British raid in which three Italian battleships were sunk at Taranto, with the loss of only two aircraft, in 1940. Such a raid by a large carrier strike force on a bottled-up U.S. fleet at Pearl Harbor seemed to promise similar results.

Some Japanese military planners wanted to concentrate all their naval strength to Southeast Asia instead of taking a chance at Hawaii, but Yamamoto's plan won out.

Onishi consulted Minoru Genda, an experienced carrier pilot and a brilliant aerial warfare tactician, who—after studying a working plan—concluded that a successful attack would be difficult but not impossible.

Yamamoto code-named the plan Operation "Z," after Admiral Togo's famous "Z" signal made on the eve of the Battle of Tsushima during the Russo-Japanese War. He selected Vice-Adm. Chuichi Nagumo to command the strike force.

Because Pearl Harbor was so shallow (45 feet), the Japanese had to devise torpedoes that would not nose into the bottom upon release from aircraft. Pilots and ordnance experts spent months on the problem. Finally, Cmdr. Mitsuo Fuchida, who was to lead the air attack, came up with an idea to place wooden fins on the torpedoes to guide them in shallow water.

Once the plan had been tentatively approved and worked out successfully on the war-game board, the best carrier pilots of the Navy were brought together for training. They were not told what the target was.

Absolute secrecy was required, for political as well as military reasons. Conceivably, the differences between the two countries might be settled only hours before the scheduled attack, thereby canceling it. If, on the other hand, there was to be war, the Japanese wanted their first blow to be a devastating surprise.

The operation was approved by Tokyo in September, and the following month the merchant ship *Taiyo Maru* sailed across the Pacific on the anticipated strike force route to make navigational observations and gather intelligence. It was happy to report that it sighted no other shipping during its mission.

For quite a while before the attack, the Japanese consulate in Honolulu had been supplying Tokyo with up-to-date intelligence about the military on Oahu.

As the fleet was secretly assembling in the remote Tankan Bay of the Kurile Islands, the Japanese made a point of showing that business between the U.S. and Japan was proceeding as usual. As late as December 2, when the attack force was well on its way, a merchant ship, the *Tatsuta Maru*, was dispatched for San Francisco as evidence of the continuing friendly relations between the two countries. But she had secret orders to turn around and sail back to Japan on the night of December 7.

A powerful task force was assembled to ensure that the attack was successful. Six carriers—*Akagi, Kaga, Soryu, Zuikaku, Hiryu* and *Shokaku*—carried 441 war planes. The screening unit comprised a light cruiser and nine destroyers. Two battleships and two heavy cruisers constituted the support force, and three I-class submarines the patrol unit. Eight tankers accompanied the force to the point of refueling. An additional 27 submarines, plus five midget submarines of the Special Submarine Attack Unit, carried orders to support the main body and to inflict damage on American warships. The task force was the mightiest fleet ever assembled in the Pacific.

A northerly course was selected, away from the normal shipping lanes. The force planned to sail within 200 miles of Oahu's northern coast and launch its planes on December 7. To hit the American fleet early on Sunday morning—a time thought to be the best for a surprise attack—the fleet would have to be at its launching point before first light.

It was a gamble, sailing so close to American fighter and bomber bases, which would surely have aircraft patrolling the seas. But the risk was considered necessary, given the

Vice-Adm. Chuichi Nagumo, commander-in-chief of the Japanese First Carrier Strike Force, which carried out the Pearl Harbor attack. Instead of sending in the third attack wave, he decided to retire to Japan. He committed suicide on Saipan in July 1944. USN

The Japanese exchange ship *Tatsuta Maru*, flagship of the NYK line, was used as a deceptive maneuver. It left Japan on Dec. 2, supposedly bound for San Francisco with American evacuees form the Orient. They were to be exchanged for Japanese nationals in the United States. The captain, however, had orders to return to Japan Dec. 7, and to observe radio silence en route. NA

short range and limited fuel capacity of the carrier planes.

On November 26 the strike force began its long journey from Etorofu Island. Tankers refueled destroyers every day until the last pre-attack fueling on December 6, then went to a rendezvous point to again refuel every day from December 8. Other ships had carried drums of fuel to feed their hungry boilers for the long round trip. No longer slowed down by the fuel-heavy tankers, the fleet picked up another 5 knots speed to make the launching point on time.

On December 2 at 5:30 p.m., Admiral Nagumo had received the signal "Climb Mount Niitaka," which meant that all the diplomatic efforts had failed and he was to proceed with the attack.

On December 7—it was already December 8 in Japan—float planes launched from the cruisers at 5:30 a.m. flew over Pearl Harbor and Lahaina roads to make sure the fleet was indeed at Pearl.

At 6:15 a.m. the first carrier aircraft were launched on their flight into history.

Japanese Monograph #97

If the destruction of enemy land-based air strength progresses favorably, repeated attacks will be made immediately and thus decisive results will be achieved.

In the event a powerful enemy surface fleet appears, it will be attacked.

2. *Organization of the Air Attack Units.*
   (See Chart 2)
3. *Targets*
   a. *The First Wave Units*
      The targets for the hi-level and torpedo Kates will be battleships and aircraft carriers; the order of targets will be battleships and then aircraft carriers.
      The dive bombers will attack the enemy land-based air strength according to the following assignments:
      The Shokaku Vals: Hangars and aircraft on Ford Island.
      The 16 Zuikaku Vals: Hangars and aircraft on Wheeler Field.
      The targets of Fighter Units will be enemy aircraft in the air and on the ground.
   b. *The Second Wave Units*
      The hi-level Kates will attack the enemy air bases according to the following assignments:
      The Shokaku Kates: Aircraft and hangars on Kaneohe and Ford Island.
      The Zuikaku Kates: Hangars and aircraft on Hickam Field.
      The targets for the dive bombers will be limited to enemy aircraft carriers. If the number of targets is insufficient, they will select targets in the order of cruisers and battleship.
      The Fighter Units will attack the enemy aircraft in the air and on the ground.
4. *Attack Procedure*
   a. *The First Wave Units*
      (1) With the element of surprise as the principle, attacks will be carried out by the torpedo unit and bomber units and then the dive bombers.
      (2) During the initial phase of the attack, the Fighter Units, in one formation, storm the enemy skies about the same time as the Kate units, and contact and destroy chiefly the enemy interceptor planes.
      In the event that no enemy aircraft are encountered in the air, the units will immediately shift to the strafing of parked aircraft as follows:
      Akagi and Kaga Fighter Units: Hickam Field and Barbers Point (Ewa).
      Soryu and Hiryu Fighter Units: Wheeler Field and Barbers Point (Ewa).
      Shokaku and Zuikaku Fighter Units: Kaneohe

Total Participants

BY DAVID AIKEN

FIRST WAVE

High-level Kates: 49 participants (fifty assigned, one mechanical abort):
Akagi: 15–Three Buntai of five aircraft each. Cmdr. Mitsuo Fuchida
Kaga: 14–Three Buntai of five aircraft each, one mechanical abort. Lt. Cmdr. Takashi Hashiguchi
Soryu: 10–Two Buntai of five aircraft each. Lt. Heijiro Abe
Hiryu: 10–Two Buntai of five aircraft each. Lt. Cmdr. Tadashi Kusumi

Torpedo carrying Kates: 40 participants (no aborts):
Akagi: 12–Two Buntai of 6 each. Lt. Cmdr. Shigeharu Murata
Kaga: 12–Two Buntai of 6 each. Lt. Kazuyoshi Kitajima
Soryu: eight–Two Buntai of four each. Lt. Tsuyoshi Nagai
Hiryu: eight–Two Buntai of four each. Lt. Hirata Matsumura

Dive bomber Vals: 51 participants (54 assigned, three mechanical aborts):
Shokaku: 26–Three Buntai of nine each, one mechanical abort. Lt. Cmdr. Kakuichi Takahashi
Zuikaku: 25–Three Buntai (27 aircraft), two mechanical aborts. Lt. Akira Sakamoto

Fighters Zero/Zeke: 43 participants (45 assigned, two mechanical aborts, 12 retained for combat air patrol):
Akagi: nine–One Buntai of nine. Lt. Cmdr. Shigeru Itaya
Kaga: nine–One Buntai of nine. Lt. Yoshio Shiga
Soryu: eight–One Buntai of nine, one mechanical abort. Lt. Masajio Suganami
Hiryu: six–Two Shotai of three each, three retained for combat air patrol. Lt. Kiyokuma Okajima
Shokaku: five–Two Shotai of three each, one mechanical abort, three retained for combat air patrol. Lt. Tadashi Kaneko
Zuikaku: six–Three Shotai of two each, three retained for combat air patrol. Lt. Masao Sato

SECOND WAVE

High-level Kates: 54 participants (no aborts).
Shokaku: 27–Three Buntai of nine each. Lt. Tatsuo Ichihara
Zuikaku: 27–Three Buntai of nine each. Lt. Cmdr. Shigekazu Shimazaki

Dive bomber/Vals: 78 participants (81 assigned, one mechanical abort and two aborts after launch):
Agaki: 18–Two Buntai of nine each. Lt. Takehiko Laihaya
Kaga: 26–Three Buntai of nine each, one mechanical abort. Lt. Saburo Makino
Soryu: 17–Two Buntai of nine each, one abort after launch. Lt. Cmdr. Takashige Egusa
Hiryu: 17–Two Buntai of nine each, one abort after launch. Lt. Shun Nakagawa

Fighters Zero/Zeke: 35 participants (36 assigned, one abort after launch).
Akagi: nine–One Buntai of nine. Lt. Saburo Shindo
Kaga: nine–One Buntai of nine. Lt. Yasushi Nikaido
Soryu: nine–One Buntai of nine. Lt. Fusata Iida
Hiryu: eight–One Buntai of nine, one abort after launch. Lt. Sumio Nono

Totals

Japanese Aircraft:
441 Aircraft aboard carriers (three spare aircraft per type).
389 Carrier aircraft used in operations.
360 assigned to attack.
Seven known mechanical aborts.
353 deck spotted.
Three aborts on launch (second wave).
350 in attack.
Plus two cruiser seaplanes (advance reconn).
352 above Oahu.
Plus four cruiser and battleship seaplanes (reconn between Niihau and task force).
39 Combat air patrol.
395 above Hawaiian waters.

Aircraft on the carriers:	Kate	Val	Zero	Total
Akagi	27+3*	18+3	18+3	73
Kaga	27+3	27+3	18+3	81
Soryu	18+3	18+3	18+3	63
Hiryu	18+3	18+3	18+3	63
Shokaku	27+3	27+3	18+3	81
Zuikaku	27+3	27+3	18+3	81
TOTAL	144+18	135+18	108+18	
	162	153	126	441

*Three spare aircraft per type

Utilized:

include CAP	Kate	Val	Zero	+CAP
Akagi	15+12=27	18	9+9=18	+3:21
Kaga	14+12=26	26	9+9=18	+3:21
Soryu	10+8 =18	17	8+9=17	+3:21
Hiryu	10+8 =18	17	6+8=14	+6:21
Shokaku	27 27	26	5 5	+12:18
Zuikaku	27 27	25	6 6	+12:18
	143	129	43+35=78	+39

TOTAL 350 attack vets
39 CAP
389 utilized

NOTES: The three spare Zeros on each carrier were available for CAP and evidently thus assigned by *Akagi, Kaga, Soryu, and Hiryu.*

The problem of the 5th CV Division is that the total aircraft aboard indicated that there should be 15 each available rather than 12. Surviving *Shokaku* records speak only of 12 assigned on CAP.

In "Japanese Naval Aces and Fighter Units in Word War II" (USNI Press 1989), page 49, Dr. Hata and Dr. Izawa speak of a "cumulative total of 29" *Zuikaku* Zeros until 1330 hours in the afternoon when the returned Zeros got into the air.

Japanese Ships Assigned to "Hawaii Operation"

Type	Name	Date and Place Sunk by U.S. Navy
CARRIERS	*Akagi*	June 5, 1942, Battle of Midway
	Kaga	June 4, 1942, Battle of Midway
	Soryu	June 4, 1942, Battle of Midway
	Hiryu	June 5, 1942, Battle of Midway
	Shokaku	June 19, 1944, Philippine Sea
	Zuikaku	Oct. 25, 1944, Leyte Gulf
BATTLESHIPS	*Hiei*	Nov. 13, 1942, Guadalcanal
	Kirishima	Nov. 15, 1942, Guadalcanal
CRUISERS	*Tone*	July 28, 1945, Kure
	Chikuma	Oct. 25, 1944, Leyte Gulf
	Katori	Feb. 17, 1944, Truk
	Abukuma	Oct. 26, 1944, Surigao Straight
DESTROYERS	*Isokaze*	Apr. 7, 1945, East China Sea
	Tanikaze	June 9, 1944, Tawi Tawi
	Hamakaze	Apr. 7, 1945, East China Sea
	Kasumi	Apr. 7, 1945, East China Sea
	Arare	July 5, 1942, Aleutian Islands
	Kagero	May 8, 1943, Solomon Islands
	Shiranuhi	Oct. 27, 1944, Luzon Area P.I.
	Akigumo	Apr. 11, 1944, Celebes Sea
	Urakaze	Nov. 21, 1944, Formosa
	Akebono	Nov. 13, 1944, Palau area
	Ushio	Surrendered at Yokosuka
	Sazanami	Jan. 14, 1944, Yap
TANKERS	*Kyokuto Maru*	Survived to surrender
	Kenyo Maru	Jan. 14, 1944, Palau area
	Kokuyo Maru	July 30, 1944, Sulu Sea
	ShinkokuMaru	Feb. 17, 1944, Caroline Islands
	Akebono Maru	Mar. 30, 1944, Palau Area
	Toho Maru	June 15, 1945, Gulf of Siam
	Nihon Maru	Jan. 14, 1944, Bismarks
	Toei Maru	Jan. 18, 1943, Rabaul area
SUBMARINES	*I-1*	Jan. 29, 1943, Guadalcanal
	I-2	Apr. 7, 1944, New Ireland
	I-3	Dec. 9, 1942, Guadalcanal
	L-4	Dec. 20, 1942, New Britain
	I-5	July 19, 1944, Guam
	I-6	July 14, 1944, Marianas I.
	L-7	July 5, 1943, Aleutian I.
	I-8	Mar. 31, 1945, Okinawa
	I-9	June 11, 1943, Aleutian I.
	I-10	July 4, 1944, Saipan
	I-15	Nov. 2, 1942, Solomon I.
	I-16	May 19, 1944, Solomon I.
	I-17	Aug. 19, 1943, Noumea
	I-18	Feb. 11, 1943, Solomon I.
	I-19	Oct. 18, 1943, Gilbert I.
	I-20	Oct. 1, 1943, New Hebridies
	I-21	Nov. 29, 1943, Tarawa
	I-22	Oct. 1942, Solomons
	I-23	Feb. 26, 1942–operational loss
	I-24	June 11, 1943, Aleutians
	I-68	July 27, 1943, Bismarks
	I-69	April 4, 1944, Truk
	I-70	Dec. 10, 1941, N.E. Oahu
	I-71	Feb. 1, 1944, Solomons
	I-72	Nov. 11, 1942, Guadalcanal
	I-73	Jan. 27, 1942, Midway
	I-74	April 3, 1944, Truk
	I-75	Feb. 5, 1944, Marshals

United States involvement in World War II was only hours away when Homer L. Kisner (right), Rochefort's radio intelligence traffic chief, warned that Japan's navy was nearly on a "war time basis." Kisner prepared his last peacetime chronology from radio intercepts gathered by his trained force of 64 radio operators. At 0755 the morning of Dec. 7, the Japanese naval task force which had been under radio surveillance by Rochefort for nearly a month, struck Pearl Harbor.
COURTESY ROBERT STINNETT

Station H
6 Dec. 1941.

CHRONOLOGY, Cont'd.

Fourth Fleet : It has been definitely established by traffic study that CinC 4th Fleet is in the Truk area. Several times traffic routing indicated that part of the Staff of CinC 4th Fleet was at Jaluit. It is possible that this command has been split-up for better administration of all operations in the South Seas. The Kamoi (with Commanding Officer, Chitose Air Corps aboard) is in the Jaluit area.

Traffic continues to be exchanged between several 4th Fleet units and Commands in the Indo-China area.

Fifth Fleet : Ominato has been heard working the flagship and at least one other unit of the 5th Fleet for the last few days. This fleet has been based at Chichijima for some time. It is probable that part of this force has remained at Chichijima; it is known that KE06 (Airron attached to 5th Fleet) is there.

General : At 0430, Tokyo was heard using 32Kcs, dual with 12330 Kcs, for UTU broadcast of traffic. This broadcast was discontinued at 1800, but 7285 Kcs (M) was immediately brought up and used until 1900, when it was secured. This broadcast was used in addition to Tokyo's regular UTU. Tokyo also broadcasted traffic on 6665 Kcs (A) during the evening.

Saipan, Takao and Ominato were also heard broadcasting traffic to units in their vicinities. The use of this method of delivering messages tends to keep unknown the positions of vessels afloat, and is probably one of the first steps toward placing the operations of the Navy on a war-time basis.

SECRET

A SPY FINDS EASY PICKINGS

In July 1941, while serving as a lieutenant commander with the staff of the Third Imperial Fleet, then blockading mainland China, I received orders assigning me to the personnel section of the ministry of the navy. This was bad news; it meant a desk job.

Two months later, in September, the office of naval operations issued me my real orders: I was to travel to Hawaii and report on Pearl Harbor. Our navy already had extensive knowledge of the American installations there, but the information at its disposal had been gathered by civilians unversed in naval matters. My task was to supplement this information with technical details. Without specifically saying so, my orders made me a spy.

The boat on which I was to travel, the **Taiyo Maru,** *was sailing from Yokohama to repatriate Japanese citizens from Hawaii. There were several hundred American families on board, going home because of the precarious political situation.*

Officially I had become the new purser of the **Taiyo Maru** *and I soon found that I was not the only secret agent on board: Commander Maejima, a specialist in submarine warfare, was traveling as ship's doctor. Besides the top executives of the shipping company, only the captain and two or three of his aides had been told of our real assignment. Maejima spent most of his time reading medical books; he was worried lest some passenger in need of medical help should call on him. I had no such problem since my job as a purser required no special knowledge.*

We weighed anchor on Oct. 20. The course we took was most unusual, for we had been ordered to sail straight north and turn eastward in the vicinity of Etorofu island, one of the Kuriles. (Today we know that the **Taiyo Maru** *was charting the route for the Japanese task force which was to attack Pearl Harbor. During the voyage the ship's doctor and purser were busy studying the winds and the atmospheric pressure, recording the pitch and the roll of the ship, and trying to find suitable areas in which to refuel a task force, a complex operation in those days).*

At 165 degrees longitude west, the **Taiyo Maru** *veered southward, maintaining a speed of 14 knots. Soon the seas became calmer. From then on I concentrated on a new phase of my work--trying to locate the likeliest spots for dispatching carrier-based planes. On the entire journey from Japan to Hawaii we did not encounter a single vessel--which constituted the most important information I obtained during the voyage, for we had expected to meet a number of American and Soviet transports.*

The **Taiyo Maru** *was directed by the Honolulu harbor command to tie up at the pier nearest Pearl Harbor. I hurried to the bridge, and there was Pearl Harbor right before my eyes. I could see everything. Luckily, the* **Taiyo Maru** *was commissioned at the time when superstructures were built high above the water line; from my vantage point on the bridge I could spot every ship entering and leaving or landing at Rogers and Hickam fields. I didn't even need binoculars. 'I turned to "Doc" Maejima: "It's too good to be true. There must be a catch. Watch out."*

Later that day we received indications that caution was indeed warranted: Members of the crew on shore leave reported they had been shadowed by policemen in uniform and followed by plain-clothesmen on motorcycles. Maejima and I agreed that it would be too risky for us to leave the ship and attempt to gather information in Honolulu and Pearl Harbor.

On board we took extreme precautions. We posted an officer on deck and put a direct telephone line from his observation point to the captain's cabin. As soon as any suspicious person approached the ship, the officer on duty would alert us. Maejima and I discussed our observations and exchanged information only in the captain's cabin. An alert from the sentinel on deck immediately stopped all conversation. We also carefully tested our telephone lines and made sure they were not tapped.

When these precautions had been taken we invited Consul General Kita to visit us on board. We explained our assignment to him and asked for his cooperation; he at once agreed. There was no difficulty about maintaining communications between the ship and the consulate; since the **Taiyo Maru** *was a reparation vessel for Japanese nationals in Hawaii, it was natural for the consul general's staff to come on board every day. And each day one staff member would act as a special courier through whom the consul general supplied us with information. We received this information in the captain's cabin and attempted to check every item that concerned the Pearl Harbor installations by going up to the bridge and looking things over with our own eyes.*

On the second morning the local newspapers gave us a rude shock. According to a front page story, a Japanese submarine had been observed operating in Pearl Harbor waters. There were other unconfirmed reports claiming that Japanese naval officers in various disguises had been seen loitering in some areas on the West Coast of the United States.

Even greater caution seemed to be called for; in the circumstances United States security officers might raid the ship at any moment. We therefore decided not to keep written records, relying exclusively on memory for both our own observations and the written reports transmitted by consular officials. We committed every line of these reports to memory before destroying this evidence of our activities . . .

On Nov. 3, just 24 hours after the alleged sighting of the Japanese submarine had appeared in the local press, it was denied by the United States Navy. Maejima and I sighed with relief . . .

Looking back, I think that in those days, the United States was easy prey for us. For example, on Nov. 3, I received an aerial photograph of Pearl Harbor that had been taken from a tourist plane stationed at John Rogers field. The picture was said to have been taken on Oct. 21, 1941, 10 days before our arrival. All this made me uneasy. Why did we receive such valuable information? I felt as if we might be walking into a gigantic trap.

From my vantage point on the bridge, I studied Pearl Harbor. I saw eight battleships, three carriers, eleven cruisers, and miscellaneous auxiliary craft, anchored at the harbor or moored to the piers. I had checked our own information, according to which 500 United States planes were based on Oahu and 114 flying boats at Kaneohe; from visual observation I was able to verify that 150 bombers were stationed at Hickam, 200 fighters at Wheeler, and 30 trainers at Bellows. Lastly, I studied the hangars and other installations. During my walks on deck I was also memorizing the schedule and the routines of the American air patrols. The hard work involved in checking, counter-checking, and double-checking every bit of information and every figure received from agents in our espionage network paid off: The data I finally pieced together turned out to be extremely accurate.

We had been scheduled to sail from Honolulu on Saturday afternoon, Nov. 4, but I wanted to see the harbor on a Sunday morning. The captain agreed to delay our departure and slowed down loading operations to justify the delay. This aroused no suspicion among the Americans. After all, it was only a delay in the sailing of a merchantman.

On Sunday I was up early. The master plan for the Pearl Harbor attack called for action on a Sunday, on the assumption that the holiday routine would relax the vigilance of the American forces. My job was to verify this assumption. And on that Sunday morning Pearl Harbor was indeed relaxed. The decks of the ships at anchor were deserted and the only movement I could detect was the fluttering of the flags. Our hunch had proved correct.

We sailed that evening, but even at sea I took no chances. Only the most important information had been put on paper. This paper was rolled into strings which lay near the ash tray in my cabin so that I could burn them at a moment's notice. My action was based on a recent incident off Tokyo Bay when a Japanese merchant vessel had been boarded by British sailors searching for German nationals. It could happen to us.

On the homeward voyage the **Taiyo Maru** *continued its charting job. Our route took us slightly south of the course we had taken on our way to Hawaii, and this was the route that was used by the Nagumo task force after the attack on Pearl Harbor.*

After an uneventful trip we arrived in Yokohama on Nov. 17. I immediately reported to headquarters and was ordered forthwith to the battleship **Hiei.** *Two days later the* **Hiei** *sailed from Kisarazu, situated at the opposite end of Tokyo Bay from Yokohama. She was to join the task force, which was then assembling in the Hitokappu (Tankan) Bay off Etorofu Island.*

It was in Hitokappu Bay aboard the carrier **Akagi,** *flagship of the task force, that the final strategy conference before Pearl Harbor was held on Nov. 23. First I reported on my "reconnaissance" of Pearl Harbor. Then I briefed our pilots, illustrating my instructions with a relief map of the city and harbor. I also gave them details on roofing materials used on the hangars--details I had obtained from some of the Japanese passengers on the* **Taiyo Maru** *who had worked on their construction.*

On Nov. 25 Adm. Isoroku Yamamoto, commander-in-chief of the Imperial Fleet, ordered the task force to sail next day.

I spent that night aboard the **Akagi.** *At 2 a.m. on Nov. 26 I was awakened by an orderly who told me that Vice-Adm. Chuichi Nagumo wanted to see me immediately.*

Admiral Nagumo looked grim. After apologizing for rousing me at such an hour, he said: "I want to be absolutely certain of one thing. Are you sure the American fleet is still in Pearl Harbor? Can you be sure that the fleet is anchored in the harbor and is not moving to an anchorage outside?"

"I feel absolutely certain, sir, that the American fleet is in Pearl Harbor. All the information I obtained supports my conviction on this point."

Later that morning the Nagumo force left the icy waters of Hitokappu Bay. I had transferred from the **Akagi** *to the gunboat* **Kunashiri** *and was returning home. The gunboat's crew kept asking me whether "the big maneuvers were now over." I replied in the affirmative. Pearl Harbor was still a tightly kept secret in Japan.*

Suguru Suzuki
former Commander of the Japanese Navy

The machine that came to be known as "Purple" broke the Japanese diplomatic and JN25 naval codes in 1941. There were only six Purple machines made in 1941. One went to London, two were in the hands of Navy Intelligence, the War Department's Signal Intelligence Service had two and the sixth went to the Philippines. The Commanders, Admiral Kimmel and General Short, did not have direct access to "Magic" intelligence. If they had, they would have had their forces in a better state of preparedness to meet the Japanese onslaught. NA

The Four Winds Code Executes

A modest-sized Netherlands East Indies Army Code Service, headed by a Captain Verkuyl, operated in early 1941 in an underground communications center at the Higher Technical College situated on Dago road in the city of Bandung, Java, N.E.I. The captain and his wife, Nancy, had lived in Japan for almost eight years and they were both fluent in the Japanese language. They had also studied Japanese cryptology and thus worked as a team for the N.E.I. code service. It was about six months before the war, in May 1941, when Nancy Verkuyl made an important discovery. She had learned how to proceed with the decipher of a major Japanese code. A Dutch-Indonesian lady had cracked codes! Because of the breakthrough found by Nancy Verkuyl the code service was enlarged as quickly as possible, but it took many more months of hard painstaking work by teams of cryptoanalysts to determine they had indeed broken an important and reliable Japanese code. By summer of 1941 the N.E.I. code service worked full shifts around the clock intercepting and decoding Japanese messages from all corners of the Far East. It was in early Oct. 1941 that through one of these intercepts it was learned that the Japanese had instructed their own units scattered throughout the Far East that from that moment on their units also had to monitor Radio Tokyo weather broadcasts. In these weather reports their would be a code-in-voice hidden, and these would only be transmitted in sudden emergencies. There would be little time left for action and therefore this code would be in-voice, in the form of wind sentences, in the middle as well as at the end of the weather report. They would mean to execute within 72 hours.

NORTH WIND CLOUDY
(Kita No Kaze Kumori) execute for: attack Russia.

WEST WIND CLEAR
(Nishi No Kaze Hare) execute for: attack British.

SOUTH WIND STORMY
(Minami No Kazi Arashi)
execute for: attack Dutch East Indies.

EAST WIND RAIN
(Higashi No Kaze Ame) execute for: attack Pearl Harbor.

Naturally, this ominous message caused considerable excitement and extra alertness at the N.E.I. code service. The tension grew.

It was on Dec. 5, 1941 (Java Time), that the message was received: Higashi No Kaze Ame (East Wind Rain) meaning that within 72 hours Pearl Harbor would be attacked. The chief military intelligence officer of the U.S. Army in Bandung was Col. E.R. Thorpe, and he states in his book *East Wind Rain* that he did send this crucial warning to Washington. He states: "I suppose the most important thing I ever did as an army intelligence officer was to notify Washington of the forthcoming attack on Pearl Harbor."

This war warning was received in Washington on Dec. 4, 1941 (it is one day earlier in Washington than in Java) as is testified to by Captain Safford, U.S. Navy and is also acknowledged by Gen. Albert Wedemeyer, U.S. Army, Chief of Army Operations.

KAREL N. RINK

Japanese Ambassador Nomura and Special Envoy Kurusu leave the White House, possibly on Nov. 26, 1941, after the proposals they hoped would avert war had been rejected. Unbeknownst to the two men, their mission would be a fruitless one on Dec. 7 when they met with Cordell Hull on the "Day of Infamy." USN

Kurusu & Nomura

Saburo Kurusu was sent by the Japanese government to help Ambassador Nomura negotiate with the United States government in November 1941. He had been the Japanese ambassador to Germany and had signed the Tripartite Partnership between Germany, Italy and Japan in 1940. He married an American, Alice Jay, in New York in 1914. She spent the war years in Japan, after the couple was repatriated there in 1942. Their son, Ryo, was in the Japanese Air Force, and after making a forced landing in Japan due to a mechanical failure on his airplane, was beaten to death by local peasants. Because of his looks, they thought he was an American. Kurusu died in 1954.

Kichisaburo Nomura was a Japanese Admiral and Ambassador to the United States during World War I and a delegate to the Versailles Peace Treaty Conference in 1917 and the 1922 Washington Naval Conference. He died in 1964.

This ad appearing in a Honolulu newspaper before the attack was attributed to a Japanese spy as a coded message. Notice how it has been decoded. This supposed message has been totally discounted.

Gen. Hideki Tojo

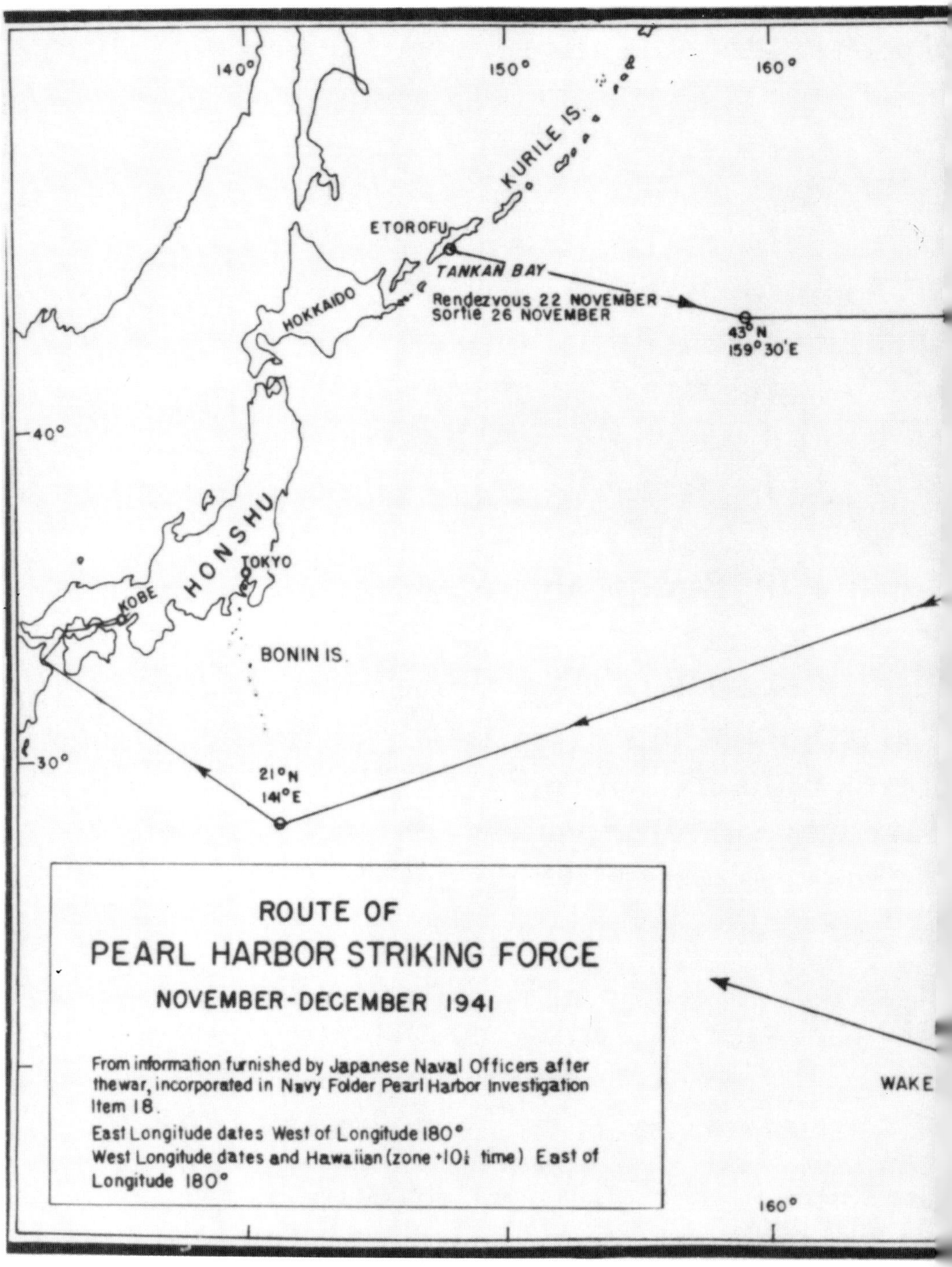

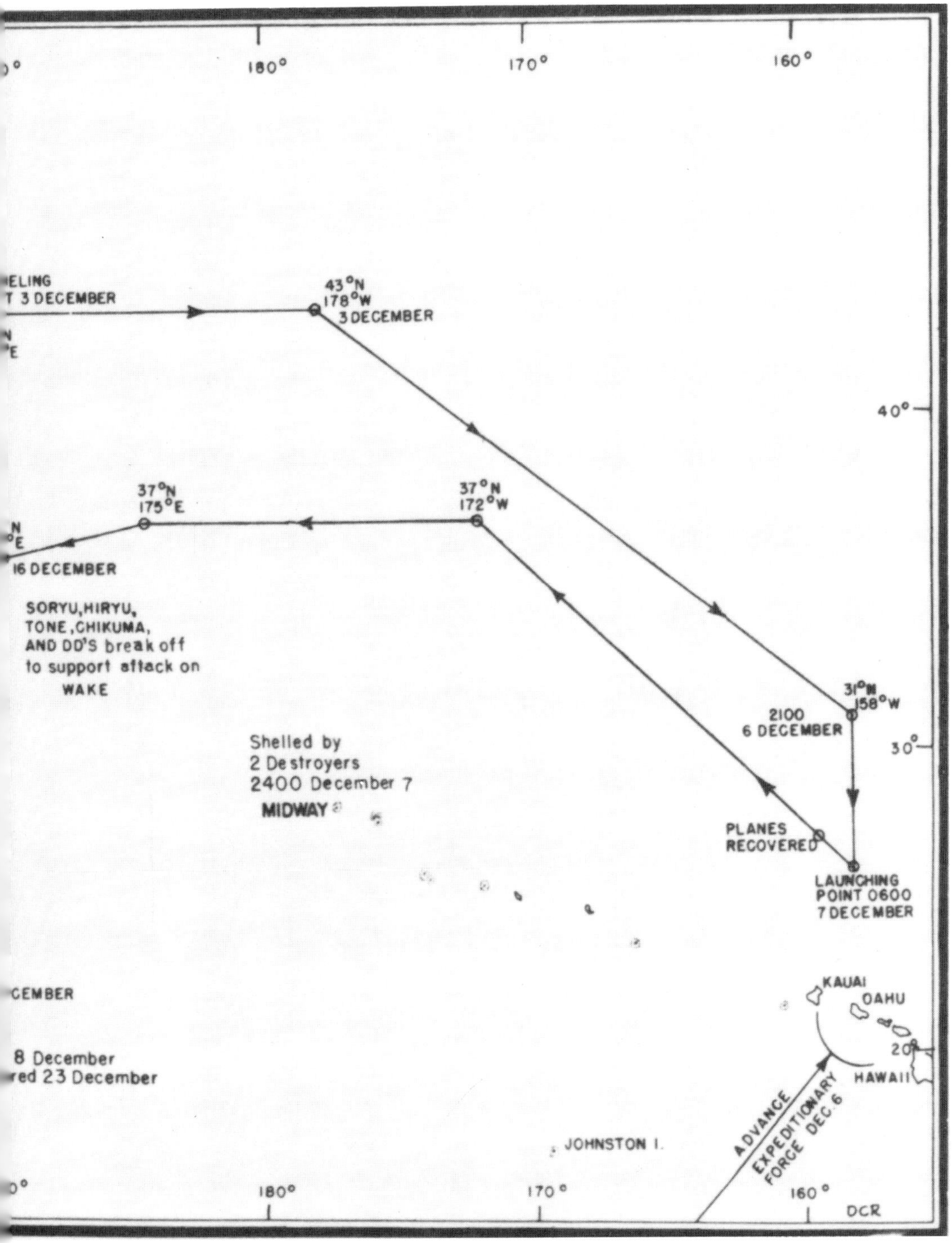

The Military Careers of Minoru Genda

From Naval Institute Proceedings, April 1990

Born in Kake, Hiroshima Prefecture on 16 August 1904, Minoru Genda entered the Naval Academy at Eta Jima in August, 1921, graduating three years later. He received his ensigns commission in December 1925 after having served nine-month tours of duty in the first-class coast defense ship *Izumo* and the light cruiser *Oi*. Following one year in the battleship *Ise*, he reported to Yokosuka for successive assignments at the Naval Gunnery School and the Naval Torpedo and Mine School. In July, 1927 he rejoined the *Izumo* as assistant navigator.

Genda's career as a naval aviator began in December 1928 when, as a second lieutenant, he reported for primary flight training at Naval Air Station (NAS) Kasumigaura, transferring one year later to NAS Yokosuka for advanced training in fighters. He joined the fighter squadron on board the carrier *Akagi* in February 1930. Returning to NAS Yokosuka as a flight instructor late in 1931. First Lieutenant Genda organized and led "Genda's Circus" of navy aerial acrobats which performed throughout Japan. In April 1933 he began 18 months of duty on the light cruiser *Ryujo*, after which he went back to Yokosuka as squadron commander and flight instructor.

Now a lieutenant commander, Genda entered the Imperial Naval Staff College in late 1935 and quickly earned the nickname "madman Genda" for his outspoken views on the supremacy of aircraft over the battleship. Immediately upon his graduation in July 1937, the war in China broke out, whereupon he served briefly on the staff of the Second Air Force and at the headquarters of the Third Fleet. He reported as wing commander at Yokosuka in January 1938, transferring in April to the Torpedo School as instructor, his genius in torpedoes now well-established. Genda reported as assistant naval attaché for air at the Japanese embassy in London the following December. At the end of this tour, November 1940, he was impressed by the British carrier-based torpedo plane attack which crippled the Italian battleship fleet at Taranto.

Reporting as air operations officer to Commander, First Carrier Squadron, later that month and in the rank of commander, Genda began developing carrier tactics for the fleet while on board the flagship *Kaga*. Early in 1941 Rear Admiral Takijiro Onishi, chief of staff of the shore-based Eleventh Air Fleet, asked his advice about a proposal by Admiral Isoroku Yamamoto, Commander in Chief Combined Fleet, for a surprise carrier raid on Pearl Harbor to initiate war with the United States. Genda studied the idea for ten days before endorsing it. In April he became air operations officer of the new fast carrier striking force. First Air Fleet, and the next month initiated the study and testing of aerial torpedoes to make short, shallow runs in the 30- to 45-foot-deep Hawaiian anchorage. He was Admiral Nagumo's key adviser on the flagship *Akagi* during the attack. Genda's carrier tactics worked equally well in the conquest of Southeast Asia, including air strikes in Ceylon and Port Darwin, Australia. He drew up the air plan for the Midway operation but was confined to sick bay with pneumonia at the outset. On strike day, 4 June 1942, he nevertheless managed to climb to the flag bridge, where, beset with fever and clothed in pajamas, he was embraced by Admiral Nagumo who followed his advice. Later in the day, however, he was evacuated from the stricken *Akagi*.

The next month Genda became air group commander on the carrier *Zuikaku*, from which he participated in the Battle of the Eastern Solomons in August. In October he moved to Rabaul as air operations officer of Eleventh Air Fleet for two crucial months of the Guadalcanal-Solomons Campaign. He transferred in December to Tokyo for duty with the air operations section, Naval General Staff and Imperial Headquarters, coordinating air defenses in Southeast Asia and making trips to the East Indies, Philippines, and Indochina between May 1943 and the end of 1944.

In January 1945 Genda took command of the 343rd Fighter Group of the last veteran navy pilots and flying new Shiden-kai ("George") fighters charged with defending Tokyo. When U.S. carrier planes from Task Force 58 struck Tokyo and Kure in March, his planes inflicted unusually heavy casualties on the Grumman F6F-5 Hellcats in dogfights. But the war was lost, and by its end in August, Genda had achieved the rank of captain. He was transferred to the reserve in November 1945.

Called upon to testify before the U.S. Strategic Bombing Survey that autumn, Genda revealed many of the details of Japan's wartime operations. To charges of inconsistencies in his accounts, he explained in 1969 that he and his peers had been called to testify with practically no food to sustain them—only a small tin of rice for each witness. Virtually starving, he had difficulty concentrating on the questions. During the hearings, he was questioned, and befriended, by U.S. Navy Commander Thomas H. Moorer, who was Chief of Naval Operations 24 years later, and arranged for Genda to visit the United States.

After the formal Treaty of San Francisco, in July 1954, Genda was commissioned a major general in the Japanese Air Self-Defense Force as Deputy Chief of Staff for Material. At the end of the following year he assumed command of the First Fighter Wing and qualified in the F-86F Sabrejet used by his command. Promoted to lieutenant general, in July 1957 Genda became commander of Japan's Air Defense Command, and exactly two years later was made Chief of Staff of the Air Self-Defense Force in the rank of general. Although he retired from active duty in April 1962, by the time of his visit to the United States he had checked out in all major Western fighters except the F-4 Phantom II.

Clark G. Reynolds

Ford Island

Holocaust at Hangar #6

In the opening minutes of the attack, one of the first bombs to fall hit Seaplane Hangar #6 on the southeast point of Ford Island. Planes parked on the ramp were set afire by other bomb hits and strafing. One bomb fell near two Dutch PBYs destined for Java. One was destroyed, one was damaged (at least one was already at Midway Island en route to Java, but it returned to aid defense of Oahu. USN

Ford Island—at one time known as Mokuumeume (Island of Strife), Rabbit Island, Marin's Island and Little Goats Island—lies in the middle of Pearl Harbor's East Loch.

Although only a mile and a quarter long and half as wide, it has played an important part in the military history of the area.

Don F. Francisco de Paula y Maria, a Spaniard who purchased the island in 1791, was the first of several owners. James Dowset bought the island in 1865 and then sold it to Carolina Jackson by trust deed for $1. In 1886, Dr. Seth Porter Ford, for whom the island would eventually be named, married Miss Jackson and assumed ownership. It was sold to the Ii estate upon Ford's death and leased to the Oahu Sugar Company until the United States entered World War I in 1917.

At that time the U.S. Army took it over and established a west-side airfield named for Lt. Frank Luke, who was credited with 18 aerial victories in 17 days during World War I.

To support the increased naval presence in the Pacific area, the Ford Island Naval Air Station was commissioned in January 1923. A seaplane hangar and other facilities were built on the southeastern side of the island.

During the 1930s, the dredging of Pearl Harbor produced enough landfill to enlarge the 334-acre island to 441 acres, and both Army and Navy facilities were expanded. But the island proved to be too small for both services and the Army transferred its operations to the newly developed Wheeler Field.

On March 20, 1936, the island was in the news as the site of Amelia Earhart's crash-landing during her attempted round-the-world flight.

In 1939, as the result of growing American concern over its defenses, many of the present steel and concrete buildings were built on Ford Island. The base was used for overhaul and repair of most of the Pacific Fleet planes and as a supply base.

The initial Japanese attacks were aimed at knocking out the planes at the naval air station to ensure that the battleships around the island could be attacked without harassment from the air. Nine enemy dive bombers took part in the attack on Ford Island itself. The most severe damage was to Hangar 6 and its seaplane ramp at the southeast corner of the island. Pounded by at least five bomb hits, the hangar and many nearby planes were soon afire. The northeast corner of the structure was burned to its steel framework, and the seaplanes were charred wrecks. There was some damage to the ramp and to Hangar 38.

A delayed action bomb apparently intended for the moored *USS California* slammed into the courtyard of the dispensary and exploded 20 feet beneath the ground, causing much damage but no casualties. Electrical, water and steam services to the building were disrupted.

When the *USS Arizona* blew up at its Ford Island moorings, the ship settled on the 12-inch main water supply pipe to the island and crushed it. A six-inch line at the south end of the island was damaged at the Navy Yard side, cutting off that supply. A pump was installed on an artesian well on the island to provide enough water to fight fires. Water from the island's elevated tank had to be rationed.

There was some damage to other buildings from misdirected bombs and fragments from exploding ships. Pilings at the small boat harbor and elsewhere were damaged by the oil fires on the water.

The *USS Neosho*, a navy tanker, had just finished discharging aviation gasoline to the tanks on the island when the Japanese planes arrived. Disregarding their own safety, the fueling detail removed the hoses from the tanker and cast off her lines, enabling the ship with its highly volatile cargo to clear the pier and avert a possible disaster.

Emergency first aid stations were set up in the mess hall, the Marine barracks and the new bachelor officer's quarters to augment the dispensary facilities, which could not handle all the 200 wounded from the ships. After the attack, the casualties were evacuated across the harbor to the naval hospital. Several thousand sailors from the bombed and sinking battleships, many covered with oil, eventually made it to the island and were given food, clothing and shelter in many buildings and homes.

Of the 70 planes at Ford Island, 33 were destroyed or damaged. At no time either during or after the attack was the naval air station out of commission. Only one individual was killed and 25 received minor injuries.

Capt. J. M. Shoemaker, Commanding Officer, NAS Ford Island, March 15, 1941, to June 8, 1942.
USN

View of Ford Island in 1925. The Army's Luke Field is to the west (left) and the Naval Air Station, commissioned in January 1923 is to the east (right). The Navy took full control of the island in November 1939 when the Army moved all its facilities to Hickam Field. NA

Seaplane base and Hangar #6 on the southeast end of Ford Island on March 5, 1926. Many of the larger aircraft, including one in the water, are Curtis F5L Flying Boats. Four of the smaller aircraft on the ramp are Martin SC-1 torpedo-bombers. USN

The Army airfield, Luke Field, on Ford Island in 1924. Operations were moved to the new Wheeler Field in the 1930s. HA

Extension of the Seaplane Beach with Hangar #6, May 11, 1934. USN

An early day view of Ford Island showing newly constructed fuel tanks. Some of the water area to the right was eventually filled in. Battleship Row is to the right. HA

This northerly view over Ford Island on Oct. 10, 1941, shows the various naval aircraft facilities situated here at the time. On the west shoreline (left) are the utility aircraft hangars. Across the airstrip (known previously to the Army Air Corps as "Luke Field"), and at lower center of photo, are the patrol squadron hangars which housed the PBY aircraft of PAT-WING-2. The first bombs to fall on Dec. 7 would destroy the large hangar #6 in the foreground. NA 80-G-279375

In this overhead view of Ford Island on Nov. 10, 1941, five battleships as well as the *Lexington* can be seen at their offshore moorings. The *"Lex"* at berth Fox-9 was, by a stroke of good fortune, at sea transporting 18 Vought scout bombers of Marine Scout-Bombing Squadron 231 to Midway Island. She would ultimately meet her fate in May 1942 at Coral Sea. NA 80-G-279385

U.S. NAVAL AIR STATION
PEARL HARBOR, T.H.

NA12/A12-1A16

JMS-10-ram
Jan. 25, 1942

War Diary of U.S. Naval Air Station, Pearl Harbor, T.H.

Sunday, 7 December, 1941

Holiday routine

0740 U.S.S. *NEOSHO* completed discharging aviation gasoline to Naval Air Station, and back pressure taken to clear fuel lines.

0750 Aircraft observed approaching Ford Island from the general direction of Merry Point and Hickam Field, but were not identified as Japanese carrier-based planes until the parking area and hangar #6 were bombed, followed by torpedo and bombing attacks on the ships of the fleet moored around Ford Island.

0757 General Quarters sounded, and word of the attack put out on all available radio and teletype circuits.

Hangar #6 set ablaze by bomb hit on eastern end and surrounding parking area damaged by five bomb hits, the largest producing crater approximately 20' in diameter by 7' deep, VP and VO-VS planes in the area destroyed or damaged by fire, fragments, and machine gun bullets. A delayed action bomb apparently intended for the U.S.S. *CALIFORNIA* at berth in Fox-3 exploded under the court of the dispensary, disrupting electrical, water and steam service to this building, but caused no injury to personnel.

Except for this initial attack on the seaplane area, none of the subsequent enemy attacks appeared to be directed at the Air Station, but fragments from A.A. projectiles, and from bombs exploding on or near ships moored around the island, machine gun bullets and 1.1 projectiles fired from the ships in the harbor, together with machine gun fire from enemy aircraft fell on the station, particularly around waterfront areas throughout the attacks. Fragments from the *ARIZONA* explosion were blown generally over the northeasterly end of Ford Island. Three delayed action bombs intended for Battleships at Berth Fox-5 and Fox-6 fell in open areas near those berths and exploded harmlessly underground.

When *ARIZONA* blew up at Berth Fox-7, she settled on the 12" water main, crushing it, and cutting off all fresh water to the Air Station, as the 6" temporary line at the south end of the island was cut off at the Navy Yard (presumably damaged). This necessitated strict rationing of water, despite the installation of a pump on the artesian well near building 167, to provide for the fire and flushing systems.

Oil fires caused damage to the fueling pier at Fox-4, where the fueling detail, Ensign D.A. Singleton, A-V(S), U.S.N.R., A.L. Hansen, C.M.M. (PA), U.S.N., and A.C. Thatcher, A.M.M.2C, U.S.N., with disregard of personal safety and with devotion to duty, ignoring enemy bombs and machine gun bullets, removed the hoses from the *NEOSHO*, cast off her lines, enabling her to clear the pier, and opened the sprinkler valves to the tanks. Other fires caused damage to the dock house, the face of Landing "A" and Berth Fox-1½.

Emergency first aid stations were set up in the mess hall, marine barracks and new Bachelor Officer's Quarters, where, together with the dispensary, about 200 wounded received medical attention. Casualties were evacuated to the Naval Hospital as soon as raids subsided. Air Station boats performed exemplary service in rescuing personnel from the waters of the harbor. Several thousand refugees from *ARIZONA*, *WEST VIRGINIA*, *OKLAHOMA*, *CALIFORNIA*, *UTAH* and other ships were given food, clothing and shelter.

0900 War Plan #46 put in effect against Japan.

1100 Last air raid ended, but personnel remained at general quarters, and preparations for repelling renewed enemy attacks continued. Station security increased preparations made for blackout.

Blackout at sunset.

2000 Air raid alarm sounded. Six *ENTERPRISE* planes attempting landing on Ford Island were fired upon by all units in Pearl Harbor; four planes lost.

Injuries to Naval Air Station personnel this date: Killed in action, CROFT, Theodore W., A.O.M.1C, USN (VP-21); 25 persons received minor injuries from burns or flying debris.

8 December, 1941

0230 Fire started by embers from burning battleships in vicinity of C.P.O. quarters; extinguished.
0245 fire broke out at landing "A"; extinguished at 0300.
0515 Air raid alarm; no attack. Continued salvage operations and preparing suitable defense facilities. Evacuated battleship personnel to Receiving Barracks. Blackout.

9 December, 1941

Continued salvage operations, improved station security.
1120 Battery "F" of the 251st Coast Artillery, Capt. C.L. Ogden, U.S.A. Commanding aboard for duty. Blackout.

Hangar #6 burning with some intact PBYs in front. The OS2U "Kingfisher" to the right foreground is one of two that got into the air that afternoon. USN

Looking over the wrecked aircraft at Hangar #6 on Ford Island, the destroyer *Shaw*'s forward magazine has exploded, sending a huge plume of fire and smoke skyward. USN

Bob Barrigan, shown here with his wife, is the sailor standing with his back to the camera on the left. His story follows on the next two pages.

Fast Action And A Lucky Break

On Friday, Dec. 5, 1941, I was assigned to a detail consisting of two other men and myself—one was Holden AMM 1/c. I can't remember the other. We were to take our two OS2U aircraft to Ford Island and remain with them until our ship the *Tangier* AV8, came back in. All, or most of the ships, including ours, was to go out to sea Saturday on maneuvers.

We went to Ford Island and were quartered in the transient bunkroom. I believe the other person with us was a first class metalsmith named Ingleman. Anyway, we all went into Pearl saturday evening, did some shopping, and I went to a PTA dance. We returned to Pearl Harbor and back to the barracks about 10:30-11:00 p.m.

Sunday morning I was awakened by a large explosion which shook the bunkroom. I jumped up as I felt a second one and ran to the window. We were on the second floor facing Diamond Head. I looked over our swimming pool down toward the No. 1 Hangar, and I could see large billows of smoke coming from it. My first thought was that one of our PBY patrol craft had hit it coming in. I then felt several other smaller explosions and saw an aircraft crossing low in the hangar area from south to north banking around and climbing. It had large red balls on the wings. I shouted to the others the Russians were attacking us.

We put on our white pants, shoes and hats and ran downstairs. As I came down the stairway, I couldn't believe my eyes—men had brooms and sticks and were breaking out all the glass frames in the doors and windows. I did not have time to dwell on it because a boatswain's mate got me and several others and ordered us to follow him. We went out the door to the street, and he shouted for us to keep low and follow him. We did, running up the street past the swimming pool. Aircraft machine gun tracers were going past us, and we could hear explosions and glass breaking. He led us to the armory. It was also very hectic there—people were opening up all kinds of ammunition boxes, rifles, gas masks, etc.

An old Chief grabbed me, threw two belts over my shoulder, a rifle and a gas mask and told me and another seaman to go up on the roof of the Operations Building. I remember running all the way over there and running up the narrow stairway to the roof. The roof was about 20′×30′ as far as I can remember; also, there was a wall around it about 24″ or 30″ high. There was a small permanent shed which held cleaning material. We ran to the side of the shed and looked around. It was an unbelievable sight. Except for the area in front of us, we had a view of everything up to the fuel dumps and the hospital on the hills. Planes were coming all across the water from the Navy Yard area. They would fly low, 50′ to 100′ over the water, drop bombs and torpedoes on the *West Virginia, California, Arizona*—all the battleships on that side; fly directly over us strafing—do the same to the *Tangier, Utah, and Raleigh*; then make a high turn over Beckoning Point and the Pan Am base and return. I saw only two aircraft hit and go down.

During this, the seaman and myself loaded our rifles and watched the waves of aircraft coming. As they approached, we would go behind the shed, fire at them as they passed directly overhead, run to the opposite side and repeat the same firing. I do remember telling the seaman I was with that we could have done better with hand grenades because the planes were so low I could see the pilot and man in the rear seat very plain. At some period during the early time on the roof, two Marines came up and uncrated a box, set up a Browning watercooled machine gun in about 2 minutes and fired it without water until the barrel was so hot the tracers were corkscrewing out.

From that point I saw the *Nevada* get under way and try to move out. I saw the destroyer *Shaw* get a direct hit and exploded. I saw the *Oglala* roll over, many whaleboats and captain's gigs got strafed, people burning in the water, and the ferry getting strafed. I saw bombs being dropped on the *Arizona.* I did not see it hit but felt the explosions.

At some period of time two men came up and told us we were relieved to go down to the mess hall to eat and be reassigned after we calmed down. We both noticed we had red marks over our right side arms and face. We did not know what the red marks were. All we had on were pants and skivvy shirts (undershirts). Our ears were also ringing and the roof deck was covered with small pieces of paper. The battleships were just below us. The *California* was laying sideways and had been firing its large guns at an angle to us. I believe what caused the red marks on us were the shell waddings hitting us during this time, but we were unaware of it.

Anyway, I don't remember the time, but I left the roof, kept my rifle, what ammunition I had left, and my gas mask. I made my way over to the messhall where I was relieved of my rifle and ammunition but kept my gas mask. I remember being in line at the mess hall, not really hungry but in line because I was told to eat. I looked around me but did not see anyone I knew. I saw men in everything I could think of. Dirty clothes, shorts to Admiral's coats, some wounded. The whole scene was unbelievable then as it still is now. I really became sick and frightened for the first time when I looked back against the mess hall—and under the tables were several rows of dead men. When I got to the head of the line with my tray, the cooks were apologizing for the cold chicken. Because the *Arizona* had set on the main Ford Island watermain, we were drinking the swimming pool water. This was later confirmed and guards were posted around the swimming pool. Anyway, when I looked at the cold chicken, orange juice, and dead men I left the mess hall without eating. And to this day, I still cannot eat cold chicken.

I was put in a truck and taken down to the hangar area. I went over to where our two aircraft were parked—in front of the second hangar from the one that had a direct hit. No more than three or four hours had past. I guess it was after 11 or 12 o'clock. Everything was burning—aircraft parts and chunks of concrete were everywhere. When I approached our area, I saw our two aircraft and the two men I came off the ship with on detail by the aircraft. Holden was sitting on the ground and Ingleman was near the wing.

Holden got me and said we were trying to get one of our aircraft flyable. One had a large chunk of cement through the right wing so we were going to take off one wing and place it on the other aircraft. All of the damage was from chunks of cement. We went into the hangar to see if we could find space to put the aircraft. I noticed that two incendiary bombs had come through the hangar roof and never exploded, but had thrown yellow powder all over the aircraft.

That night I was put on a .50-caliber gun crew to help load ammunition by the hangar. During the day we had several false alarms of new air raids and we always ran to the runway area where a trench was dug for some reason. We all jumped in there till it was clear.

That night on the gun crews, with guys from the other ships, was my worst time. As it grew dark, we became more apprehensive since the rumors were that the Japanese transports would be landing at night and air raids were expected prior to that. What all gun crews were told was that if an attack was imminent condition red would be indicated by the fire station who would sound a continuous blast. So we waited; it got dark; it was very quite; and we were nervous. I had to rest my knees against the sandbags to keep them up. Sometime, I don't know just what time it was, but we heard aircraft coming in up the channel from the direction of Diamond Head; their formation lights were blinking; we didn't know what they were. Suddenly, some ship out in the bay near the dry docks opened fire just for a few minutes; then every gun in the Pearl Harbor area joined in. You couldn't even hear a yell and not even a bird could have survived. The tracers lit the sky, several aircraft were hit. I saw them go down burning—one to the south and two on up the hill toward the Navy hospital. We sadly later learned they were F4Fs from the *Enterprise.* No one slept that night.

The next morning—second day—we went back to work on our aircraft. The Executive Officer of Ford Island came by and told us that he wanted us to notify our ship's captain that we would be working around the clock on the aircraft. I was elected to go. I made my way back to the quay where the *Tangier* was docked. I went up on the quarter deck and spoke to Capt. C.F. Spraque. I repeated to him the message. I cannot repeat what he said—but, in no uncertain terms, he told me to get the rest of the men, forget the aircraft, and be back on the ship within a half hour. We came back.

We moved out in the bay the next day. After that a lighter came alongside, and for two days and nights loaded ammunition, guns, bombs, aircraft parts and about 100 marines. We left about Dec. 15 and met a task force—*Saratoga,* destroyers and other cruisers. We never really knew where we were going. One afternoon and the 2nd or 3rd day we all were circling. What happened was that a destroyer had been refueling from the *Saratoga* and had gotten its crossmast hooked into the walkway around the *Saratoga*'s stack. We could see them working with cutting torches—after dark—I believe we lost several hours. The next day we steamed steady. I had every four hour fantail watch to watch the distance of the ship directly aft. I went off watch about 12 midnight and went back on at 4:00 a.m. I looked at the compass and noticed we were going in the opposite direction, and most of all, we had only one ship, the destroyer *Blue* with us.

We ended up going to Midway Island. This was funny—we stopped outside for the pilot—took him aboard and proceeded into the bay. We picked up a tug just inside the bay and he put a steel line on our fantail—we proceeded in. The dock was several hundred yards to our port ahead. We were to make a hard left turn and the tug was to assist pulling us hard to increase the turn.

We started our turn fast, too fast to throw off the tug line. We were pulling the tug sideways. Our 1st Lieutenant cut the wire with an ax and we went about 20 feet up the center of the dock tossing civilian workers and their bags in the water on each side of the dock. They had been waiting for us to take them back to Pearl Harbor.

What we later found out was that our ship was to reinforce Wake Island. Captain Sprague had orders to run the ship aground to assist the Marines if we did not have time to unload. Because of the coral reefs they had to use a donkey engine and lighter to get supplies ashore. So because of the problem with the destroyer and the *Saratoga* refueling episode, that delay most likely saved the *Tangier* crew because Wake Island was taken over by the Japanese during that time.

Bob Barrigan
1441 SW 68th
Oklahoma City, Oklahoma 73159

A burned-out section of Hangar #6, a few days after the attack. The structure was damaged by at least five bombs, the largest producing a crater 20 feet wide and 7 feet deep. A sandbagged gun emplacement was established on the ramp. USN

Hangar #6 was abandoned years ago and torn down in the late 1980s.

Oil and debris from the bombed battleships washed up on the east shore of Ford Island. Note the shack and the H-shaped structure where the dredge pipeline meets the shore. This is the Ford Island ferry slip, which is still in use today. NA

Smoke from burning fuel oil obscures the battleship *California* moored at Fox-3 opposite the Headquarters Building, Ford Island. NA

Cleanup has already begun at the Seaplane Base on Ford Island. Smoke at center is from the destroyer *Shaw* in YFD #2. Toward the right rear can be seen the fore and aft masts of the *Nevada.* AMC

Re-arming clips and belts on Ford Island. NA 80-G-32497

In a hastily set up bunker, a .30-caliber machine gun crew, awaits a follow-up attack by enemy aircraft, possibly on Dec. 9. This view is looking west across a sea plane ramp to Beckoning Point and Middle Loch. Note two TBD-1 Devastators parked on left. The two men without helmets are probably survivors from one of the sunken ships. NA 80-G-32543

Machine gun emplacements such as these along the ramp on the south end of Ford Island proliferated in the wake of the Japanese attack on Dec. 7. Curtiss SOCs from cruiser-based VCS units are in the background, along with a pair of PBYs, one of which (visible behind the hangar at right) has its engines warming up. *Nevada*, beached off Waipio Point, is in the background (left), visible beyond the three SOCs. NA 80-G-324-92

The dispensary as it looks today.

Lt. Comdr. Art Humphries in the courtyard of the Ford Island dispensary, where a Japanese bomb exploded.

Dispensary on Ford Island that was hit by a delayed action bomb probably intended for the *California* Berth Fox-3. It landed in the inner court and exploded, causing slight structural damage to the building and cutting electrical, water and steam services. No one was injured.

Smoke still billows from the stricken *Arizona* in this northeasterly view taken a day after the attack from the highest point on Ford Island, the control tower atop the water tower. Aircraft below are Sikorsky JRS-1's and Vought OS2U's. New utility hangar still under construction can be seen in right foreground. USN

Scene at the Seaplane Base following the attack. Several PBYs are parked near a burned hangar. In the left background is the beached *Nevada*. NA 80-G-32505

A wrecked seaplane. This is all that remains of a Vought OS2U-2 Kingfisher observation plane destroyed on Ford Island during the attack. AMC

View of the abandoned air-field on Ford Island in 1981. At one time, Ford Island was the site of the Army's Luke Field as well as the Naval Air Station. There are plans for the eventual demolition of the field and unused support facilities, to make room for much needed housing for military personnel stationed at Oahu. Plans also include a causeway or bridge, possibly from Aiea to Ford Island, thus eliminating the ferry.

Buildings on Ford Island.

In this aerial view taken on Dec. 10, the damaged *Shaw* (bottom) is still in the sunken floating drydock. The bomb damage to the seaplane base and Hangar #6 on Ford Island (top left) is visible. Docked to the right is the seaplane tender *Curtiss* also damaged in the attack. The dark streaks seen in the waters is fuel oil that is leaking from the broken and battered ships of Battleship Row.
NA 80-G-387579

View from the water tower at NAS Pearl Harbor, Dec. 8, 1941; in front of hangars at top left are three SBDs from the *Enterprise* Air Group. Various utility aircraft sit scattered around the mat in foreground, including some whose wings appear to have been hastily camouflaged. Identifiable ships include the seaplane tender *Tangier* (AV-8), heavy cruiser *Chester* (CA-27), the damaged light cruiser *Raleigh* (CL-7) and the hospital ship *Solace* (AH-5). NA 80-G-32482

Copy of a memorandum from Lt. Comdr., E.B. Wilkins,
Operations Officer, Naval Air Station, to his Commanding Officer.

NA12/

MEMORANDUM:

U.S. NAVAL AIR STATION
PEARL HARBOR, T.H.

From: Operations Officer
To: Commanding Officer

10 December, 1941

During the early evening of Dec. 7, 1941, I received word that friendly planes, were approaching to land on Ford Island. Reliable men were sent out in cars, motorcycles, etc. to warn all riflemen, machine gun nests, etc. to hold fire. After several false alarms as to the immediacy of the approach of these planes, word came through which led me to believe the planes would be landing in a very short time. I again ordered the word passed to the defense forces, having particular regard to men stationed adjacent to the southwest portion of the field, from which direction the planes would normally approach. I then drove to the Luke Field side and took position well out on the warming up platform at hangar #133 in order to direct planes to their parking area and give what service might be needed. After a few minutes I saw the planes approaching from Hickam Field. At first I saw only four planes in sections of two each. An instant later I saw that one section had three planes and heard one of the men with me say "There's six of them." I never saw the sixth plane. All running lights were burning brightly and the planes appeared to be flying up the Pearl Harbor Channel. I believe they must have been in the close vicinity of Hospital Point when I heard the first shots fired. In less than five seconds the entire Pearl Harbor area was firing. The planes flew up drydock channel at an estimated 300 feet altitude until they disappeared from my view at a point a little northeast of the administration building.

/s/ E.B. Wilkins
Lt. Comdr., U.S.N.

---

10 December 1941

U.S. NAVAL AIR STATION
PEARL HARBOR, T.H.

INCIDENT OF *ENTERPRISE* AIRPLANES, ATTEMPT LANDING.

I was in the landplane control tower when the six *Enterprise* planes were fired upon. Lt. Comdr. Young, Commander of the *Enterprise* Air Group was also present and assumed control to bring the planes in. Two flood light trucks with lights on were stationed at the southwest end of the runway and green lights were placed at the northwest end to mark the corner of the runway. The following is the traffic that passed between the tower and the planes:

TOWER: Turn on your running lights, make approach from Barber's Point. Come in as low as possible.

PLANE: (Believed to be Blue 18): Am making one pass at the field.

TOWER: Do not make pass at field. Turn on running lights and come in as low as possible.

BLUE 18: (To planes in formation): Close in, I am going to make one pass at the field. (The planes were then approx. over drydock channel).

TOWER: Do not make pass at field, come straight in. (At this time firing started apparently from surface vessels).

ONE OF THE PLANES: What the hell is wrong down there.

TOWER: Turn off lights and beat it. (One plane got on the field during the firing). Later instructions were again given to approach low from Barber's Point with running lights on and come straight in. Only one other plane from this group managed to get in.

/s/ F.A. ERICKSON
Lt., U.S.C.G

I was to be second-in-command of a flight of six F4F-4 fighters from the **U.S.S. Enterprise** *that were to escort 19 torpedo planes and six scout planes on our way to find the Japanese Fleet, which a report said had been located.*

Unfortunately, the report was erroneous, as we later found out. However, we were launched and went out some 200 miles.

It was dark when we returned to the ship and my flight leader talked to the **Enterprise***, and asked for permission to land. The ship said, "Hell, no. We're not going to light up for you. Go into Pearl Harbor," and gave us a coded direction.*

We turned on the heading toward Pearl. Everything was blacked out except burning ships, which we thought were burning cane fields. It was 8:30 Sunday night.

As we passed Diamond Head we turned toward Ford Island in a loose formation and were given permission to land. Most of our gauges had been indicating we were running out of fuel for the last 20 minutes.

When we broke formation in preparation for landing, everything in Pearl Harbor opened up on us with their anti-aircraft batteries. The sky was ablaze with gun tracers.

Lt. (j.g.) Fritz Hebel, the squadron commander, took off towards Wheeler Field but was shot down and killed when he tried to land. Ens. Herb Menges crashed and was killed at Pearl City. Ens. Gayle Hermann's plane took a 5-inch shell through his engine, and spun in right on the Ford Island golf course. He survived. Ens. David Flynn bailed out over Barbers Point and we found him 10 days later at Tripler Army Hospital with a broken leg. Ens. Eric Allen was killed by a 50-caliber machine-gun bullet after parachuting from his crippled plane.

I called the Ford Island tower and told them I was coming in. I put my wheels down and headed back right over the harbor about 50 feet over the water.

I roared right past the foretop of the **Nevada**. *They turned all their guns on me but nothing connected.*

Moments later I touched the runway. I overshot. There were two crash trucks in front of me at the end of the runway. I slammed on the brakes and spun around in a full circle on the first green of a golf course just beyond the field.

I taxied back up the field. A Marine gunner sprayed the plane with bullets. He just missed my head.

Of the six planes and pilots I was the only one to land intact; three others were killed.

After this frightening experience, I went to the BOQ to find a bed. I could see and hear the **Arizona** *still burning. I wanted to call my wife who was staying east of Pearl City but assumed that with all the damage around that there would be no telephone service. I picked up the phone anyway, and to my surprise got a dial tone. To my complete surprise I dialed my number and got through to my wife.*

I was the luckiest man in the Navy on Dec. 7, 1941.

Capt. Jim Daniels, Ret.
Kailua, Hawaii

An F4F-4 carrier fighter. This was the type that flew into Ford Island from the *Enterprise* on the night of the attack. USN

The Fleet

The Pride of the Navy

Prewar sailors on the Waikiki Beach.

Ninety-six ships of all types, constituting almost one-half of the U.S. Pacific Fleet, were moored, berthed, anchored, drydocked or under steam at 7:55 a.m. on Sunday, Dec. 7, 1941, at Pearl Harbor. The other half of the fleet was scattered over the Pacific from Alaska to South America and from Wake, Midway and the Samoan islands to shipyards and naval bases on the West Coast of the United States.

Seven of the fleet's nine battleships—*Nevada, Arizona, Tennessee, California, West Virginia, Oklahoma* and *Maryland*—were moored along Battleship Row on the eastern side of Ford Island. The *Pennsylvania*, flagship of the fleet, was in Drydock I in the Navy yard. The only Pacific Fleet battleship not at Pearl was the *Colorado*, undergoing repairs at Puget Sound Navy Yard near Seattle.

Three light cruisers—*St. Louis, Honolulu* and *Helena*—were berthed at the Navy Yard docks and a fourth, the *Phoenix*, was moored northeast of Ford Island.

The light cruisers *Raleigh* and *Detroit* were moored on the western side of Ford Island. Twenty-eight destroyers swung at anchor to the north and west of Ford Island. Three more were being repaired or refitted—the *Downes* and *Cassin* in Drydock I and the *Shaw* in Floating Drydock 2. One destroyer, the *Ward*, patrolled the harbor entrance and the *Helm* was in the main channel, about to turn up the West Loch.

Three submarines were docked at the sub base and a fourth was at 1010 Dock in the Navy Yard.

One gunboat was tied up at a Navy Yard dock, and 20 minelayers were berthed or moored along the Navy Yard docks or at Middle Loch.

Repair ships, oilers, tenders, store ships and tugs were scattered throughout the harbor.

All three Pacific Fleet aircraft carriers were out of port on various assignments. The *Enterprise* of Task Force 8, which included cruisers and destroyers, was returning from Wake Island after delivering Marine Corps fighters and was 200 miles off Oahu when the attack occurred. The *Lexington* of Task Force 12 was en route to Midway Island with a squadron of Marine Corps scout bombers. The *Saratoga* was docked at the San Diego Naval Base. The *Yorktown* and *Hornet* had been transferred earlier to the Atlantic Fleet.

Twelve Cruisers, 36 destroyers and 18 submarines were out of port on Sunday morning.

Newly invented radar equipment had been installed on the *Pennsylvania, California, West Virginia* and the seaplane tender *Curtiss*, but it was not in operation in the harbor because of interference from the mountains surround-

The *Solace*, a new hospital ship, just commissioned on Aug. 9, 1941, was anchored at the north end of Ford Island during the Dec. 7 attack. For the heroic work that day of her doctors, nurses and crew, many of them young women who had never seen anything worse than a traffic accident casualty, the ship was cited by Ad. Chester W. Nimitz and awarded the Navy Unit Citation. This photo was taken about 0800 just as enemy planes were beginning their attack. NA

ing it.

Adm. Kimmel, having no knowledge of the Japanese force steaming toward Oahu, ordered most of the ships operating in the area to return to Pearl for the weekend.

The channel at the entrance to Pearl Harbor was 400 feet wide and 40 to 50 feet deep. It was protected by an outer anti-submarine net reinforced on top with crossed spikes to prevent surface craft from entering the harbor, and an inner net, unreinforced. No anti-torpedo nets were put around the moored battleships.

The facilities at the Navy Yard comprised a repair basin capable of repairing the largest ships afloat, two standard drydocks and a floating drydock. The naval base included the submarine base, a harbor control facility, the Fourteenth Naval District headquarters, the Naval Air Station Ford Island and the headquarters of CINCPACFLT-Commander-in-Chief, Pacific Fleet.

The *Lexington* was ordered as a large battle cruiser in 1917, but her keel was not laid down until 1921. On July 22, when 33 percent complete, she was converted to an aircraft carrier and commissioned Dec. 14, 1927. On Fri., Dec. 5, 1941, she had cleared Pearl Harbor on her way to Midway Island to deliver 18 Vought SB2U-3 Scout Bombers. But the *Lexington* and Task Force 12 turned back for Pearl Harbor when word came of the Japanese attack. They arrived on Dec. 10. USN

The *Enterprise*, the "Big E" of WWII fame. In 1941 she was the flagship of Adm. William "Bull" Halsey. On the morning of Dec. 7, the *Enterprise*, after delivering 12 Grumman F4F-3 fighter planes to Wake Island, was returning to Pearl Harbor with Task Group 8. At 0618, when she was about 250 miles due west of Oahu, she commenced launching 18 Douglas SBD's to scout sectors 150 miles ahead and then fly on to land at NAS, Ford Island. The pilots were unaware they would be flying headlong into the middle of the attacking Japanese Naval Air Fleet. USN

The *Oklahoma* "Oakie," was built by the New York Shipbuilding Corp., Camden. N.J. and commissioned May 2, 1916. Hit by as many as 9 torpedoes on the morning of Dec. 7, the ship capsized within 20 minutes after the attack began with the loss of 415 men. The decision to raise her would become an epic chapter in the history of marine salvage. She was finally raised two years later, in Dec., 1943, but restoration was impractical. She was sold to Moore Drydock Co., Oakland, Calif. She denied the scrappers their due when she sank 540 miles northwest of Oahu while in tow for the West Coast. USN

The *California*, the "Prune Barge," was built by the Mare Island Navy Yard, Vallejo, Calif. and commissioned on Aug. 10, 1921. She was the flagship of Vice Ad. W.S. Pye, Commander, Battle Force in 1941. She sank on an even keel on Dec. 7 from torpedo and bomb damage. The ship was salvaged and on Oct. 10, 1942, under her own power, steamed to the West Coast for repairs and modernization. She rejoined the fleet ready for action in Jan., 1944. On Feb. 14, 1947, her flag was hauled down for the last time at Philadelphia where she was mothballed. She was later sold to Boston Metals Co., Baltimore, MD for $860,000 and broken up for scrap. USN

The *Tennessee*, the "Big Tenn," was built at the New York Navy Yard and commissioned June 3, 1920. *Tennessee* received moderate damage on Dec. 7 and returned to Bremerton, Wash. on Dec. 29, 1941, for permanent repairs. In 1943 she underwent a major rebuilding, emerging a virtually new and modern ship. She earned 10 Battle Stars during the war, seeing action from Pearl Harbor to the final victory. *Tennessee* was placed in reserve at Philadelphia in 1945. In July 1949 she was sold to Bethlehem Steel Corp., Baltimore, and was scrapped. USN

The *West Virginia*, the "Wee Vee," was built by the Newport News Shipbuilding and Drydock Co., Newport News, VA. and was commissioned Dec. 1, 1923. After the Dec. 7 attack, she was left a flaming wreck by nine torpedo hits and two bombs. She settled on the shallow bottom. Raised in May, 1942, and after temporary repairs, departed Pearl Harbor on May 7, 1943 for the West Coast. After a complete overhaul and modernization, she rejoined the fleet and served in the Pacific Theatre from Oct. 1944 through VJ-Day. Her proudest moment came when she sailed into Tokyo Bay with the U.S. Fleet. She was de-commissioned on June 18, 1946 and scrapped in 1951 by Todd Shipyards, Seattle, Wash. USN

The *Nevada*, the "Cheer-up Ship," was built at the Fore River Shipbuilding Co., Quincy, Mass., and commissioned March 11, 1916. She was severely damaged by a hale of bombs as she made her heroic attempt to standout to sea during the attack. Two men, Machinist Donald K. Ross and Chief Bosn. Edwin J. Hill would receive the Medal of Honor for their actions. After repairs and modernization she would serve in both the Atlantic and Pacific Theatres of War. In June, 1946, she was chosen as the target ship for the atomic bomb tests at Operation Crossroads. The ship was painted an embarrassing bright orange to aid recognition for the crew of the bombing plane. She survived the tests and was sunk July 31, 1948, 66 miles south of Oahu. USN

The *Maryland*, "Old Mary," was built by the Newport News Shipbuilding and Drydock Co., Newport News, VA. and commissioned July 21, 1921. On Dec. 7, she received moderate damage from two aerial bomb hits and lost only four men. After repairs and upgrading at a West Coast yard, she rejoined the fleet in Feb. 1942. In the many amphibious campaigns of the Pacific Theatre, the gunfire support of *Maryland* and her sister ships would play a major role. At war's end, on July 15, 1946, she was placed in reserve. She was sold in 1959 and broken up at Todd Shipyards, San Pedro, Calif. USN

The *Pennsylvania*, "Pennsy," was built at the Newport News Shipbuilding and Drydock Co., Newport News, Va., and commissioned June 12, 1916. On the morning of Dec. 7, she was sitting in drydock with her propellers removed. She was moderately damaged by one bomb hit, but lost 24 men. Repaired at Hunter's Point Navy Yard in March 1942, she would serve valiantly in many of the Pacific Island campaigns from the Aleutians to the Philippines. She won a Navy Unit Citation for her exploits. At war's end she was used as a target ship for the Bikini A-bomb tests. She survived and was later sunk off Kwajalein in 1948. USN

The *Arizona* was built at the New York Navy Yard and commissioned Oct. 17, 1916. On the fateful morning of Dec. 7, 1941, she was hit by two 800 kg armor piercing bombs dropped by horizontal bombers from the carriers *Kaga* and *Hirya*. One bomb, at about 0810, penetrated the *Arizona*'s forward magazine and in a tremendous blast virtually destroyed the ship with the tragic loss of 1,177 men. USN

The *Utah* was built at the New York Shipbuilding Co., Camden, NJ and commissioned Aug. 31, 1911. In 1931 Utah was converted to a radio controlled mobile target ship. She became a gunnery training school for the fleet in 1935, fitted out with various 5-inch gun mounts and assorted anti-aircraft weapons. On Dec. 7, she was moored on the west side of Ford Island at a berth normally used by a carrier. Hit early by two torpedoes that caused her to list rapidly, she capsized at 0810. Fifty-four men are still entombed in the *Utah*. One of them, Chief Watertender Peter Tomich, received the Medal of Honor posthumously. The *Utah* was partially righted and now serves as a war memorial at Pearl Harbor. USN

The *Tangier*, a large seaplane tender, commissioned Aug. 25, 1941, was assigned as tender to Patrol Wing Two (Pat Wing 2) based at the Naval Air Station, Ford Island. She was berthed at Fox-11 when the attack began. Her guns were in action by 0800 assisting in the shooting down of three enemy planes that day. The mission of *Tangier* and her brood of PBY-Catalina seaplanes throughout the Pacific Theatre were patrol duties and search and rescue operations. USN

In 1941, the *Oglala*, a minelayer, was the flagship of Adm. William R. Furlong, in Command of Minecraft, Battleforce. On Dec. 7, she was moored outboard of the cruiser *Helena* at 1010 Dock. A torpedo explosion on the *Helena* and a near miss by a bomb ruptured *Oglala*'s hull, causing extensive flooding. The ship was moved astern of *Helena* where she later capsized. She was salvaged in December 1942 and was restored to active duty in 1944 as an engine repair ship. USN

The *Raleigh*, a light cruiser, was built by the Bethlehem Steel Co., Quincy, Mass., and commissioned Feb. 6, 1924. In the opening minutes of the attack Dec. 7 she was hit portside, amidship by a torpedo from the *Hiryu/Soryu* Air Group. The ship began to list rapidly and it was feared she might capsize, but valiant damage control efforts of her crew saved the ship. *Raleigh* earned three Battle Stars in WWII. She was sold for scrap at Philadelphia in February 1946. USN

The light cruiser *Phoenix* was commissioned Oct. 3, 1938, at the Philadelphia Navy Yard. The ship luckily, was not damaged in the attack. She would go on to earn nine battlestars for her wartime service. At war's end she was decommissioned and placed in the reserve fleet. She was transferred in 1951 to Argentina and renamed *General Belgrano* in 1956. She was sunk by the submarine HMS *Conqueror* on May 2, 1982, during the Falkland Island War with Great Britain. USN

St. Louis, the "Lucky Lou," was built by the Newport News Shipbuilding and Drydock Co. and was commissioned May 19, 1939. The ship was docked outboard of *Honolulu* at the Navy Yard for overhaul on Dec. 7. Undamaged during the attack, she moved away from the pier at 0931 and headed for South Channel and the open sea. As the ship cleared the harbor entrance, a midget sub fired two torpedoes that just missed and exploded on a coral reef 200 yards from the *St. Louis*. Decommissioned June 20, 1946, she was transferred to the Brazilian Navy on Jan. 29, 1951 and renamed *Tamandare*. She was stricken in 1975. USN

Shaw was commissioned Sept. 18, 1936, and was in the floating drydock for repairs along with the yard tug *Sotoyomo*. *Shaw* took three bomb hits at about 0850 and blew up in a spectacular explosion at 0930 that also sunk the *Sotoyomo* and the drydock. *Shaw*'s stern structure was salvaged and fitted with a temporary bow. On Feb. 9, 1942, she steamed to the West Coast for a complete rebuilding. *Shaw* earned 11 Battlestars and was scrapped in 1947. USN

The *Allen*, last of the Pre-World War I destroyers, was recommissioned Dec. 9, 1940. She joined the *Ward Chew* and *Schley* to form Destroyer Division 80 based at Pearl Harbor. *Allen* was moored between the *Chew* and the ex-*Baltimore* at Buoy X-Ray 5 in the East Loch and was not damaged in the attack. *Allen* would operate in the Hawaiian area for the duration of the war until she was scrapped in 1946. USN

The *Honolulu*, the "Blue Goose," was built by the New York Navy Yard and commissioned on June 15, 1938. During the Dec. 7 attack she suffered severe flooding from her hull as the result of a near miss by a 250 kg. bomb that exploded less than 20 feet away. She was repaired by Jan. 12, 1942, and would go on to earn eight Battlestars and a Navy Unit Citation. She was decommissioned Feb. 3, 1947, at Philadelphia and sold for scrap in 1949. USN

Monaghan (DD-354), with Lt. Cmdr. William P. Burford in command, was the Ready Duty destroyer on Dec. 7 and got underway at 0827 hours. As the ship proceeded down the west side of Ford Island, the *Curtiss* signaled the destroyer of the presence of a submarine in the harbor. *Monaghan* rammed the sub and dropped two depth charges, sinking the intruder. *Monaghan* was lost on Dec. 18, 1944, when she capsized in the fury of typhoon "Cobra" off the Philippines. USN

Downes (DD-375) was on blocks alongside the *Cassin* (DD-372) in Drydock #1, forward of the *Pennsylvania*. At approximately 0850 a group of Aichi D3A1 dive bombers of Lt. Cmdr. Takashige Egusa's air group concentrated their attack on the drydock area and the *Nevada* moving down the channel. The *Downes* was virtually destroyed by three 250-kg. bombs. Vital machinery and equipment was all that could be salvaged. These would be installed in a new hull and by November 1943, the resurrected *Downes* was ready for sea duty. USN

Whitney, a destroyer tender, was built by the Boston Navy Yard, and commissioned on Sept. 2, 1924. On Dec. 7, she was moored at Anchorage X-ray 8 in East Loch. She was supplying steam, electricity and fresh water to her nest of ships of Destroyer Division Six, the *Conyngham* DD-357, *Tucker* DD-374, *Case* DD-370, *Selfridge* DD-357 and *Reid* DD-369 tied up alongside. These ships opened fire at the attacking aircraft by 0804. The *Whitney* was scrapped in 1948. USN

The *Neosho* (AO-23), a large fleet oiler, arrived at Pearl Harbor on Dec. 6, 1941, to offload a cargo of high octane aviation fuel at the Naval Air Station, Ford Island. Luckily, the ship was not hit during the attack. Her explosive cargo would have posed a more serious peril to the already devastated ships of Battleship Row. *Neosho* was with Task Force 17 at the Battle of the Coral Sea and was sunk by enemy aircraft on May 8, 1942. USN

Curtiss, a large seaplane tender, commissioned Nov. 15, 1940, was moored off the entrance to Middle Loch. At 0836 she spotted a midget submarine and commenced firing. The sub launched a torpedo that missed the *Curtiss* and hit a dock at Pearl City. *Curtiss* scored a direct hit with her 5-inch gun through the sub's conning tower. The destroyer *Monaghan* finished off the sub a few minutes later. USN

The *Helena* hoisted her commission pennant at the New York Navy Yard on Sept. 18, 1939. She was assigned to the Pacific Fleet in 1940. On Dec. 7 she was moored at the Navy Yard's 1010 Dock, a berth normally assigned to the battleship *Pennsylvania*. Three minutes into the attack, the *Helena* was hit amidships by a single torpedo that passed underneath the minelayer *Oglala* that was tied up alongside. The ship did not sink and continued firing her antiaircraft guns until the attack was over. The *Helena* was lost on the night of July 6, 1943, in the Battle of Kula Gulf during the Solomon Islands campaign. EA

Avocet (AVP-4), a small seaplane tender, was moored on the east side of Ford Island at the Naval Air Station dock (near Fox 1A). She opened fire immediately. An early round from her 3-inch, .50-caliber antiaircraft gun scored a hit on a Japanese torpedo plane attempting to evade after launching a torpedo at the *California*. The aircraft burst into flames and crashed in the vicinity of the Naval Hospital. EA

The *Tern* (AM-31), a "Bird"-Class minesweeper of World War I vintage, was moored at the end of 1010 Dock inboard of the yard oiler YO-30. Able to get underway by 0943, *Tern* moved into the harbor and rescued 47 men from the oily waters. She then fought fires continuously on the blazing *West Virginia* and *Arizona* for the next 48 hours until the fires were under control. USN

Moored at the Coast Guard Base in 1941 at Honolulu was the CG-8, a former rumrunner of the prohibition era. Astern of her is the USCG *Kukui*, a buoy tender. The Coast Guard Base was not bombed by the Japanese attackers. EA

The *Pelias* (AS-14) was originally the *S.S. Mormacyork*, a C-3 freighter for the Moore-McCormick Steamship Lines. The ship was acquired by the U.S. Navy for conversion to a submarine tender and was the Navy's newest ship at Pearl Harbor having commissioned on Sept. 5, 1941. Tied up at the sub base, the ship was not damaged during the attack. *Pelias* was sold in 1971. USN

The *Rigel* of 1922, a repair ship, was berthed at the Navy Yard repair basin for an extensive refit and conversion. On the day of the attack her superstructure was incomplete and covered with scaffolding. Her crew, unable to fire at the attackers because there was no armament on board the vessel, assisted other ships in rescue and salvage work. *Rigel* received minor damage and returned to service on April 7, 1942. USN

WAR EXTRA! WAR EXTRA! WAR EXTRA!
U. S. FLEET IN ACTION
Destroyers Attack Jap Raiders
104 DIE IN HAWAII
Seattle Post-Intelligencer
SUNRISE EDITION
SEATTLE, MONDAY, DECEMBER 8, 1941
All Military Posts In Seattle Region Go on War Basis
JAPS DECLARE TWO AMERICAN WARSHIPS SUNK
WAR EXTRA
WAR DECLARED!
U. S. FLEET SAILS!
BATTLESHIP BOMBED
2ND RAID ON HONOLULU!
The Seattle Daily Times
America's Best Evening Newspaper
SEATTLE, WASHINGTON, MONDAY, DECEMBER 8, 1941.
3RD SUNDAY EXTRA!
PRICE FIVE CENTS
MANDAN
TODAY'S NEWS TODAY
PRICE FIVE CENTS
MANDAN, NORTH DAKOTA
U.S. CONGRESS DECLARES WAR
3000 Casualties In Hawaii
Only One Vote Cast Against War With Japan--Manila Heavily Bombed Today
Several Jap Planes And Submarines Destroyed Active Fighting Continues
Reinforcements Being Rushed To Islands--Planes From Frisco Arrived While Attack Was In Progress--Attacking Planes Came From Carriers Which Are Being Sought By Navy
Terrific Damage Is Reported In Air Raid On Manila -- Nichols Airfield Is Target -- Gasoline Supplies Burning -- Guam Is Reported Ablaze
Battle In Pacific Flames Over Wide Area -- Britain Takes Quick Action And Declares War -- Losses Reported At Singapore And Hongkong -- Thailand Sues For Peace

Japanese Midget Submarines

The Objective Was Not Accomplished

Ens. Kazuo Sakamaki's abandoned Type A midget submarine aground at Waimanalo Bay, approx. 600 yards from Bellows Field, about 40 miles from Pearl Harbor on the morning of Dec. 8. Ens. Sakamaki's sub was one of five that formed the "Special Attack Unit." They were transported to within 10 miles south of Pearl Harbor, each secured to the deck of an I-Class mother submarine. They were released at midnight on Dec. 6-7 and would attempt to gain entry through the nets protecting the harbor entrance. USN

The most bizarre element of the Pearl Harbor attack was the use of midget submarines. They were employed, despite the skepticism of several Japanese admirals, in the hope that they could damage inner-harbor ships that the attacking planes missed. As it turned out, the mini-subs constituted Japan's only failure in the remarkably successful surprise attack that crippled the United States fleet.

Having experimented with midget submarines since the 1930s, the Japanese Navy had developed them well enough to convince Yamamoto himself to employ five in the Pearl Harbor attack. Five I Class submarines, the largest in the Japanese fleet, were hastily fitted to carry the midget Type A subs aft of their conning towers in piggyback fashion. The group was designated the Special Attack Unit.

Since the midgets were driven by small electric motors with short-lived batteries, they had to be launched close to their targets. Eighty feet long, six feet in diameter at their widest point and displacing 46 tons, each boat carried two 18-inch torpedoes and was controlled by a two-man crew. Top speed was 23 knots on the surface, 19 knots submerged.

On Nov. 25, 1941, five I Class submarines and their attached midget subs left Kure Naval Base for the Hawaiian Islands. Slowed by their 46-ton cargo, the group did not follow the carrier strike force route to the north, but instead set a direct course for Pearl Harbor.

The larger submarines were to approach within 10 miles of Pearl Harbor, fan out before the entrance and launch their midget submarines early on the morning of Dec. 7. The mother boats would then retire west of Lanai Island where they would pick up the midgets that returned from the attack.

For their part, the midgets would penetrate Pearl Harbor, sail counterclockwise around Ford Island and launch their torpedoes at the capital ships when the air attack began.

From the moment of launching, nothing went right.

Because of an inoperative gyrocompass, the midget from I-24 lost its way, drifting around the other side of Oahu and finally beaching itself on a coral reef off Bellows Field on the night of the 7th. Ens. Kazuo Sakamaki, the submarine's commander, attempted to blow up his boat, but it was captured intact. Both crewmen tried to swim ashore,

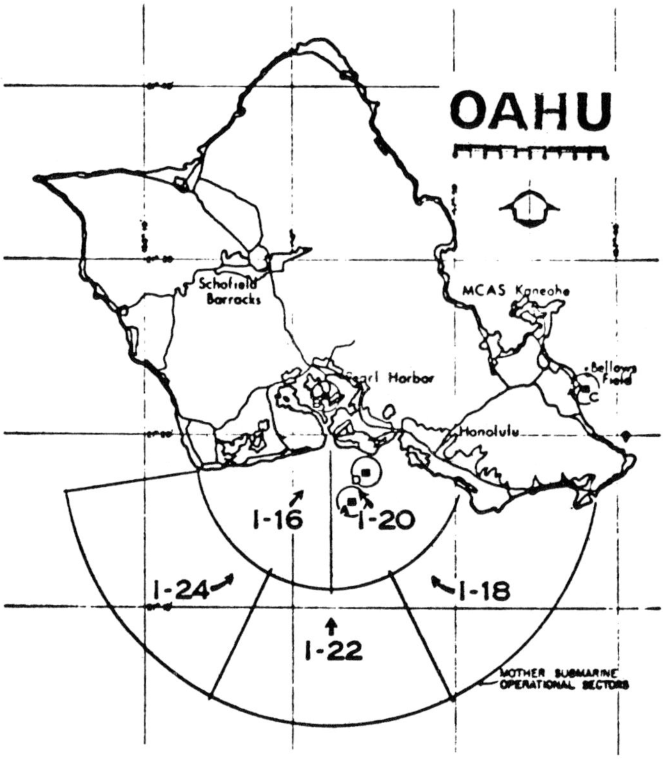

Operational sectors of the five I-Class submarines around the entrance to Pearl Harbor at the time of the attack.

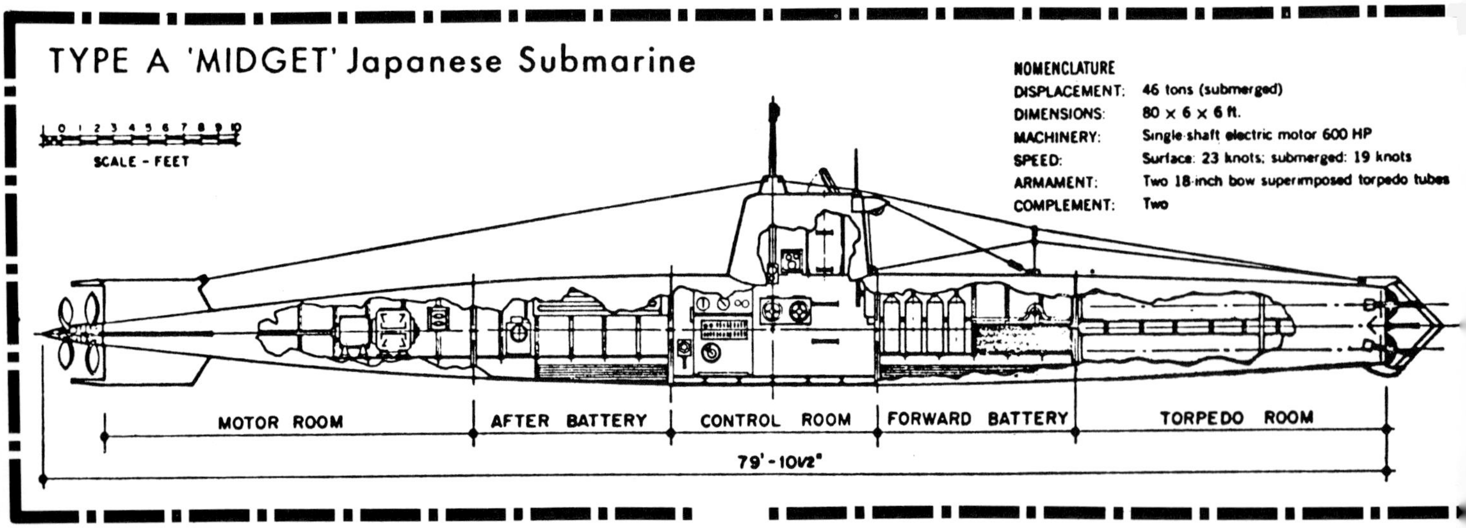

but only Sakamaki made it. He was captured—America's first Japanese prisoner of the Second World War.

Another midget was sighted outside the harbor by the destroyer U.S.S. *Ward* one hour before the air attack. Shelled, depth-charged and sunk in 1,200 feet of water, the little sub became the first Japanese casualty of the Pearl Harbor attack.

One midget did penetrate the harbor and was sighted by the seaplane tender U.S.S. *Curtiss* after the air attack had begun. The submarine launched a torpedo at the *Curtiss*, but it missed the tender and instead struck a dock at Pearl City. The sub also fired a torpedo at the U.S.S. *Monaghan*, which was racing to clear the harbor, but the shot missed and the destroyer rammed, depth-charged, and finally sunk the Japanese boat. It was raised after the attack and used as fill material for a new pier at the submarine base at Pearl.

The fourth midget was apparently sunk outside the harbor by depth charges after she fired torpedoes at the U.S.S. *St. Louis*. In 1960, she was accidentally discovered by Navy SCUBA diver trainees and brought to the surface by the U.S.S. *Current*. Because no human remains were found inside the boat, it was surmised that the crew might have escaped alive, swam to shore and assimilated into the Japanese population on Oahu.* The boat later was transferred to the Japanese Navy and is now on display at the Maritime Self-Defense Force Service School at Eta Jima, Japan.

The last midget is presumed to have been sunk outside the harbor on the 7th or 8th. Several American destroyers reported attacking enemy subs on those days.

Thus, all five midget submarines and their crewmen were lost. The Special Attack Unit inflicted no damage on the American fleet.

*There has been no evidence to prove this supposition.

Nine of the midget submariners who attempted to attack Pearl Harbor painted on silk by an unknown Japanese artist. The tenth, Kazuo Sakamaki, was stricken from Japanese records and officially ceased to exist. Names, left to right were: PO 1/c Yoshio Katayama, PO 1/c Naoshi Sasaki, PO 1/c Shigenori Yokoyama, Sub. Lt. Masaji Yokoyama, Lt. Naoji Iwasa, Sub. Lt. Shigemi Furuno, Ens. Akiro Hirowo, PO 2/c Sadamu Ueda and PO 2/c Kioshi Inagaki. USN

A Japanese I-Class submarine, with one of the midget submarines on its deck, heads toward its launch site near Pearl Harbor. DRAWING BY PAUL BENDER

Mother Sub	Captain	Midget Sub Captain	Midget Sub Crewman
I-16	Commander Isao Yamada	Sub Lieutenant Masaji Yokoyama	PO 2/c Sadamu Ueda
I-18	Commander Seikyo Ohtani	Sub Lieutenant Shigemi Furuno	PO 1/c Shigenori Yokoyama
I-20	Commander Takashi Yamada	Ensign Akiro Hirowo	PO 1/c Yoshio Katayama
I-22	Commander Kiyashi Yoda	Lieutenant Naoji Iwasa	PO 1/c Naoshi Sasaki
I-24	Commander Yoshita Hanabusa	Ensign Kazuo Sakamaki	PO 2/c Kioshi Inagaki

"Flank Speed An' Ram It"
USS *Monaghan* DD-354

On Sat., Dec. 6, 1941, the *Monaghan* had the "Ready Duty," meaning all hands had to be on board, steam up in two boilers, engines warm and jacking over and all navigational and communications equipment energized and operating. At approximately 0645 on the morning of Dec. 7, 1941, the *Monaghan* got orders to get underway and proceed outside the entrance of Pearl Harbor to assist the USS *Ward*, which had sighted a submarine in restricted waters. Reveille was held immediately and all hands manned their Special Sea Detail stations. My Special Sea Detail Station, as well as my Battle Station, was in the Interior Communications Room, located under the Bridge, as far down in the ship as you could go.

I proceeded to my station—there was very little to do since all systems were ready to get underway. Lines were singled up and as we were ready to back out of the nest, orders came through to cancel. We later learned that the *Ward* had sighted another Japanese midget submarine and had sunk it. Since we were to be relieved of the Ready Duty at 0800, the Captain ordered all systems be secured and set up for the regular port watch.

After securing the gyrocompass, navigational and communications equipment, I went up on the main deck to await breakfast due at 0800. After a few minutes on deck, we could first hear, then see, low flying airplanes coming in from the north. As they got closer, we could see the Japanese insignia on the wings and fuselage and also the torpedo slung under the belly of the plane. Instinctively, we knew this was an attack and all hands rushed immediately to their Battle Stations.

I proceeded to the Interior Communication Room and began energizing all systems which had been secured only a few minutes earlier. Obviously, I could not see anything from my station, but I did have communication with all major stations and could hear what was going on. We were able to get underway very quickly since all main propulsion systems were still warm.

As we were proceeding down the back side of Ford Island, a lookout reported a submarine conning tower almost dead ahead. The Captain ordered the forward guns to fire, but they could not be depressed low enough. He then ordered the helm to aim and ram the submarine. At about this time, a lookout reported that the sub had fired a torpedo at us. The torpedo ran parallel to us and we later learned it had traveled across the bay and mired in the mud but did not explode. We made contact with the submarine, orders were given for the engines to back full (so we would not run on the beach) and to drop two depth charges. Between the ramming and depth charges, the sub never had a chance. Of course, while all this was going on we were constantly firing at the Japanese planes.

After backing away from the beach, we proceeded out of Pearl Harbor and ultimately several other ships joined us. We were constantly sounding for submarines and did get some contacts and dropped several depth charges.

We remained at sea until about noon Wed., Dec. 9, 1941. We returned to Pearl Harbor to take on fuel, ammunition and supplies. At that time I was able to see the devastation of the fleet. It really made your heart sink but increased your determination to win the war. We left early that same evening with a task force and the USS *Enterprise*.

Bill London

The U.S.S. *Ward* puts a shell through the conning tower of a midget submarine attempting to slip into Pearl Harbor. More than an hour before the air raid began, the *Ward* sent the message "We have attacked, fired upon, and dropped depth charges upon submarine operating in defensive sea area. . . ." Paul Bender

Monuments in front of the club at Bellows Field commemorating the beaching and capture of the Japanese midget submarine.

Flags found in Ensign Kazuo Sakamaki's captured midget submarine. The large flag is probably Sakamaki's personal one. To the right is the Japanese naval ensign. The U.S. flag was intended to confuse any observers if the submarine was spotted. NA 80-G-13033

The midget submarine beached near Bellows Field on the east end of Oahu on the night of Dec. 7. The next day the sub was towed up to the beach, separated into three sections (it was bolted together) and trucked to Subase at Pearl Harbor where all its vital equipment was removed for study and then put back together. USN

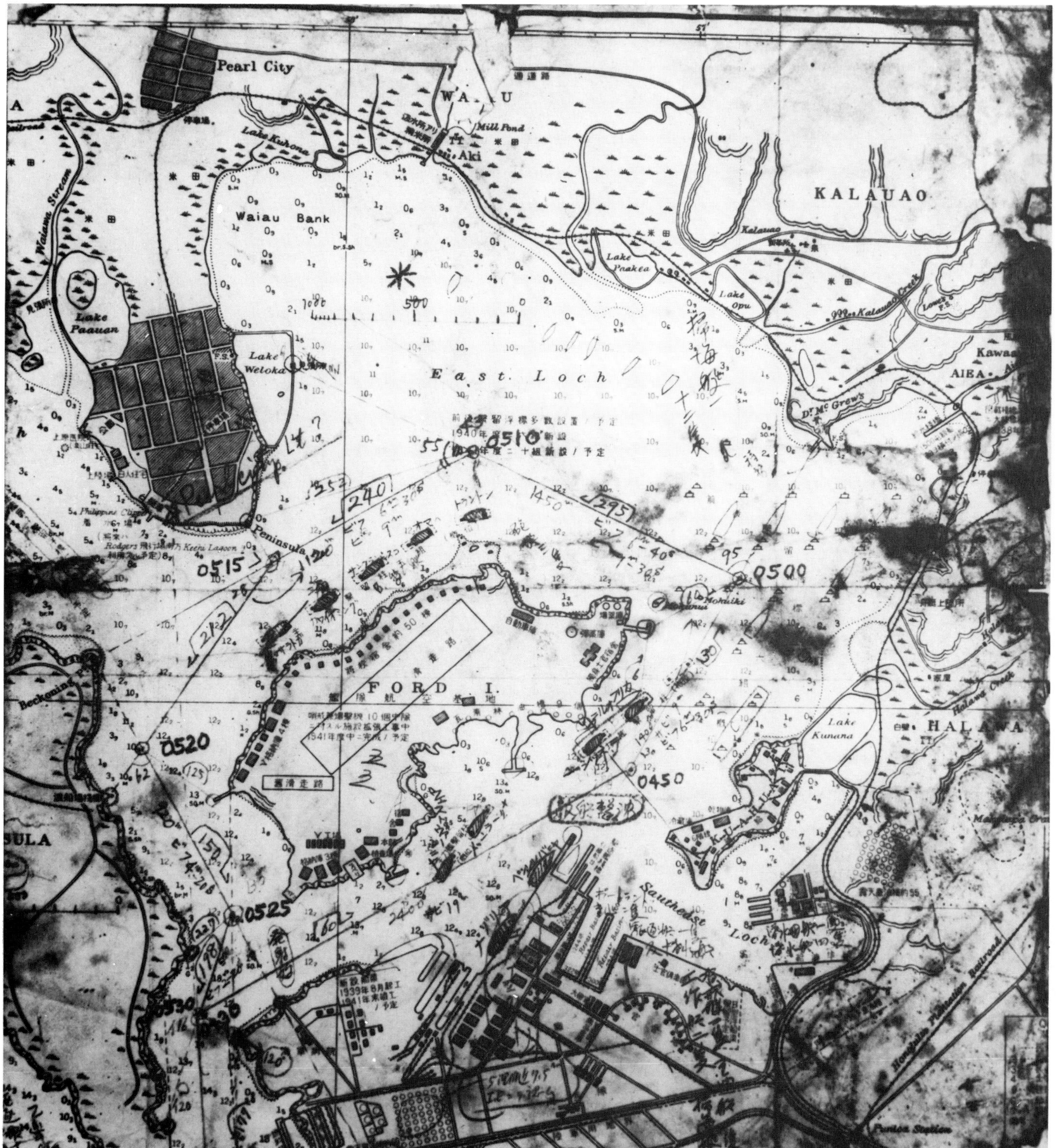

A captured Japanese chart of Pearl Harbor, found in Ensign Kazuo Sakamaki's Type "A" midget submarine that beached near Bellows Field after several unsuccessful attempts to enter Pearl Harbor. NA 80-G-413507

TOP: Conning tower of the Japanese midget submarine that was forced to beach at Bellows Field on the eastern shore of Oahu on Dec. 8. BOTTOM: Midget sub's control room, showing gyrocompass whose malfunction caused the vessel to miss the Pearl Harbor entrance. USN

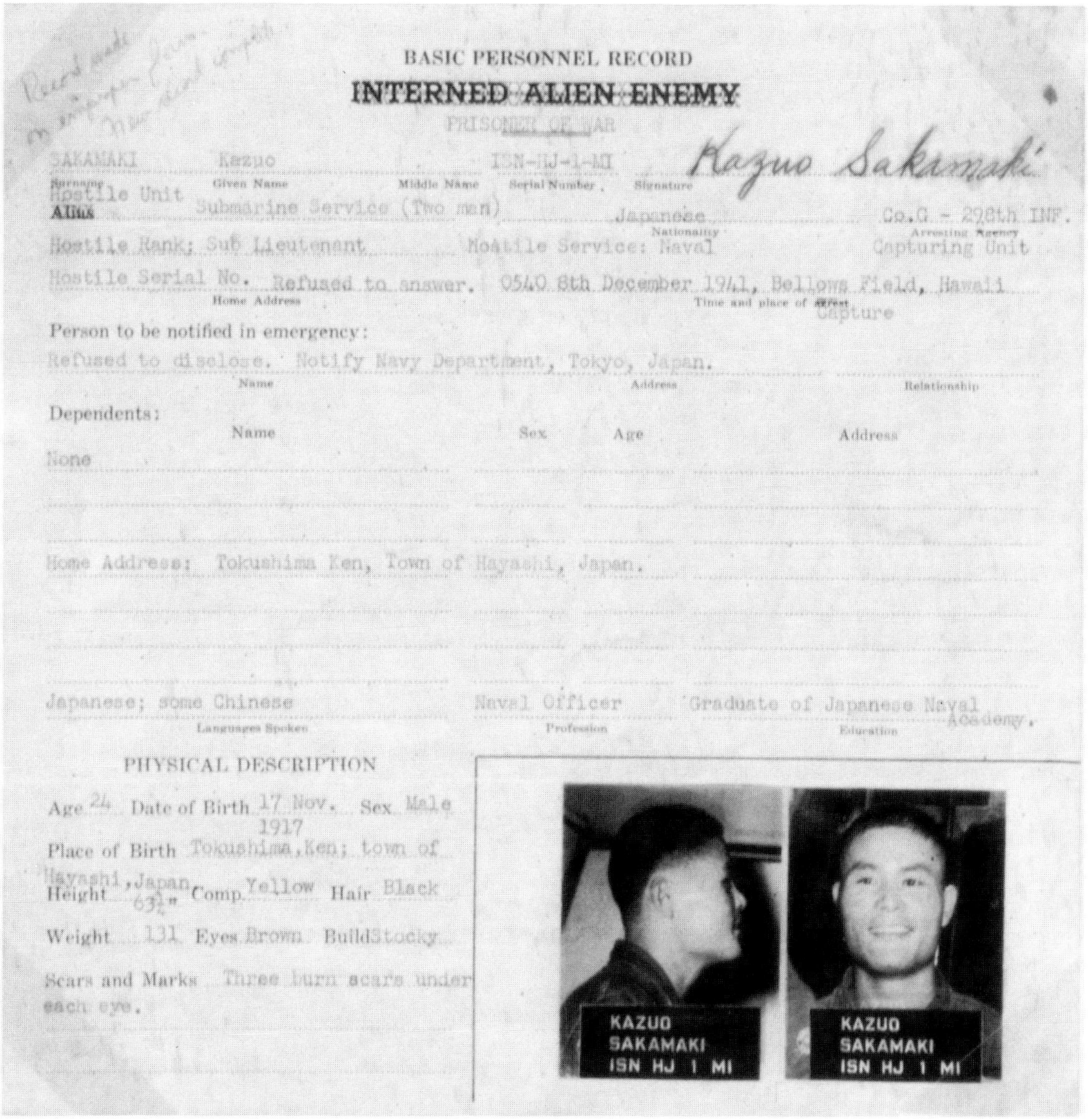

BASIC PERSONNEL RECORD

~~INTERNED ALIEN ENEMY~~

PRISONER OF WAR

Record made on improper form. New record complete.

SAKAMAKI (Surname) — Kazuo (Given Name) — (Middle Name) — ISN-HJ-1-MI (Serial Number) — *Kazuo Sakamaki* (Signature)

Hostile Unit (Alias): Submarine Service (Two man) — Japanese (Nationality) — Co. G - 298th INF. (Arresting Agency) Capturing Unit

Hostile Rank: Sub Lieutenant — Hostile Service: Naval

Hostile Serial No. Refused to answer. (Home Address) — 0540 8th December 1941, Bellows Field, Hawaii (Time and place of Capture)

Person to be notified in emergency:

Refused to disclose. Notify Navy Department, Tokyo, Japan. (Name / Address / Relationship)

Dependents:

Name	Sex	Age	Address
None			

Home Address: Tokushima Ken, Town of Hayashi, Japan.

Japanese; some Chinese (Languages Spoken) — Naval Officer (Profession) — Graduate of Japanese Naval Academy. (Education)

PHYSICAL DESCRIPTION

Age 24 Date of Birth 17 Nov. 1917 Sex Male

Place of Birth Tokushima Ken; town of Hayashi, Japan

Height 63½" Comp. Yellow Hair Black

Weight 131 Eyes Brown Build Stocky

Scars and Marks Three burn scars under each eye.

KAZUO SAKAMAKI ISN HJ 1 MI

KAZUO SAKAMAKI ISN HJ 1 MI

Prisoner of War report for Kazuo Sakamaki, U.S. Prisoner of War No. 1.

Ensign Kazuo Sakamaki before the Pearl Harbor attack.

Mr. Kazuo Sakamaki and one of his captors the night of Dec. 7, former Lt. Steve Weiner of Los Angeles, meet for the first time in 50 years at the Admiral Nimitz Museum in May 1991. Mr. Sakamaki went to work for the Toyota Motor Company after the war, eventually becoming president of Toyota of Brazil. He is now retired in Japan.

COURTESY ADMIRAL NIMITZ MUSEUM.

The sub was brought to Wilmington, Del., on April 1943.
DELAWARE STATE ARCHIVES

Ensign Kazuo Sakamaki's captured midget submarine on display in New York City's Times Square for a war bond drive. The submarine toured cities in 41 states around the country to help sell war bonds for America's war effort. It was mounted on a trailer and had 22 small windows installed around the hull with two mannequins dressed as Japanese sailors inside. EA

HA 19, America's first war prize, on temporary exhibit at the Admiral Nimitz Museum State Historical Park in Fredricksburg, Texas (1991). After its capture the sub was put on display at Subase Pearl Harbor and then taken to the mainland where it spent the war years touring the country, promoting war bond sales. At the end of the war it wound up in Chicago and eventually was sent to the submarine base in Key West, Fla. In 1964 it was put on display at the Lighthouse Museum in Key West. In 1991, it was moved to the Admiral Nimitz Museum. It will be placed on permanent display at Pearl Harbor in the future.
ADMIRAL NIMITZ MUSEUM

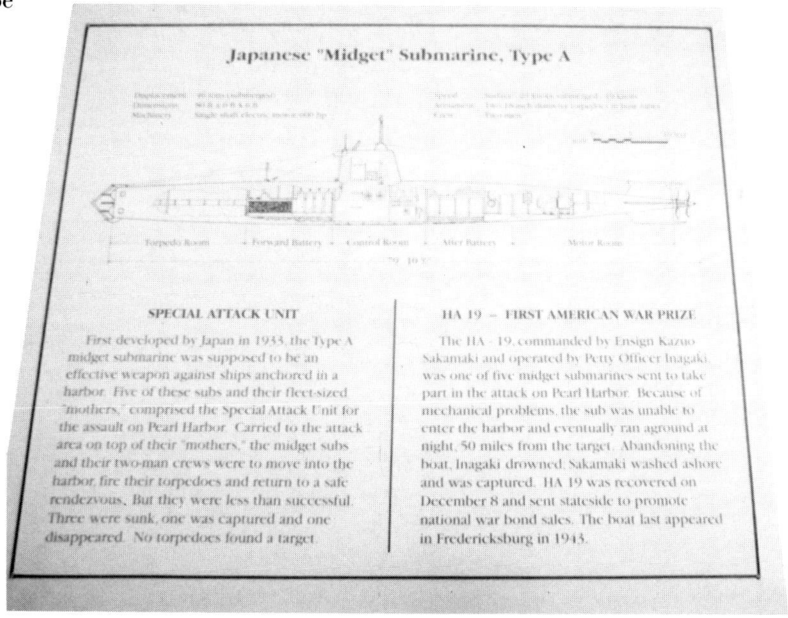

On June 13, 1960, a Navy scuba diver, SK/1 C.F. Buhl, discovered a midget submarine 75 feet below the surface of Keehi Lagoon, about four miles from the entrance to Pearl Harbor. The next day, *Current* was assigned the task of recovery and brought the sub to the Naval Base. The live torpedo section was removed for disposal at sea. The remainder of the submarine was returned at the request of the Japanese government and is now a war memorial at Eta Jima, Japan's Naval Academy. USN

The remains of the midget sub that entered the harbor on the morning of the Dec. 7 attack. It was rammed, depth charged and sunk by the *Monaghan*. The sub was salvaged two weeks later. Officials decided to use the sub as land fill material for a new pier at the submarine base. A military funeral was given by the U.S. Navy for the Japanese two-man crew, still aboard, before she was buried. NH 54302

The First Shot

The first shot of World War II for the United States can be credited to an old World War I "four-piper" destroyer, the U.S.S. *Ward*. Her skipper, Lt. William W. Outerbridge, had just taken command on Dec. 5, and most of her crewmen were reservists from St. Paul, Minn., who had been on the ship less than a year.

At 3:32 a.m. on Dec, 7, four U.S. minesweepers were routinely searching for magnetic mines off the Pearl Harbor entrance when one of them, the Condor, sighted the conning tower of a submarine 50 yards off her bow. The harbor's submarine net had been opened to let in the Condor. As all American submarines were to surface before entering the harbor, any submerged vessel was to be considered hostile. Not equipped to attack a sub, the Condor notified the *Ward*, which was patrolling in the area: SIGHTED SUBMARINE ON WESTERLY COURSE SPEED FIVE KNOTS. The *Ward* began a search, but made no contact.

Hours passed without incident. Then, at 6:30 a.m., a patrolling PBY seaplane spotted a submerged object approaching the harbor entrance, whose sub net had been opened to allow several U.S. vessels to enter.

At 6:40 a.m. the *Ward* also made contact and sounded general quarters. Five minutes later she opened fire on the enemy sub at a range of 100 yards. The first shot missed, but No. 3 Gun scored a direct hit on the conning tower. When the sub dove, the *Ward* dropped four depth charges, and the PBY several more. it was assumed that the two-man vessel sank in 1,200 feet of water.

A message was sent to the commandant, at 6-53 a.m.: WE HAVE ATTACKED, FIRED UPON, AND DROPPED DEPTH

Condor, the minesweeper that spotted the Japanese midget submarine off the entrance to Pearl Harbor and notified the destroyer *Ward*.

CHARGING IN DEFENSIVE SEA AREA. STAND BY FOR FURTHER MESSAGES.

The duty-ready destroyer U.S.S. *Monaghan*, inside the harbor, was ordered to the scene to investigate, but she did not get under way until after the 7:55 a.m. attack had begun.

Thus, one hour before the surprise air raid the fleet had some warning of the impending attack, but owing to message-decoding delays and the relaxed atmosphere that prevailed on this Sunday morning, no mobilization occurred.

Exactly three years later to the day, the *Ward* was sunk by a Kamikaze plane off Leyte in the Philippines. No. 3 Gun, which fired the war's first American shot, had earlier been removed during the ship's conversion to a high-speed transport. It was placed on the grounds of the Minnesota State Capitol in St. Paul in 1958, in celebration of Minnesota's Centennial.

The *Ward*, a World War I destroyer, was recommissioned Feb. 13, 1941, after 20 years in the reserve fleet. The morning of Dec. 7, with Lt. William W. Outerbridge in command, she was on patrol outside the harbor entrance. At 0645 she fired at and dropped four depth charges on a midget submarine as it attempted to sneak into Pearl Harbor an hour before the first wave of the Japanese Air Fleet began their attack. The *Ward* was lost Dec. 7, 1944, in the Philippines in an enemy air attack. USN

Ward's number three four-inch gun on the lawn of the Minnesota state capitol, St. Paul. This gun fired the first shot in the war for the United States as the *Ward* attacked a Japanese submarine trying to enter Pearl Harbor behind the supply ship *Antares*. Eighty-five of *Ward*'s 119-man crew were Naval Reservists from the St. Paul, Minn., area. MINNESOTA HISTORICAL SOCIETY

Aerial Activity

America's First Air Heroes

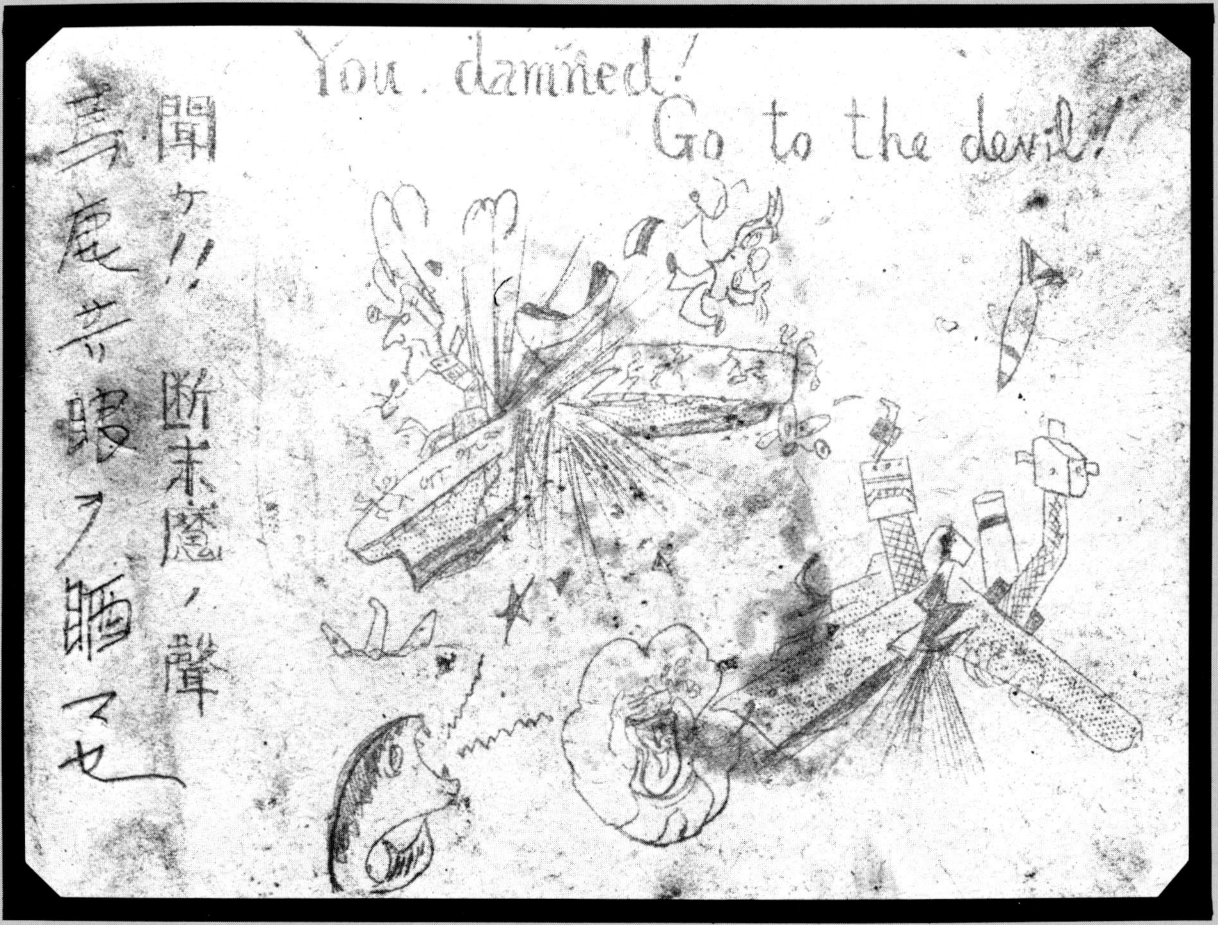

A Japanese drawing found on a dive bomber shot down during the attack. Translated it says, "Hear! The voice of the moment of death. Wake up you fools." NA 80-G-32891

Pearl Harbor remains as the classic example of a tragic result of a nation's unpreparedness. The popular historical emphasis on the destruction of the Pacific Fleet battleships and the general chaos of the event has led to confusion and neglect in the chronicling of the American air response to the Japanese attack. The Japanese strike plan included initial attacks on all the air bases which resulted in American air interference with Japanese sorties over Battleship Row being nil. The Japanese strategy was so successful that only token aerial resistance was met rendering their carriers and returning aircraft safe from counterattack.

The Japanese launched 353 aircraft (three aborted on take-off) in two attack forces from six carriers (*Akagi*, *Kaga*, *Soryu*, *Hiryu*, *Shokaku* and *Zuikaku*). The first attack wave, led by Lt. Cmdr. Mitsuo Fuchida, consisted of 185 aircraft of which 89 were to attack the U.S. Pacific Fleet while the remainder were to attack the airfields. Forty-five A6M2 "Zero" fighters of the "Air Control Force" under Lt. Cmdr. Shigeru Itaya were to gain air superiority and then strafe the fields: Ford Island (USN), Wheeler (USAAF), Hickam (USAAF), Kaneohe (USN), Ewa (USMC), and Bellows (USAAF). The Zeros were followed by 51 Type 99 Aichi D3A1 "Val" dive-bombers under Lt. Cmdr. Kakuichi Takahashi. Each Val was to drop a single 550 lb. bomb on hangars and aircraft on the ground at Ford Island (9), Hickam (17), and Wheeler (25).

The Japanese aerial armada passed off Kahuku Point, north Oahu at 0740 proceeding over the Army air field at Haleiwa at 0749. Japanese intelligence had overlooked this auxiliary field on the northern coast. The 47th Pursuit Squadron, 15th Fighter Group, from Wheeler Field was using the field for gunnery practice and had P-40s, P-36s and a few obsolete P-26s there. At 0755–0800, the six U.S. Air Bases were attacked with devastating results. Kaneohe was attacked by eleven Zeros destroying 26 and damaging a PBY Catalina patrol bomber (three were out on patrol). At Ford Island, 9 Vals damaged or destroyed 33 of 70 aircraft. At Ewa, the 49 Marine aircraft which were parked wingtip-to-wingtip to protect against sabotage were easy targets for the strafing Hiryu Zeros, which came in over the mountains to destroy 33 aircraft. At Hickam, 18 Zeros and 17 Vals attacked from different quadrants, first attacking the parked aircraft, knocking out 18 of 30, and then the hangar line. Wheeler was strafed by eight Zeros and then attacked by 25 Vals which dropped 250 kg. bombs from 200-250 feet. A total of 43 of 83 aircraft were destroyed and 29 others damaged. At 0830 a single Zero strafed Bellows damaging three of 12 fighters there.

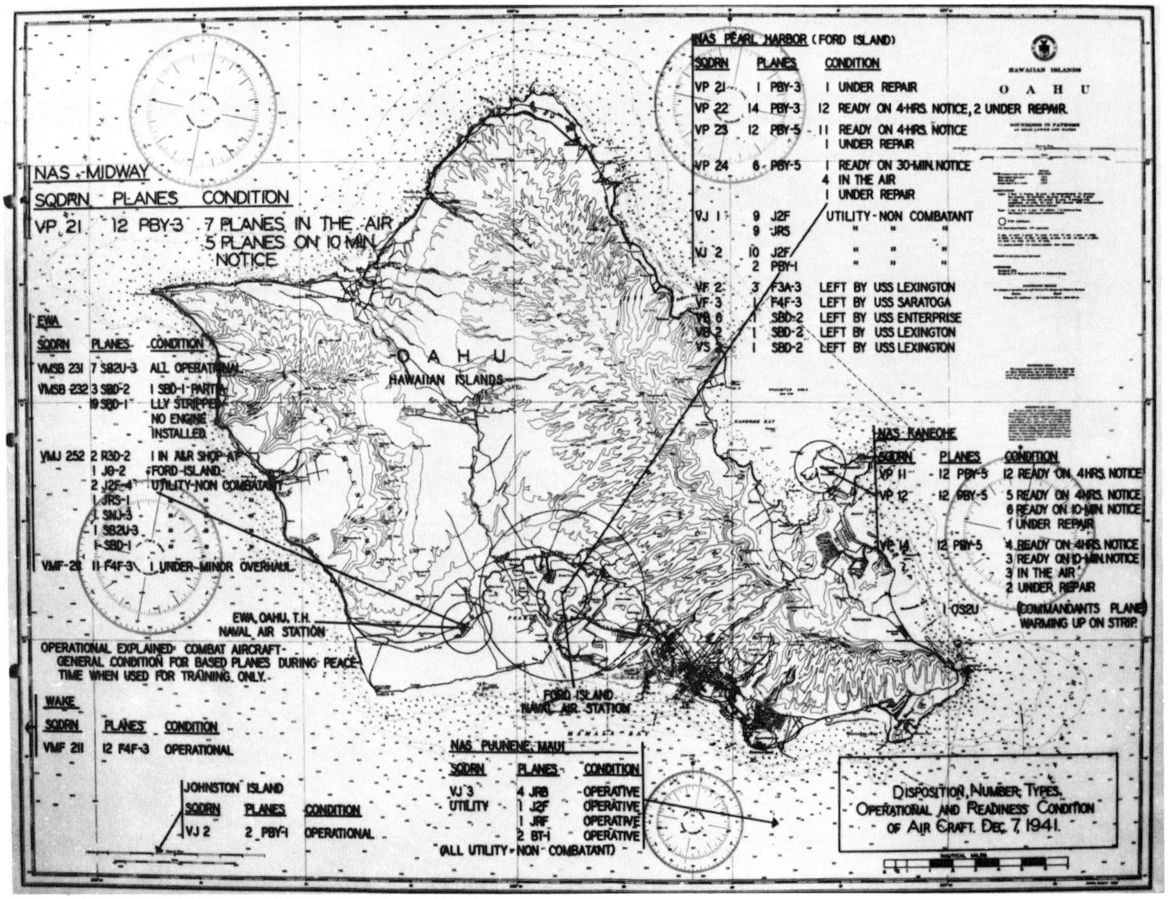

DEPLOYMENT OF JAPANESE AIRCRAFT OVER OAHU

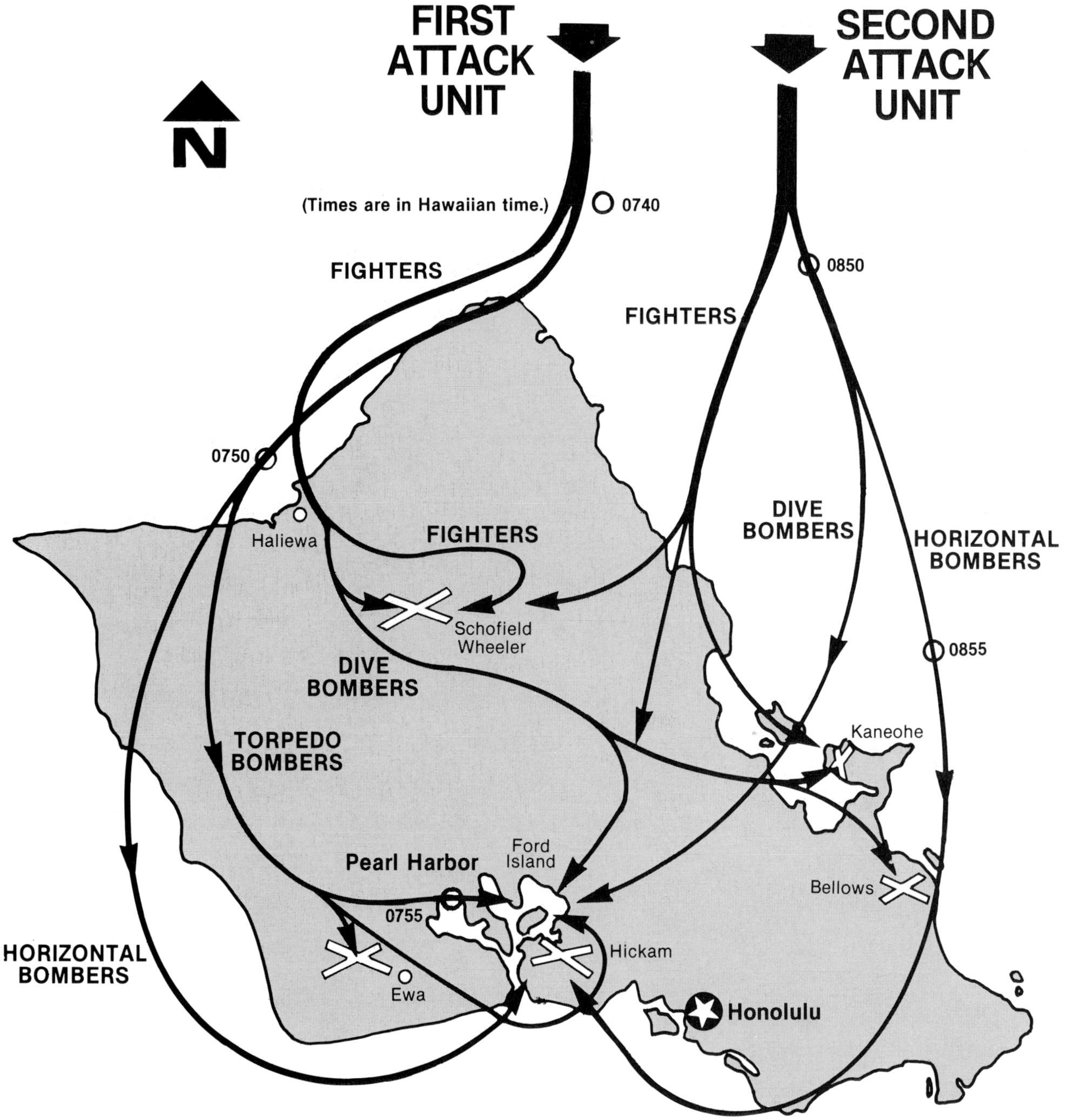

Haliewa Field, July 4, 1941.

Ewa Marine Corps Air Station, Oct. 1, 1941.

Bellows Field, Oct. 1, 1941.

Kaneohe Naval Air Station, Oct. 1, 1941.

P-36s of the 6th Pursuit Squadron at Wheeler Field. They were ferried to Hawaii by aircraft carriers and later repainted in olive drab. HARRY BROWN

Nine SBD-2s and -3s of Scouting Six over the Pacific on a tactics hop. Oct. 27, 1941. 6-S-14 an SBD-3, nominally assigned to Ens. Edward T. Deacon, VS-6's engineering officer, would be shot down by American antiaircraft fire from Fort Weaver. NA

P-40 fighters over Hawaii in August 1941. USAF

B-18 bombers on the flight line at Hickam Field. By the time of the attack these planes were obsolete. HA

These P-36 fighters are shown at the 1939 Cleveland Air Races in various paint schemes. This unit was later transferred to Hawaii. USAF

A Navy PBY-5 "Catalina." These planes flew regularly out of Oahu on patrol duty. Most were destroyed on the ground at Ford Island or Kaneohe Naval Air Station in the initial stage of the attack. NA

Sikorsky JRS-1 utility amphibian, the "One-Jig-One" of Utility Squadron One (VJ-1) was one of 10 JRS-1s based at the Naval Air Station, Ford Island, in 1941. Powered by two 750 h.p. Pratt & Whitney "Hornets," she cruised at 166 mph with a range of 775 miles. On the afternoon of Dec. 7, the 1-J-1 flew a five-hour mission in search of the Japanese carriers. NA 80-G-463233

The "One-Jig-One" is one of the surviving aircraft (in original condition) that was present during the attack. It is currently on display at the storage facility of the National Air and Space Museum in Silver Hill, Md.
ROBERT BRACCI

America's First Air Heroes

The attack on Wheeler Field caught most of the P-40 and P-36 fighters of the 7th Fighter Command on the ground. Six pilots, however, managed to get their planes into the air.

Overwhelmingly outnumbered, they scored the first American victories of the war, shooting down 12 enemy planes.

Three P-36 pilots of the 46th Pursuit Group—1st Lt. Lewis M. Sanders, 2nd Lt. Philip M. Rasmussen and 2nd Lt. Gordon M. Sterling, Jr.—were each credited with shooting down an enemy plane. John Thacker's guns jammed.

Three P-40 pilots of the 47th Pursuit Squadron—2nd Lt. George S. Welch, 2nd Lt. Kenneth M. Taylor and 2nd Lt. Harry W. Brown—shot down nine enemy planes among them. Welch (4 kills) and Taylor (4 kills), whose fighters had been based temporarily at Haleiwa, each registered four kills; Brown was credited with one.

Some of the planes of the 47th Pursuit Squadron from Wheeler Field were on field training at Haleiwa auxiliary field on Oahu's northern coast on Dec. 7. Among them were P-40s, P-36s and some outdated P-26s. When the enemy planes swooped down on Wheeler, 2nd lieutenants George Welch and Ken Taylor jumped into a car and hurried to Haleiwa where they got their P-40s into the air. Spotting a large number of enemy planes over Ewa to the south, the two pilots pounced on the attackers, shooting down five planes over the Marine base. They flew to Wheeler to get more ammunition, landing in front of Hangar 4, which was in flames from the first attack.

Taylor was still on the ground when more enemy divebombers appeared. As his ground crew dashed for cover, the lieutenant gunned his engine and took off straight into the formation of attacking aircraft, his guns blazing. When an enemy pilot got Taylor in his sights and fired a burst into the American's cockpit, Lt. Welch, also airborne, came in from behind and shot down the Japanese plane.

Both Welch and Taylor landed at Wheeler once to replenish their ammo. By the time the Japanese retired, the two Americans claimed at least four enemy planes. Taylor thought he might have destroyed five, but in the heat of battle, he said, it was hard to know for sure. The wreckage of two of his downed planes was found later. Having followed the returning Japanese planes out to sea, Taylor thought he knew the location of the enemy fleet, but in the confusion back at the base, he could get no one to listen to him. Anyway, few planes were available for pursuit.

Both Army pilots were awarded the Distinguished Service Cross in January 1942 for their heroism on that historic morning.

The abandoned Haleiwa airstrip on the north coast of Oahu. Lieutenants Welch and Taylor took off from here in their P-40s during the attack and shot down four Japanese Zeros each.

Second lieutenants Ken Taylor (left) and George Welch, America's first World War II air aces.
BRIG. GEN. KEN TAYLOR, RET.

Second lieutenants Welch and Taylor received the Distinguished Service Cross in January 1942 at Wheeler Field for the heroism during the Pearl Harbor attack. Welch is on the left and Taylor on the right.
BRIG. GEN. KEN TAYLOR, RET.

You Flew in the Clothes You Were Wearing

In 1941 life at Wheeler Field was "Alice in Wonderland!" We were bivouacked at Haleiwa Beach, flying off a grass strip while we strove to qualify in air-to-air gunnery. A P-36 was great for this work because it had a .30 cal and a .50 cal machine gun (the solenoid for the .50 cal was disconnected so that only the .30 cal would fire) synchronized to fire through the prop. You can set yourself up on a pursuit curve, pull the throttle and prop pitch back and squeeze-off rounds one-at-a-time, a practice which considerably improved your score. Johnny Dains and I finished qualification and were free to return to civilization so we spent Saturday night, Dec. 6, in Honolulu celebrating. We returned to Wheeler in the wee hours and finished the night yakking.

We were sitting there having a nightcap when we heard the snarl of an airplane in a dive, followed by an explosion. The Navy had a practice of sometimes rousing the base on Sunday morning as an extension of the intense inter-service rivalry that existed, by aggravating any hangovers we might have. A big explosion followed, shaking the building we were in. I assumed that the harassing pilot had clobbered himself and started outside to watch someone tidy up the mess. Upon reaching the door, I looked up and saw that the sky was full of airplanes -all of which were laying bombs and then machine-gunning on their pull-ups. Someone shouted "Japs! They're Japs!" Another explosion almost knocked me off my feet. I ducked instinctively and ran back inside. Johnny was wildly looking for his socks. I yelled, "Let's go," but he insisted on delaying the war until he could find those socks. When he finally succeeded, we dashed for my car and started for the flight line. A plane dropped his bomb and then zeroed in on my distinctively-colored car for the kill. His aim was high and his machine-gun blew out the second-story windows of a residence we were passing.

The flight line was, of course, utter chaos! All airplanes had been pushed to one end of the quadrangle to open space for troops to form for "Saturday Morning Inspection" (SMI), a ritual observed weekly, and of course the domino effect started when the first bomb among them triggered a massive amount of destruction. Nevertheless, there were brave men there, valiantly doing there best to strike back in defense, some of them literally throwing racks at those deadly planes. I saw one brave soul courageously stand his ground until a burst of machine-gun fire literally blew him in two! Johnny yelled "Haleiwa!" and I turned in the direction of the exit. A bomb nearly ended the war for me right there. The impact of the explosion nearly upended my car. On the way to the exit from Wheeler, we passed Lt. Bob Rogers' residence in the married officers quarters section and stopped for him. Shortly we headed for the exit from Wheeler, another Japanese aircraft picked us up and began strafing us. He'd come down across the cane fields and shoot, then chandelle as his rear gunner fired at us. Rogers was shouting, "The cane fields! Hide in the cane fields!" but, for some reason, Johnny found something funny in the situation and was laughing uproariously. We saw speeds in excess of 100 m.p.h. And, of course, we led our pursuer straight to a hitherto undiscovered airfield! I dove under the wing of a parked P-36 and then remembered I was sitting under a tankful of 100 octane gasoline. That Japanese pilot promptly set about shooting up the airplanes parked on the field while I made a mad dash for a tree. I was convinced by now that the pilot had a dedicated mission in life to get me personally! One of the ground crew and I were trying to load the guns on a P-36 and that was the one that seemed to be attracting most, if not all, of the fire. However, after shooting up a couple of airplanes, he left for parts unknown. I jumped into the P-36 and was quickly airborne. As I got into the air, I heard some reference to Bellows Field on the radio and started in that direction but could see no reason. I had just started back in the general direction of Kahuka Point when I saw another plane. I started to pounce only to see that it was another P-36. I closed on his wing and saw that it was Rogers. He motioned downward and there was the enemy! I couldn't understand why Rogers didn't attack! Finally, reluctantly, he started his dive, got within maybe 300 yards and fired. When he pulled up, I closed on the target. He rolled out, headed downward, then pulled almost vertical. He hammerheaded to the left and headed for the deck. I had built up a lot of speed and passed him, getting only a quick shot as I went by. By the time I was horizontal again he was way below me and I dove. Suddenly, he chopped his throttle and dropped his dive-flaps. I roared past and quickly realized I was in trouble! I was in a vertical dive at excessive speed and I could distinguish individual white-caps below! I pulled on that stick as hard as I could and, by the time I was horizontal again, I was completely blacked-out. I instinctively rolled out in a kind of sloppy Immelman turn but never saw my adversary again.

I could hear Rogers shouting on the radio but couldn't ascertain what he was saying. I started a slow turn to the right and suddenly there were three planes over Kaena Point. I started for them and, as I closed, could see that two Japanese planes were in hot pursuit of a P-36, presumably Rogers. They were slightly below me and I dove toward the second one. He snap-turned inside me, leav-

A P-40 that had thrown a rod at Kaena Airstrip.
HARRY BROWN

Harry Brown's P-40 right after the attack. His two enemy kills have already been added to the fuselage.
HARRY BROWN

ing me almost on the tail of that first one. He made a mistake! He tried to turn away from me and, of course, flew right through my line of fire. I wasn't more than 10-15 feet behind him and I couldn't have missed him. I saw the rear gunner crumple and the left wing begin to burn so I snapped to the right and climbed to set myself for another pass. I saw the plane I had hit go into the water almost vertically. I turned left looking for the one I had missed and found myself looking right down the throat of a covey of about 10-12. I think I must have surprised them as much as I had been surprised because they burst in all directions as I flew right through the middle of them. I saw what I thought was a straggler and started for him only to find it was another P-36. I closed with him thinking it was Rogers. It turned out later to be a man named Mike Moore. (Interestingly enough, I only saw him once after that to exchange experiences but a little more than a year later our paths crossed again in New Guinea on a day when I was escorting a squadron of C-47s led by him and I got three kills over Tsli-tsli.)

Mike later told me that I was shouting so loudly over the radio that I was unintelligible. I was, of course, telling him of the airplanes below us. At any rate, he aggressively jumped that plane with me trying hard to follow. We went all over the sky but Mike was so close that I couldn't get a shot. Finally, he broke off, having used all his ammunition. I then started after him and got in three good passes before I, too, was out of ammo. I know I inflicted heavy damage on my first pass. I saw the pilot's canopy shatter and the engine take some hits. The last time I saw him he was headed out over Kaena Point in the general direction of Kauai trailing a column of black smoke and rapidly losing altitude.

I didn't get confirmation of that second kill until almost

two years later. Even now, the ambiguity in the citation awarding me a medal for action that day has plagued me. I've always attributed the delay to the fact that my medal was awarded to Harry "M." Brown and whoever inverted that middle initial from the correct "W." rendered me into two different people in a world where someone with a name like Harry Brown has a constant fight to escape anonymity. I really don't care so much for myself since I know what I did that day and whether my total is recorded as six or seven won't significantly affect anything. However, for the record, a radio transmission which was initiated to consolidate my records with the Seventh and Fifth Air Forces gives me credit for two (General Order No. 193, Hq Fifth Air Force, APO 925, 10 Sept. 1943). Moreover, that it was accepted by my peers is a demonstrated testimonial which I also received from the C.O. when I was to return to the States. He confirmed my total as seven. Also, I would have been hoorawed off the field when I painted two rising suns on my P-40 in Hawaii if there had been any doubt on the part of my associates.

Recently, students of that event have asked about the coloring of the Japanese aircraft engaged. I can only give impressions for I have no definite memory. I believe that each of the two for which I claim credit had a blue belly band, and one of them had a single yellow or orange stripe, raked, on the vertical stabilizer. Both were Kates although my Form 5 records them as Vals.

I returned to Haleiwa and landed. A servicing crew chief teasingly pointed to how I was dressed. Only then did I realize that I had flown my first combat mission dressed in pajama tops, tux trousers, houseshoes, and helmet and goggles! While the airplane was serviced, I changed into a flight suit. Taylor and Welch took off on another search. About five minutes later Johnny Dains taxied out in a P-36 and I gave him a thumbs-up as he taxied by. That was the last time I saw him alive because, as he was hurrying to join Taylor and Welch, our own ground troops opened up and shot him down! I suppose all that excited people could see was that his P-36 differed in appearance from the P-40s he was trying to catch! I flew one more brief mission that day without seeing any action.

Harry Brown now lives in Alamo, Calif.

Harry W. Brown

America's first World War II air heros. Left to right: Lew Sanders, Phil Rasmussen, Ken Taylor, George Welch and Harry Brown.
HARRY BROWN

I Won't Be Back

Following the destruction of the P-40s on the ramp at Wheeler, I saw many dead in the base barracks and tent areas. Some had attempted to escape the strafing by digging through wooden tent floors with their bare hands. Hands and fingers were lacerated, and in many instances finger nails torn out. It was a poignant sight.

Only one fighter of my 46th Squadron had been damaged, and I proceeded to get my P-36 and three others into the air. I had selected three veteran pilots, but when we were in the air I noticed that one was a young inexperienced pilot who somehow had taken over a plane.

In a slight dive at near maximum throttle we sighted a formation of 11 enemy fighters headed north, and came in at an overtaking speed from about level flight. Firing at the leader, I watched my tracers enter the fuselage, saw him pull up slightly and then fall off to the right, smoking, I also saw one of our planes hit, and spiral toward the ocean, trailing smoke. Later, when we returned to Wheeler, Lt. Rasmussen, Lt. Thacker and I were shot at by our own ground personnel who thought we were the enemy, but we managed to land safely. Rasmussen's plane was pitted with 54 elongated holes from 20-millimeter fire, both on the wings and the fuselage. It appeared that a heavy axe had been used to make them.

During the debriefing I learned that Lt. Norris, one of the pilots I had originally selected for the mission, had returned to the parachute truck for a smaller chute when young Lt. Sterling, who had been standing nearby with chute and life vest, jumped into the waiting plane. Sterling handed his wristwatch to the crew chief with instructions to have it sent to his mother because he wouldn't be back. It was his plane I saw spiraling into the ocean.

The price was high when one considers that this single action cost us a pilot and two planes, in exchange for three confirmed and one probable enemy plane losses. Although acceptable in this particular context, it also illustrated the cost of being unprepared.

All the pilots received Silver Stars for their gallant action that day.

COL. LEWIS SANDERS, USAF, Ret.,
Lillian, Alabama

(A lieutenant at the time of the attack, Sanders is credited with shooting down one of the first Japanese plane of the minutes-old war.)

HAWAIIAN AIR FORCE AS OF DEC. 7, 1941***

TOTAL STRENGTH
754 officers, 6,706 enlisted men.

CASUALTIES	KILLED	MISSING	WOUNDED
HICKAM	121	37	274
WHEELER	37	6	53
BELLOWS	5	0	9
TOTAL	163	43	336

PLANES

AIRCRAFT	TOTAL	DESTROYED	USABLE
B-17D	12	4	4
B-18A	33	12	11
A-20A	12	2	5
P-40C	12	5	2
P-40B	87	37	25
P-36A	39	4	16
P-26	14	0	14
TOTAL	223****	64	77

***Courtesy--Office of Information, 15th Air Base Wing (PACAF) Hickam AFB, Hawaii

****Plus an assortment of observation and training planes.

Ken Taylor is retired and living in Anchorage, Alaska.

JAPANESE AIRCRAFT TYPES USED IN THE PEARL HARBOR ATTACK

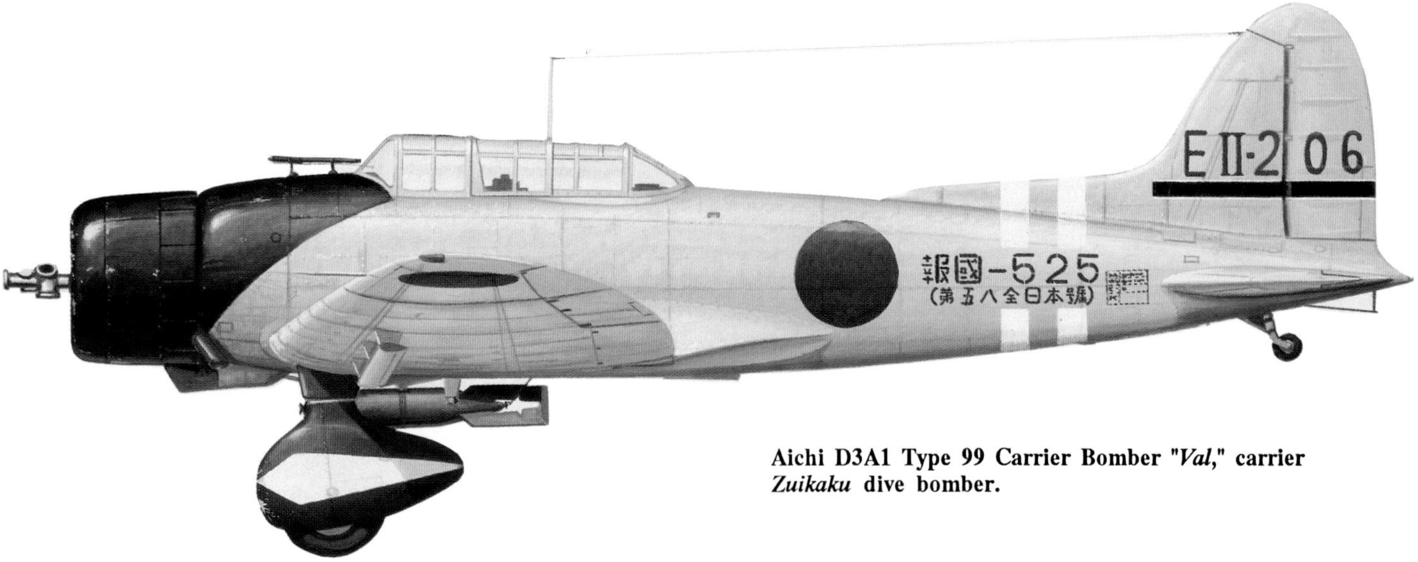

Aichi D3A1 Type 99 Carrier Bomber "*Val*," carrier *Zuikaku* dive bomber.

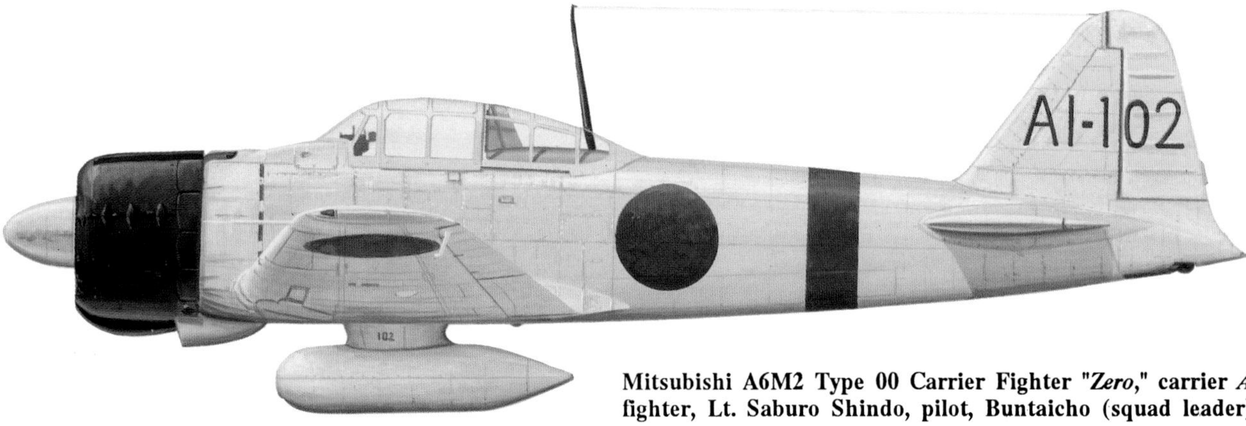

Mitsubishi A6M2 Type 00 Carrier Fighter "*Zero*," carrier *Akagi* fighter, Lt. Saburo Shindo, pilot, Buntaicho (squad leader).

Nakajima B5N2 Type 97 Carrier Attack Plane "*Kate*," carrier *Hiryu* torpedo bomber. Lt. Hirata Matsumura, pilot, Buntaicho.

Nakajima B5N2 Type 97 Carrier Attack Plane "*Kate*," carrier *Akagi* horizontal bomber; Cdr. Mitsuo Fuchida's aircraft, April 9, 1942.

AMERICAN AIRCRAFT PRESENT DURING THE PEARL HARBOR ATTACK

Curtiss P-36A flown by 2nd Lt. Philip M. Rasmussen from the 46th Pursuit Squadron, Wheeler Field.

P-40B *Tcmahawk* from the 47th Pursuit Squadron, Haleiwa Field.

SBD-3 *Dauntless* flown by Lt. Clarence E. Dickinson from VS-6, *USS Enterprise.*

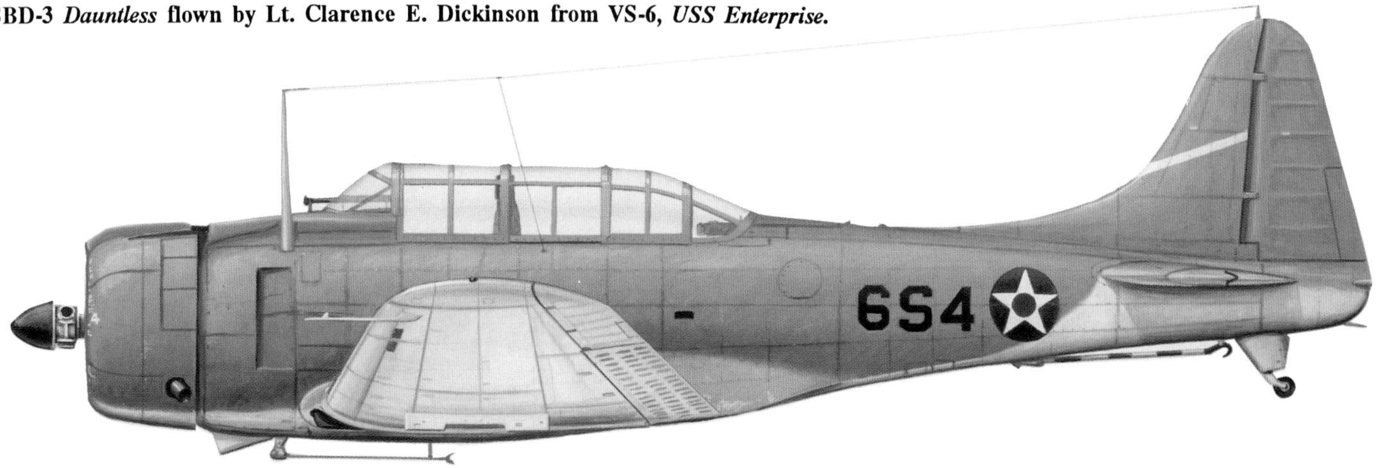

B-17C *Flying Fortress* flown by Lt. Robert H. Richards. Arriving inbound from California during the attack, Lt. Richards made a forced landing at Bellows Field.

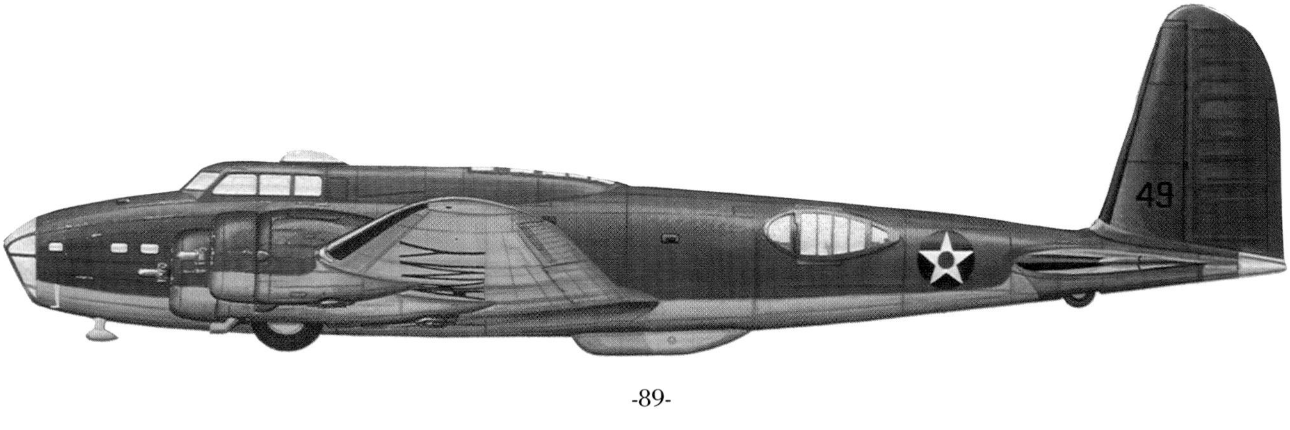

Aichi D3A1 Type 99 EI-204 piloted by Lt. (jg) Iwakichi Mifuku. This plane attacked Hickam Field in the first wave. MICHAEL WENGER

A damaged second wave fighter. The Japanese lost 20 aircraft in the last attack. NA 80-G-19931

A navy photographer took the closest photo of an attacking Japanese dive bomber. NA 80-G-33013

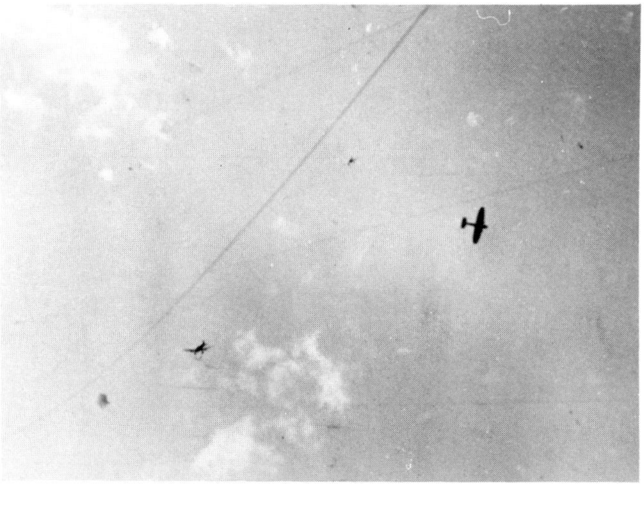

Three Aichi D3A1 Type 99 "Val" carrier bombers from the *Kaga* attack the battleship *Nevada*. This photo was taken from Ford Island. NA

Japanese Airmen Killed or Missing In Action During the Attack*

Nagaaki Asahi	*Kaga* D3A II
Shunichi Atsumi	*Soryu* A6M II
Toshiaki Bando	*Kaga* D3A II
Hajime Goto	*Akagi* D3A II
Ippei Goto	*Kaga* A6M II
Toru Haneda	*Kaga* A6M I
Takeshi Hirano	*Akagi* A6M I
Fumio Hirashima	*Kaga* D3A II
Kinsuke Homma	*Akagi* D3A II
Fusata Iida	*Soryu* A6M II
Fukumitsu Imai	*Kaga* D3A II
Tomio Inenaga	*Kaga* A6M II
Saburo Ishii	*Soryu* A6M II
Kunio Iwatsuki	*Shokaku* D3A I
Satoru Kawasaki	*Soryu* D3A II
Hirokichi Kinoshita	*Akagi* D3A II
Syuzo Kitahara	*Kaga* B5N I
Isamu Kiyomura	*Hiryu* D3A II
Kenichi Kumamoto	*Kaga* B5N I
Tetsusaburo Kumazo	*Shokaku* D3A I
Hideyasu Kuwabara	*Soryu* D3A II
Kazuyoshi Kuwabata	*Kaga* D3A II
Yoshiharu Machimoto	*Kaga* B5N I
Saburo Makino	*Kaga* D3A II
Kenji Maruyama	*Soryu* D3A II
Yoshizo Masuda	*Kaga* B5N I
Isamu Matsuda	*Kaga* B5N I
Tsuneo Minamizaki	*Kaga* D3A II
Tsuneki Morita	*Kaga* B5N I
Hajime Murao	*Hiryu* D3A II
Izumi Nagai	*Kaga* B5N I
Shigenori Nishikaichi	*Hiryu* A6M II
Nafikatsu Ohashi	*Kaga* B5N I
Iwao Oka	*Kaga* D3A II
Shigenori Onikura	*Kaga* D3A II
Toshio Onishi	*Kaga* B5N I
Seiichi Ota	*Akagi* D3A II
Toshio Oyama	*Akagi* D3A II
Noboru Sakaguchi	*Kaga* D3A II
Kiyoshi Sakamoto	*Akagi* D3A II
Seinoshin Sano	*Kaga* A6M I
Chuji Shimakura	*Akagi* D3A II
Yoshio Shimizu	*Kaga* B5N I
Yoshio Shimizu	*Hiryu* D3A II
Koreyoshi Sotoyama	*Hiryu* D3A II
Shigeharu Sugaya	*Akagi* B5N I
Sueo Sukida	*Kaga* D3A II
Mitsumori Suzuki	*Kaga* B5N I
Ryochi Takahashi	*Soryu* D3A II
Hidemi Takeda	*Kaga* B5N I
Tomoharu Takeda	*Kaga* B5N I
Nobuo Tsuda	*Kaga* D3A II
Yonetaro Ueda	*Kaga* B5N I
Nobuo Umezu	*Kaga* B5N I
Doshi Utsuki	*Akagi* D3A II

*Includes their carrier, type of aircraft and if they were in the first or second wave.

Lt. Shoichi Ogawa of Kaga's dive bomber aircraft. He lost his two wingmen during his attack on the *Nevada*. USN

An Aichi D3A1 Val noses over with dive brakes in use. NA 80-G-32708

One of two *Kaga* dive bombers shot down in Wahiawa city limits, just outside Wheeler Field. AMC

This *Kaga* torpedo bomber, AII-356, flown by Lt. Mimori Suzuki crashed in the waters of the southeast loch of Pearl Harbor. USN

This Val is another *Kaga* loss. This crash was used by U.S. technical intelligence. The *Kaga* lost four Zeros, five Kates and six Vals, more than any other Japanese carrier that day. NA 80-G-32441

This Akagi Zero, AI-154, crashed into the Fort Kamehameha ordnance building killing the pilot and three soldiers. NA 80-G-13040

Sam Tooney, a sugar cane plantation executive, points out to radio announcer Ken Carney the tail section of a Japanese dive bomber that crashed in a macadamia nut grove and exploded. HA

Other pieces of the plane came down nearby. HA

A corpse of a Japanese airman is raised from his downed aircraft after several days in the water. His face was eaten by crabs prior to recovery. NA 80-G-32465

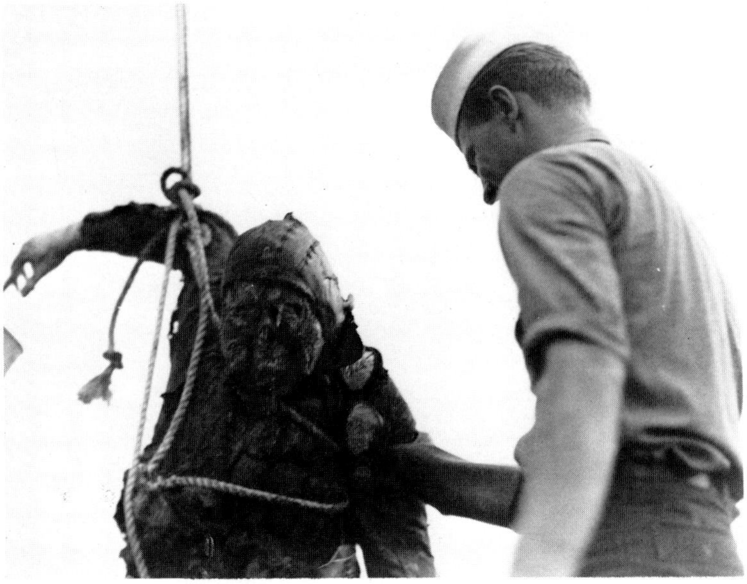

The tangled wreckage of a Japanese plane is wrapped around a tree. NA 80-G-32567

The body of a Japanese airman is retrieved from the oily waters of Pearl Harbor. NA 80-G-32553

This *Kaga* torpedo plane crashed near the Pearl Harbor base hospital. The first plane to crash, the wing section was stripped for souvenirs soon after the attack was over. The tail code can only be reconstructed thus far to read AII-35x, the last digit is unknown. FORREST SMITH

A Japanese plane retrieved from the waters of Pearl Harbor. USN

Destroyed SBDs of Scouting Six from *Enterprise* (CV-6)

Tail of Ens. "Charlie" McCarthy's SBD-2 (BuNo 2158), Dec. 26, 1941. The rear gunner, killed in the crash, is still listed as missing-in-action. USN

Tangled wreckage of Ens. Vogt's SBD-2 (BuNo 2160), one block off Belt Road, Ewa Beach Road, Dec. 26, 1941. USN

Burnt and twisted wreckage are all that remains of the SBD-3 (BuNo 4570) flown by Lt. Dickinson on Dec. 7. This view was taken by crash investigators, Dec. 26, 1941. USN

Wright R-1820 engine from Lt. Dickinson's SBD-3, Dec. 26, 1941. The stencilled card reads NAVY CRASH 7 DEC. 1941 INVESTIGATION COMPLETED DO NOT REMOVE THIS SIGN. USN

Aerial Vets of Dec. 7, 1941

Between 0620-0950 the following aircraft are known to have been in the air during the Japanese attack. The air crew roster is still incomplete. Some of post attack recon flights had combat with the Japanese Combat Air Patrol north of the Hawaiian Islands. This roster is also incomplete. Aircraft type, unit and pilot are listed.

Myers OTW; Gambo Flying Service; Mrs. Marguerite H. Gambo, instructor
Interstate 'Cadet'; Andrew Flying Service; Miss Cornelia C. Fort, instructor
Aeronca 'Tandum'; Hui Lei Lei Flying Club; Tommy Tomerlin, instructor
Aeronca 'Tandum'; Gambo Flying Service; Roy Vitousek, renter
"Cub"; K-T Flying Service; M. F. Poston, student solo (shot down/bailed out)
"Cub"; K-T Flying Service; Robert Tyce, instructor (killed after landing)
"Cub"; K-T Flying Service; Clyde Brown, renter (MIA)
"Cub"; K-T Flying Service; Henry Blackwell, renter (MIA)
Boeing A-314; PanAm "ANZAC" Clipper; H. Lanier Turner (California to Hilo, HI)
B-17E; 38th RS, 19th BG; Truman H. Landon (California to Hickam Field)
B-17E; 38th RS, 19th BG; Karl T. Barthelmess (California to Hickam Field)
B-17C; 38th RS, 19th BG; Raymond T. Swenson (California to Hickam Field) destroyed
B-17C; 38th RS, 19th BG; Bruce G. Allen (California to Hickam Field)
B-17C; 38th RS, 19th BG; Earl J. Cooper (California to Hickam Field)
B-17C; 38th RS, 19th BG; Robert H. Richards (California to Bellows Field) destroyed
B-17E; 88th RS, 7th BG; Richard H. Carmichael (California to Haleiwa Field)
B-17E; 88th RS, 7th BG; Harold N. Chaffin (California to Haleiwa Field)
B-17E; 88th RS, 7th BG; Robert Thacker (California to Hickam Field)
B-17E; 88th RS, 7th BG; Frank Bostrom (California to golf course)
B-17E; 88th RS, 7th BG; Harry N. Brandon (California to Hickam Field)
B-17E; 88th RS, 7th BG; David G. Rawls (California to Hickam Field)
SBD-2; Enterprise; Howard L. Young (to Ford Island)
SBD-2; Enterprise; Perry Lee Teaff (to Ford Island)
SBD-3; Enterprise; Hallsted L. Hopping; (to Ford Island)
SBD-2; Enterprise; John H. L. Vogt, Jr. (KIA Ewa area)
SBD-3; Enterprise; C.E. Dickinson, Jr. (shot down/gunner KIA)
SBD-2, Enterprise; John R. McCarthy (shot down/gunner MIA)
SBD-3; Enterprise; H. Dale Hilton (to Ford Island)
SBD-2; Enterprise; E.J. Kroeger (to Ford Island)
SBD- ; Enterprise; Carlton Fogg (to Ewa Field)
SBD-2; Enterprise; C.J. Dobson (to Ford Island)
SBD- ; Enterprise; Earl Gallaher (to Ford Island)
SBD- ; Enterprise; William West (to Ford Island)
SBD-3; Enterprise; Frank Patriarca (to Barking Sands Field, Kauai)
SBD-2; Enterprise; Walter Willis (MIA)
SBD-3; Enterprise; Ed Deacon (shot down by Fort Weaver fire)
SBD-2; Enterprise; W.E. Roberts (to Hickam Field)
SBD-2; Enterprise; Manuel Gonzales (MIA)
SBD- ; Enterprise; Fred Weber (to Ford Island)
PBY-5; VP-14 (Kaneohe); William P. Tanner
PBY-5; VP-14 (Kaneohe); O.F. Meyer, Jr.
PBY-5; VP-14 (Kaneohe); T.W. Hillis
PBY-5; VP-24 (Ford Island); John P. Fitzsimmons
PBY-5; VP-24 (Ford Island); Stuart White
PBY-5; VP-24 (Ford Island); Gene Tatom
PBY-5; VP-24 (Ford Island); Charles Hibbard

PBY-5; VP-23 (Ford Island); Joseph Kellam
P-40; 47th PS (Haleiwa); George S. Welch
P-40; 47th PS (Haleiwa); Kenneth M. Taylor (WIA)
P-40/P-36; 47th PS (Haleiwa); John Dains (KIA by Schofield Barracks fire)
P-36; 47th PS (Haleiwa); John J. Webster (WIA)
P-36; 47th PS (Haleiwa); Harry W. Brown
P-36; 47th PS (Haleiwa); Robert J. Rogers
P-36; 46th PS (Wheeler); Lewis M. Sanders
P-36; 46th PS (Wheeler); John M. Thacker
P-36; 46th PS (Wheeler); Phillip M. Rasmussen
P-36; 46th PS (Wheeler); Gordon H. Sterling, Jr. (MIA)
P-36; 46th PS (Wheeler); Malcolm A. Moore
P-40; 45th PS (Wheeler); Fred B. Shifflet (damaged by Hickam Field ground fire)
P-40; 45th PS (Wheeler); Woodrow B. Wilmot
P-36; 45th PS (Wheeler); Henry W. Lawrence
P-36; 45th PS (Wheeler); William F. Haney (damaged by Pearl Harbor fire, glided to Wheeler)
P-40; 44th PS (Bellows); George A. Whiteman (KIA)
P-40; 44th PS (Bellows); Samuel M. Bishop (WIA)
0-47; 86th OS (Bellows); Charles B. Stewart
TBD-1; "Pearl Harbor, Battle Force" (Ford Island); Theodore W. Marshall (VP-21)
B-18; 17th AB (Wheeler); Gordon H. Austin (Molokai to Wheeler)
SBD- ; Enterprise; Leonard Check (Inner Air Patrol)
SBD- ; Enterprise; Edward L. Anderson (Inner Air Patrol)
F4F- ; Enterprise; Francis F. Hebel (Combat Air Patrol)
F4F- ; Enterprise; Eric Allen (Combat Air Patrol)
F4F- ; Enterprise; John C. Kelley (Combat Air Patrol)
F4F- ; Enterprise; James G. Daniels, III (Combat Air Patrol)

Post-Combat Reconnaissance Mission Action

SOC; St. Louis; Malcolm Reeves
SOC; St. Louis; Fred Covington (battle with Combat Air Patrol, 1135 to 1155 north of Niihau Island)
JRS; VJ-1 (Ford Island); Wesley H. Ruth (battle with Combat Air Patrol at 1310, about 50 miles west of the Japanese Fleet)
JRS; VJ-1 (Ford Island); John P. Edwards (flew closest to the Japanese fleet, about 30-35 miles west, but did not see it)

2nd Lt. Gordon Sterling, a P-36 pilot, killed in aerial action on Dec. 7. He is credited with one destroyed enemy aircraft.
JOHN LAMBERT

Attack

The Messenger Came Late

This remarkable photo, taken from Aiea Heights at about 0845, shows the concentrated antiaircraft fire the second wave of attacking Japanese planes had to fly through. The large plume of smoke (center) is from the ships of Battleship Row damaged in the first wave. USN

One of the great natural harbors of the world, Pearl Harbor has been an important naval base for the U.S. Navy for many years. Before anyone thought of it as a naval installation, it was a favorite place for the Hawaiians to gather oysters and their byproduct—pearls. King Kamehameha the Great used the harbor's pearl revenues to enlarge his treasury.

The British, French and Russians had cast covetous eyes on the harbor, but it was the Americans who eventually developed its potential.

Commodore Charles Wilkes of the American navy surveyed the harbor in the late 1830s and reported: "If the water upon the bar should be deepened, which I doubt not can be effected, it would afford the best and most capacious harbor in the Pacific."

Army Maj. Gen. J. M. Schofield made another survey in 1873 and was influential in obtaining authorization for U.S. use of the harbor. In 1877, King Kalakaua granted the United States exclusive rights to establish a coaling and repair station for the U.S. fleet in exchange for certain trading privileges.

Construction of the naval base did not begin until after Hawaii became a U.S. Territory in 1898. The shore facilities began to go up in 1901, and the first major U.S. warship, the *California*, entered the harbor in 1909. The original drydock was started in 1901, but—partly as the result of a major construction accident—it was not turned over to the navy until 10 years later. The submarine base was begun in 1919; in the 1920s and '30s more base facilities were added, or existing installations expanded. With war clouds on the horizon in 1939 and 1940, thousands of mainland workers were brought to Oahu to upgrade facilities at Pearl as well as those at other military bases.

Fort Kamehameha, the major Army fort guarding the entrance to Pearl Harbor, had been established in 1913 and other forts and coastal artillery batteries had sprouted

This photo was taken in 1919 by Chinese photographer Tai Sing Loo, just prior to the dedication of Drydock #1. Mr. Loo had climbed one of the 760-foot radio towers for a better view of the dock. This so impressed visiting Secretary of the Navy, Josephus Daniels, that it led to the appointment of Mr. Loo as the official photographer of the Pearl Harbor Navy Yard, a position he held for 30 years until his retirement in 1949. USN

Testing the new 200-ton crane at the Navy Yard, Pearl Harbor, July 1935. USN

up around the island since. The Army was charged with the defense of naval ships while they were in port, but at the time of the Japanese attack, few anti-aircraft guns had been placed around the harbor. The Army's main concern was providing an adequate coastal artillery defense against a possible invasion.

For all its advantages, Pearl Harbor was not an ideal place to base a large fleet. There was only one entrance to the harbor, and it was narrow enough to be bottled up easily. Because of the limited space, ships were clustered rather than dispersed while in port, and harbor defenses were inadequate. Moreover, Hawaii was far from sources of supply and fuel. Base facilities were not always able to meet the diverse needs of the fleet, and housing for naval base personnel was inadequate.

Citing these problems, the commander-in-chief of the fleet, Adm. James O. Richardson, had protested vigorously against the basing of the fleet at Pearl Harbor; he suggested the ships operate out of California. But Roosevelt's decision to base the fleet at Pearl had been a political as well as military decision, and the admiral's complaints were listened to and dismissed. On Feb. 1, 1941, Richardson was relieved of his command and replaced by Adm. Husband E. Kimmel.

The main gate into Pearl Harbor in the middle 1930s. HA

Aerial view taken Oct. 13, 1941, of Southeast Loch with many fleet subs in port at the submarine base (right) and the fleet supply depot on Kuahua (center). Across the top, looking toward Pearl City and Aiea, are the north end of Ford Island, Battleship Row and the fleet anchorage in East Loch. NA 80-G-411193

The Japanese fleet moves into final position during the night of Dec. 6, 1941. Sailing a northern route and maintaining complete radio silence, the six carriers and their escorts arrived undetected in Hawaiian waters. PAUL BENDER

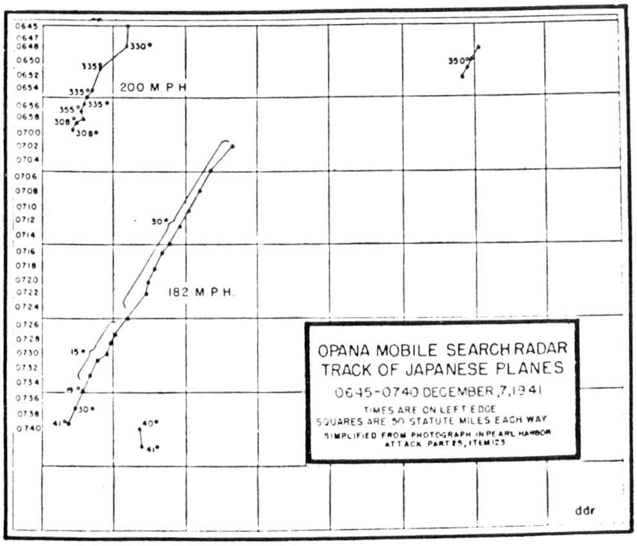

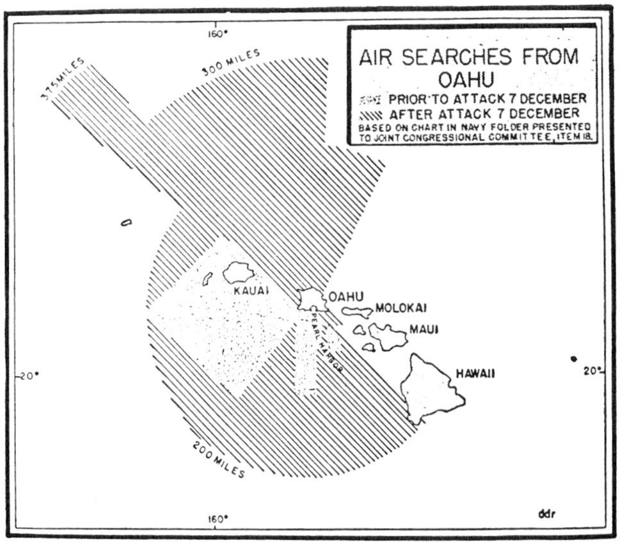

View looking northeast across West Loch to Ford Island in the opening minutes of the attack at approximately 0758. The destroyer *Helm* has just rounded Waipio Point. At extreme left, the *Utah* has taken a torpedo hit; center, the large plume of smoke is burning Hangar #6 on Ford Island and right center, smoke from torpedo explosion on the *Helena*. EA

On Sunday morning, Dec. 7, 1941, at least 96 ships of the U.S. Pacific Fleet were inside the harbor or patrolling just outside the entrance. The atmosphere aboard the moored ships was relaxed— many sailors had enjoyed shore leave the night before and were looking forward to a quiet Sabbath. Everything on the island seemed normal. Listening to Hawaiian music on the radio, Honolulu residents were getting ready to go to church, play golf or enjoy a picnic.

All ships in the harbor were in Readiness Condition Three at the time of the attack (a quarter of the anti-aircraft batteries and control stations were manned). Condition Three required that a ship be able to get underway within 12 hours.

At the Opana mobile radar station at Kahuku Point on the northern tip of Oahu, the operators were supposed to cease operations at 7 a.m., but they kept the station on a little longer for practice. When a large echo appeared on the oscilloscope, the station reported the contacts to the control center at Fort Shafter, but everyone assumed the echo was a large flight of B-17s due in from California that Sunday. No one guessed the truth—that the radar had picked up the first wave of 183 Japanese planes that had been launched starting at first that the attacking planes were U.S. aircraft practicing bombing runs. It was not until the red balls became visible on the wings and fuselages, and the bombs started falling, that they realized it was the real thing. Several radio operators immediately sent out the famous message—"AIR RAID PEARL HARBOR THIS IS NO DRILL."

Fuchida, seeing that his planes had obtained complete surprise, sent back his equally famous message to the Japanese fleet—"TORA, TORA, TORA," the code words for a successful surprise attack. Three minutes after the attack had begun, torpedo bombers hit Battleship Row. Every outboard battleship received torpedoes in the four attacks constituting the first phase of the strike.

The battleship *Arizona* had absorbed two high-level bombs before a high-level bomber dropped two more, one next to the 14-inch powder magazine. The result was a spectacular explosion and fire that sent the ship to the bottom with more than 1,000 men on board. The old battleship was gone before the battle was 15 minutes old.

The *Vestal*, a repair ship, was tied alongside the *Arizona*. When the *Arizona* blew up, the *Vestal*'s captain was blown overboard. After swimming back to the vessel, he learned that orders had been given to abandon ship and countermanded them. He let go the line to the *Arizona*, got his ship underway and managed to beach the *Vestal* at Aiea, thus saving it from burning up or sinking.

Taking torpedoes, the battleship *Okalahoma* listed rapidly to 30 degrees. When more torpedoes hit her, she rolled until her masts struck the bottom. She lost 415 men.

Both heavy bombs and torpedoes ripped the battleship *West Virginia*, which settled to the bottom, her decks awash. When a large fire raged out of control amidships, she was abandoned.

Screaming in from the west, five Japanese planes let loose with torpedoes that sped toward the cruiser *Helena* and the minelayer *Oglala*, moored together at the 1010 dock. One torpedo passed beneath the *Oglala* and hit the *Helena*, doing harm to the minelayer as well. After a second wave Val bomb exploded between the two ships, causing further damage, a tug helped move the crippled *Oglala* away from the *Helena* and secured her to the dock. But at 10 a.m., *Oglala* capsized after taking in too much water.

Other planes directed their attack toward the west side of Ford Island where the *Tangier*, *Utah*, *Raleigh* and *Detroit* were moored. The *Tangier* and *Detroit* escaped damage, but the torpedoed *Raleigh* was in danger of capsizing before lines were run out from the mooring quays to keep he stable.

Struck by two torpedoes, the *Utah* listed dangerously to port. She finally capsized and had to be abandoned. This old battleship, stripped down to serve as a target ship, was hardly a threat to the Japanese, but they apparently mistook her for an aircraft carrier. Fortunately for the United States, no aircraft carriers were in the harbor that morning.

Back at Battleship Row, the *California* had been badly damaged. Ravaged by an amidships fire, she was abandoned. The *Nevada*, *Maryland* and *Tennessee* were also hit, with less devastating results. The cruiser *Honolulu* was slightly damaged.

By 8:25 a.m. the first wave of the attack was over. All the torpedo damage had been done. Only a few scattered attacks marked the 30-minute second phase, but at 8:55 the second wave started with intensive bombing runs at Kaneohe NAS.

At 9:02 a.m. the second wave attacked Pearl Harbor. The *California* was hit again and began to sink, though it would take her three days to settle to the bottom. A bomb blasted the main deck of the seaplane tender *Curtiss*, killing 20 men. *Curtiss* gunners brought down an enemy plane, only to have it crash into their ship and cause more damage.

Tied up near the *California*, the oiler *Neosho* hurriedly cut her moorings and steamed toward Merry Point with her hull full of highly flammable fuel. Luckily she was not hit or the disaster at Battleship Row would have been even worse than it was.

Though the *Nevada* was torpedoed once, she managed to get underway and headed toward the harbor entrance with dive bombers attacking her furiously. Fearing his ship would be sunk in the entrance, thus blocking the harbor, the captain grounded her at Hospital Point. Later, with help from tugs, he backed her across the channel to Waipio Point.

The battleship *Pennsylvania*, Pacific Fleet flagship, was in Drydock #1 undergoing repairs along with the destroyers *Cassin* and *Downes*. After all three ships had taken bomb hits, the flagship's captain ordered the drydock flooded in an effort to put out the fires. It was a mistake. Oil slick fires floated up with the water, igniting the magazines of the destroyers. The explosions caused the *Cassin* to tumble over onto the *Downes*.

In Floating Drydock #2 with her ammunition still on board, the destroyer *Shaw* was rocked by a bomb, possibly meant for another ship. When the resulting fire reached the forward magazines, the explosion ripped off the bow and sunk both the ship and the drydock. Several ships managed to get underway in the midst of the attack, and made it outside the harbor. Undergoing repairs at a Navy yard dock, the cruiser *St. Louis* cut her moorings and cleared the yard at 9:31. Other ships—the *Phoenix*, *Detroit*, *Monaghan*, *Tucker*, *Bagley*, *Dale*, *Henley* and *Phelps*—also made it to open sea, where they began fruitless searches for the enemy fleet.

Those ships that could get their anti-aircraft guns in operation were returning fire only a few minutes after the attack began. The *Pennsylvania* alone put up more than 50,000 .50-caliber rounds, though the ships' gunners downed only two enemy planes. More than 275,000 rounds were fired from the ships during the one hour and 50-minute attack.

At Fort Kamehameha, a few anti-aircraft batteries shot down several enemy planes, but strafing aircraft killed seven fort personnel and wounded 12.

The B-17s that arrived from California during the attack were forced to land wherever they could. The unarmed bombers dropped onto runways at Hickam (eight) and Haleiwa (2). One crash-landed on the golf course. Eighteen navy SBDs from the carrier *Enterprise* also flew in during the attack.* Rearmed and refueled, nine carrier aircraft took off at 12:10 p.m. to look for the Japanese fleet.

Casualties started arriving at the U.S. Naval Hospital at Hospital Point about 9 a.m. They came in all manner of vehicles, both civilian and military. Emergency first-aid stations and nearby sugar cane plantation hospitals also treated the wounded. More than 500 casualties were admitted to the Naval Hospital on Dec. 7; 313 dead were placed in a temporary morgue in the basement.

Military casualties included 2,251 killed and 1,119 wounded. About 65 percent of the officers and 95 percent of the enlisted men were on board their ships when the attack began. The rest were either on shore leave or en route to their ships.

Heroism did not go unrecognized. The Army awarded five Distinguished Service Crosses and 65 Silver Stars; the Navy recommended 15 Medal of Honor and awarded 60 Navy Crosses.

Adm. Kimmel watched the first moments of the attack from the front lawn of his home, which was about five minutes away from the naval base. Gen. Short saw the planes from his quarters at Fort Shafter. Neither man knew they were watching their military careers go up in smoke. At 11:45 a.m., an RCA messenger rode up to Fort Shafter on his motorcycle with a cable—received at 7:33 a.m. in downtown Honolulu—for the general. It took until 2:58 p.m. to get it decoded and sent to Gen. Short and Adm. Kimmel. From Gen. George C. Marshall in Washington, the message explained that the Japanese were to present an ultimatum at 1 p.m. EST (7:30 a.m. in Honolulu) and added "Just what significance the hour set may have we do not know, but be on the alert accordingly." It was a little late. . . .

*Six landed at Ford Island, four at Ewa, one at Kauai (Burns Field), and one at Hickam. Four were shot down by Japanese Zeros and one by ground fire and one by a Val.

Anti-aircraft fire above Pearl Harbor. USAF

Aerial view of NAS, Ford Island, at the height of the attack on Battleship Row. Smoke from the stricken *Arizona* (middle, center) obscures all but the *California*. On the top (left), *Utah* has capsized. Of the many vessels berthed at the Navy Yard (lower left), most escaped with little or no damage as this area was not a prime target of the attackers. EA

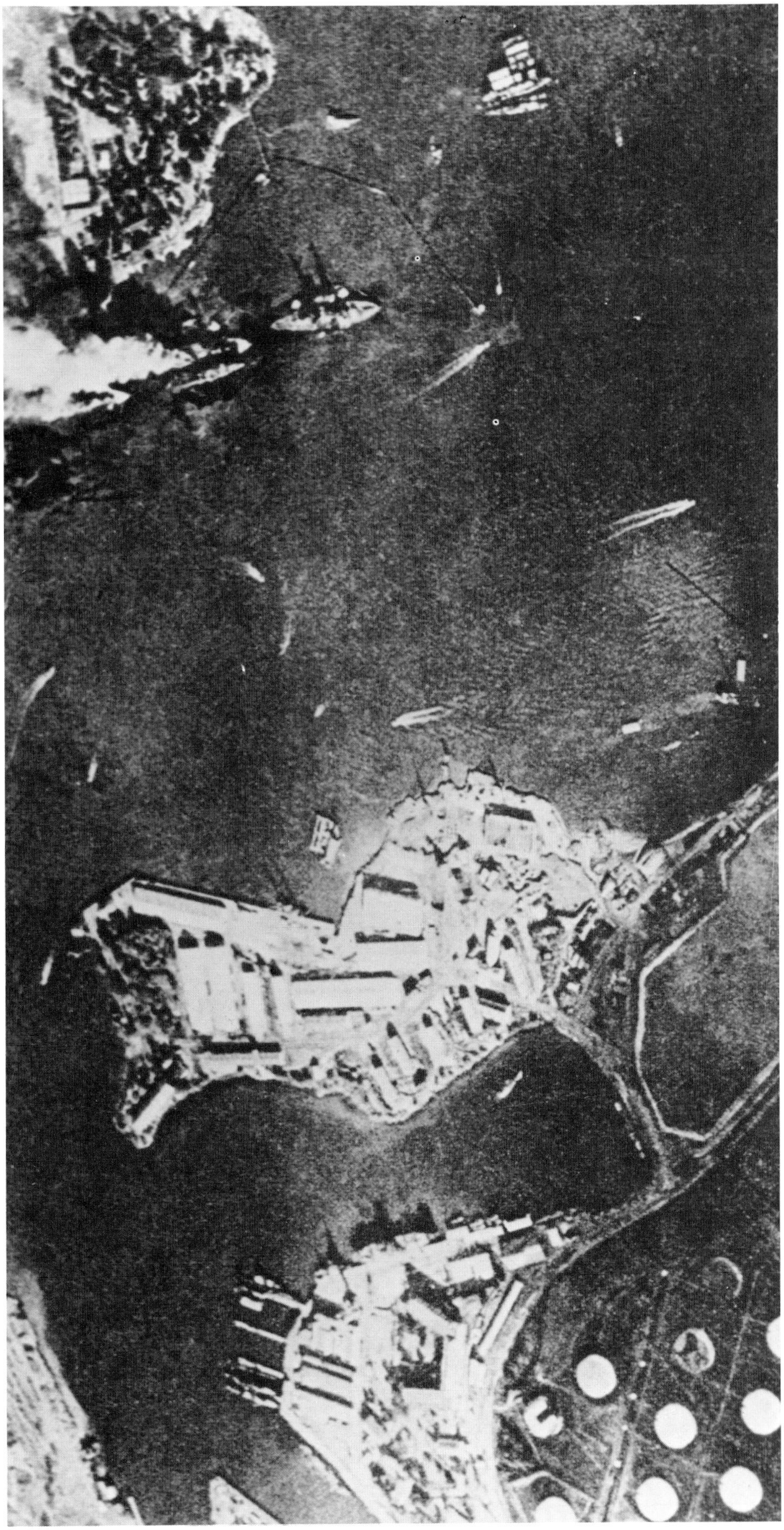

Direct overhead view of the Fleet Supply Depot on Kuahua early in the attack at about 0815. On the bottom is the Submarine Base and tank farms. At top, the northern end of Ford Island with battleships *Nevada* and burning *Arizona*. EA

The *Antares* (AKS-3) had arrived off the entrance to Pearl Harbor two hours before the attack began. She was returning from a mission to Canton Island with a barge in tow. At approximately 0630 *Antares* spotted a submarine in the restricted area. She notified the destroyer *Ward* which took offensive action resulting in the sinking of a two-man Japanese midget sub. USN

Signal Log of U.S.S. *Antares*, Dec. 7-8, 1941*

– Lying to, off Pearl Harbor entrance, transferring barge to U.S.S. *Keosanqua.*

0600 – Exchanged calls with U.S.S. *Ward* on patrol duty.

0630 – Sighted unidentified submarine on starboard quarter. Patrol plane investigating.

– At this point the U.S.S. *Antares* sent a visual signal to the U.S.S. *Ward* telling her of the suspicious submerged submarine. U.S.S. *Ward* approached the submarine.

0645 – U.S.S. *Ward* opened fire on unidentified sub (first shot of the war).

0647 – U.S.S. *Ward* ceased firing gun and dropped three depth charges. Submarine sank slowly.

– Submarine was sighted by A.E. Chiappari, S.M. 2/c and G.R. Vargo, B.M. 2/c.

0750 – C.G. #400 stood out of Pearl Harbor.

0758 – Three loud explosions in Navy Yard. Sighted a great number of Japanese planes dropping bombs in Navy Yard, Pearl Harbor afire.

0800 – U.S.S. *Antares* fired on (strafed) by Japanese aircraft, several bombs dropped nearby.

0811 – U.S.S. *Ward* dropping depth charges and firing anti-aircraft and main batteries. Ships in Navy Yard opened up with anti-aircraft batteries. Shells falling around ship.

0824 – U.S.S. *Antares* received visual signal from shore signal station: "BT under no circumstances enter harbor."

– *Antares* was scheduled to dock at earl Harbor Navy Yard but on receipt of this signal headed for Honolulu Harbor.

Note: Counted four separate groups of enemy bombers, nine in each group.

0848 – All ships and shore batteries ceased firing.

0855 – Enemy planes approaching, anti-aircraft batteries opened up. Sighted eight groups of Japanese planes (bombers) three in each group, passing overhead, headed for Pearl Harbor.

0905 – Destroyers – U.S.S. *Dale*, U.S.S. *Faragut* and five others stood out of Pearl Harbor with all anti-aircraft batteries in action and dropping depth charges.

0925 – Three coastal minesweepers and two destroyers stood out of Pearl Harbor.

0930 – All firing ceased at Pearl Harbor.

0937 – One destroyer stood out of Pearl Harbor.

0950 – Two destroyers stood out of Pearl Harbor.

1010 – One cruiser (*Minneapolis* type) stood out of Pearl Harbor.

1057 – Anti-aircraft batteries opened up at Pearl Harbor.

1059 – Anti-aircraft batteries ceased firing.
1135 – Anti-aircraft batteries opened up.
– One Dutch merchantman opened up on Japanese planes with anti-aircraft batteries. This Dutch vessel was tied up to dock in Honolulu Harbor.
1140 – U.S.S. *Antares* entered Honolulu Harbor.
1200 – Two light cruisers stood out of Pearl Harbor.
1235 – Two destroyers stood out of Pearl Harbor.
1245 – (RDO) Enemy flight from southeast direction headed for Pearl Harbor.
1305 – (RDO) More Japanese transports off Barber's Point.
1314 – (RDO) Dog-fight, southeast direction.
1316 – (RDO) Enemy landing party between OP9 and Nanakuli.
1324 – Motor torpedo boats out of Pearl Harbor.
1328 – One destroyer out of Pearl Harbor.
1350 – (RDO) 21 Japanese vessels 35 miles off shore flying American flags are firing on American ships.
1540 – PBYs and aircobras returning to Ford Island airfield.
1912 – Radio reports say Pearl Harbor is being bombed again.
2105 – Anti-aircraft batteries at Pearl Harbor opened up.
2109 – Anti-aircraft batteries ceased heavy barrage. Light anti-aircraft firing continuing.
2122 – All anti-aircraft firing ceased.
2114 – Glare from fires in Pearl Harbor getting brighter. Fires apparently gaining in intensity.

8 Dec. 1941

0436 – (RDO) 30 enemy planes reported heading this way from Kauai.
0440 – Tracer bullets sighted in Hickam Field area. Anti-aircraft firing at Pearl Harbor.
0455 – (RDO) Enemy planes south of Wheeler Field. OP3 overhead many high.
0500 – Enemy reported heading for Pearl Harbor.
0505 – Signal from commandant 14th naval district: –"All ships stand by – enemy planes overhead.
0507 – Planes from Honolulu – headed toward Pearl Harbor. 18,000 feet altitude.
0510 – (RDO) Many high, northeast, enemy planes heading towards Pearl Harbor.
0515 – Enemy parachute troops reported at Kaliki Valley – (via police radio).
0517 – (RDO) Submarines sighted off Diamond Head. Unidentified.
0518 – (RDO) OP12, Many high, heading towards Pearl Harbor.
0518 – Planes overhead believed to be ours.
0523 – (RDO) OP10, Many high, unidentified, Northeast.
0524 – (RDO) OP12, Few high, circling.
0524 – (RDO) OP1, Many high, unidentified.
0525 – Unknown flight over Schofield Barracks.
0532 – Saboteurs reported at Hickam Field.
0535 – Planes overhead believed to be ours.
0540 – U.S. Planes have been taking off from Pearl Harbor, Wheeler Field, Hickam Field and Ford Island.
0547 – Anti-aircraft firing at Pearl Harbor – Appears as if P.H. is being bombed.
0550 – All ships ceased firing.
0600 – Signal from commander battleships to all ships: –"Exercise more control over Anti-aircraft firing.
0630 – (RDO) Army assumes there are no enemy planes within 200 miles.
0645 – (Police Radio) Things back to normal in Honolulu, workmen are being permitted to go back to work. Citizens urged to stay at home. Schools closed.
2100 – (News Broadcast) San Francisco reported blacked out tonight. Enemy planed intercepted or shot down 20 miles from coast.

This signal log of the U.S.S. *Antares* gives a good early perspective, even before the actual attack began, of the days events, but it also indicates the confusion after the attack, into the night and the next day.

The U.S.S. *Helm* at Pearl Harbor, December 7, 1941

On the afternoon of Fri. Dec. 5, 1941, the U.S.S. *Helm* (DD388), a 1500-ton destroyer of the U.S. Pacific Fleet, returned with the other ships of her division to the Pearl Harbor Naval Base after a week of operations at sea. During that week, as in the several weeks preceding, ships of the fleet operating in Hawaiian waters had been on a war footing. Hostilities with Japan were believed imminent. Orders from the Commander-in-Chief, Pacific Fleet, called for ships at sea to keep armament and detection equipment continuously manned. The *Helm* was in "Condition III," which meant that one-third of her armament (guns, torpedoes, depth charges) was manned around the clock; sonar and fire-control was in continuous operation with reduced crews. Ready ammunition was in place at all gun mounts.

For some reason, probably linked unconsciously to the distance of Hawaii from Japan, and the believed impossibility of surface warships approaching undetected, the focus of attention in the *Helm* and elsewhere in the fleet was on the more stealthy submarine threat. Japan had a substantial submarine fleet, quite capable of an attack in force against Pacific Fleet ships at sea. During the week just ending, the *Helm* had dropped a number of depth charges against what were thought to be sonar submarine contacts. No corroborating evidence developed, however, and it later seemed more than probable that these "contacts" were false ones.

Upon entering Pearl Harbor that Friday afternoon, a subtle change took place in the mental attitude of all on board the *Helm*. Pearl Harbor was landlocked, protected from submarines by a net and boom across its one narrow entrance. Air defense of the Naval Base was the responsibility of the Hawaiian Department of the U.S. Army. The orders from higher authority requiring "condition watches" when at sea did not extend to time in port. In spite of the looming war clouds, normal peacetime routine prevailed within the harbor.

Peacetime safety precautions called for live ammunition above decks to be struck below to the magazines when ships were in port. The Chief Gunner's Mate of the *Helm* came to the Executive Officer, Lt. Allan L. Reed, USN, and asked whether or not to send ammunition below. Perhaps he had some unconscious premonition that it might be needed. Lieutenant Reed, not having any premonitory feelings, and being an officer who "went by the book," told the Chief to go ahead and strike the ammunition below. The unfortunate nature of this decision was forcefully brought home some forty hours later.

Safely moored with other ships of the division in East Loch, the crew of the *Helm* prepared for weekend liberty. The Commanding Officer, Lt. Comdr. Chester E Carroll, USN, planned to be with his wife and 13-year-old son in Honolulu. Lieutenant Reed intended to spend Saturday moving his family from one rented house to another in Honolulu. Others had their own plans. The "duty section," consisting of about one-fourth of the crew, remained on board.

There was, however, one circumstance which differentiated the *Helm* from other ships of the fleet on this weekend. *Helm* was scheduled to move early Sunday morning from her berth to a pier in West Loch (another arm of the sprawling harbor), where she would undergo a de-

USS *Helm*, a destroyer, was the only major warship underway when the attack began. She was en route to the Deperming Station in the West Loch when her crew saw the first explosion on Ford Island. Lt. Cmdr. Chester E. Carroll saw Admiral Furlong's signal for all ships to sortie and by 0817 had cleared the harbor entrance doing 25 knots. At 0915, *Helm* was attacked by two *Hiryu* dive bombers. Two near misses caused flooding forward from ruptured hull plates. Repairs were completed Jan. 15, 1942, on the Navy Yard's Marine Railway. NA 80-G-321525

magnetizing procedure known as "deperming." In this process, designed to neutralize the ship's acquired magnetism as a protection against magnetic mines and torpedoes, large cables were passed entirely around and under the ship's residual magnetic "signature." In preparation for deperming, all clocks and other items which could be adversely affected by the magnetic field were removed from the ship on Saturday.

Arrival at the deperming station in West Lock was set for 0830, Sunday, Dec. 7th. Lt. Commander Carroll ordered that all hands be back aboard by 0600 that morning, in order to be ready to get underway at 0700. The wardroom officers asked the captain if he would let the duty section get the ship underway and shift berths; it was not a difficult maneuver, and to do so would allow the rest of the crew to enjoy uninterrupted weekend liberty. The captain said, "No," he wanted a full crew on board.

So it came about that everyone returned to the ship Saturday night or in the early hours of Sunday. The engineer officer, Lt.(jg) Gerald Christie, picked up Lieutenant Reed, who lived near him, at 0500 and after picking up one or two others drove the few miles to Pearl Harbor on dark, deserted roads. Lieut. Comdr. Carroll was also on his way back, bringing with him his son for what promised to be a real treat for the youngster—a ride across Pearl Harbor, with the boy on the bridge watching his dad maneuver the ship. Clearing the nest of destroyers at the East Loch buoy about 0700, the *Helm* proceeded slowly around Ford Island toward Waipio Point, a tongue of land near the entrance, to the west of which lay the channel to West Loch. Waipio Point was the site of a small and little-known naval ammunition storage. The *Helm*'s two motor whaleboats had not been hoisted for this brief "cruise," but followed in the ship's wake. The "special sea detail," which had got the ship underway, remained on station to attend to mooring at the deperming dock. The turn around Waipio Point into West Loch was a sharp one, nearly 180 degrees. The *Helm* was well into this turn with full right rudder, when Lieutenant Reed, standing on the bridge with his back to the pilothouse bulkhead, saw through the pilot house windows several airplanes diving steeply toward Ford Island. Reed just had time to think, "This is an odd time for our carrier planes to be holding dive bombing practice," when the first of the diving planes turned broadside and the rays of the rising sun illuminated the big red "meatballs" on its wings. Almost immediately a large hangar at the southwest end of Ford Island lighted up inside with a fiery red glow and then collapsed like a house of cards. Reed's next thought was, "This is it!!" He reached behind him and pulled the handle sounding the general alarm, calling the crew to battle stations.

The captain and the others on the bridge, of course, witnessed this "opening shot" of our entry into World War II. Lt. Commander Carroll's first action was to back all the engines emergency full to get the ship out of her tight turn and out into the main channel. Next he sent his son below to the wardroom, where for safety's sake the boy spent the next hour or so in life jacket and steel helmet, wondering what was happening.

The main concern of the executive officer was to get the ship's guns firing. The sky was full of Japanese planes, some passing at fairly close range on their attack runs against "battleship row." But only the *Helm*'s .50-cal. machine guns were firing. There was no ready ammunition at the five-inch gun mounts, and it quickly developed that the keys to the magazine hatches could not be found. Precious minutes were lost in this "snafu" before bolt cutters were brought up and the padlocks securing the hatches were severed. The executive officer's bitter regret at his decision on Friday to return the ready ammunition to the magazines was scarcely lessened by this "missing key" foul-up. It later developed that the keys were in the pocket of the "in-port" Officer-Of-The-Deck, who had forgotten to turn them over to a "underway O.O.D." and had gone to his battle station without realizing that he still had them.

Meanwhile, the ship had backed out into the main channel and was heading for the harbor exit to get clear of those confined waters. Their .50 cal. machine guns fired continuously at enemy planes as the ship rushed down the channel. By the time the *Helm* was clear, 5-inch shells were at the guns and the gunnery officer, Lieut.(jg) Victor A. Dybal, was firing at the periscope of a mini-sub creeping across the inshore waters too shallow for *Helm* to close with depth charges.

The ship's boats, with admirable presence of mind, had promptly beached themselves amid the heavy foliage on Waipio Point. (Had they known of the ammunition dump there, they might not have chosen that particular refuge). For the next two or three days, these *Helm* boat crews worked without rest and with little food rescuing survivors from the oil-blackened waters and shattered ships in the harbor.

Emerging into the relatively open water of Honolulu harbor, near the famed "Aloha Tower" of the Matson Line Pier, Captain Carroll had two main preoccupations. One was to get his son ashore as soon as possible, back to his mother, who would of course be distraught once she learned what had happened at Pearl Harbor. After a good many fruitless radio calls, *Helm* finally succeeded in getting a promise from the Coast Guard Station to send a boat. True to their word, they did so in spite of the obvious hazards (Japanese planes seemed to be everywhere) and at about 0930, an hour and a half after the attack started, the boy was taken ashore and sent home. The captain's other preoccupation was the safe navigation of the ship. The compensating spheres, Flinders bars, and other magnetic elements of the magnetic compass had been removed in preparation for deperming. In any event, the gyrocompass, unaffected by magnetic fields, was always used for navigation and piloting. But the sudden full-scale reversal of the propellers at Waipio Point had induced violent vibrations throughout the ship, which caused the gyro to "tumble." This meant that a period of some hours must pass before the gyro, set back on its proper axis, "settled down" to deliver reliable direction. With no means of getting accurate bearings, or even of knowing the ship's heading, the Captain had to exercise extreme care to keep from going aground.

At this point, while steaming around waiting for other ships to emerge and trying to stay in deep water, the *Helm* suffered her only real damage of the day. A small Japanese plane appeared undetected from astern and dropped a 100-lb. bomb at low altitude. Fortunately, it was a near-miss, perhaps 50 feet off the starboard bow, and there were no personnel casualties, but again the ship was subjected to a violent vibration, whipping and flexing her whole structure. The forward peak tank, a void space directly abaft the stem, quickly filled with water, but the transverse bulkhead held, and no further flooding occurred. Of more import was the effect on the main battery fire control system. The gun director, weighing several thousand pounds, was mounted above the pilothouse atop a steel tube about three feet in diameter which extended directly down through the superstructure to the below decks plotting room. The whipping of the ship from the near-miss had cracked the welded seam which secured the upper part of the fire-control tube to the deck below the director. The captain sent the executive officer down to the plotting room to climb up the whole length of the fire control tube to assess the damage. Nearing the top of this vertical black tunnel, a few feet below the director, Lieutenant Reed could see a crack of daylight around two-thirds of its circumference.

There was only one thing to do – shore up the gun director on blocks to take the heavy weight off the weakened fire control tube. Otherwise, there was a grave risk that in a seaway the entire mass of the director might come toppling down. The shoring-up of course made rotation of the director impossible, and resulted in total loss of central control and automatic direction of gunfire.

In this sorry state, then, with a bent and twisted bow, water in the forward tank, only local control of her guns, an uncertain and delicate gyrocompass, and with no clocks, chronometers and few watches aboard, the *Helm* joined a hastily formed task force of cruisers and destroyers to spend the next three days in a fruitless search for the Japanese. Returning to the scene of death and desolation that was Pearl Harbor, *Helm* welcomed and praised her boat crews for their valiant work, and set about getting ready in earnest for the long war to come. After a week or two, *Helm* was hauled out on a marine railway at Pearl Harbor where temporary repairs to the bow were made. The cracked fire-control tube was rewelded. But final repairs to the hull, including a new bow section, were not made until the following June or July at a drydock in Sydney, Australia.

The *Helm*'s wartime career, including her participation in the disastrous Battle of Salvo Island at Guadacanal, is another story, but she emerged from Dec. 7, 1941, with a unique cachet – "the only ship in Pearl Harbor fully-manned and underway when the war began."

This is a personal memoir written by

Rear Admiral Allan L. Reed
USN (retired)
written to mark the 40th Anniversary of the "day of infamy."

Berthed at buoy X-Ray 5 in East Loch with a nest of barges and two destroyers, *Allen* (DD-66) and *Chew* (DD-106), was the 51-year-old hulk of the Spanish-American War cruiser, the ex-*Baltimore*, which had been out of service since 1922. The sunken *Arizona* is at right. NA 80-G-32735

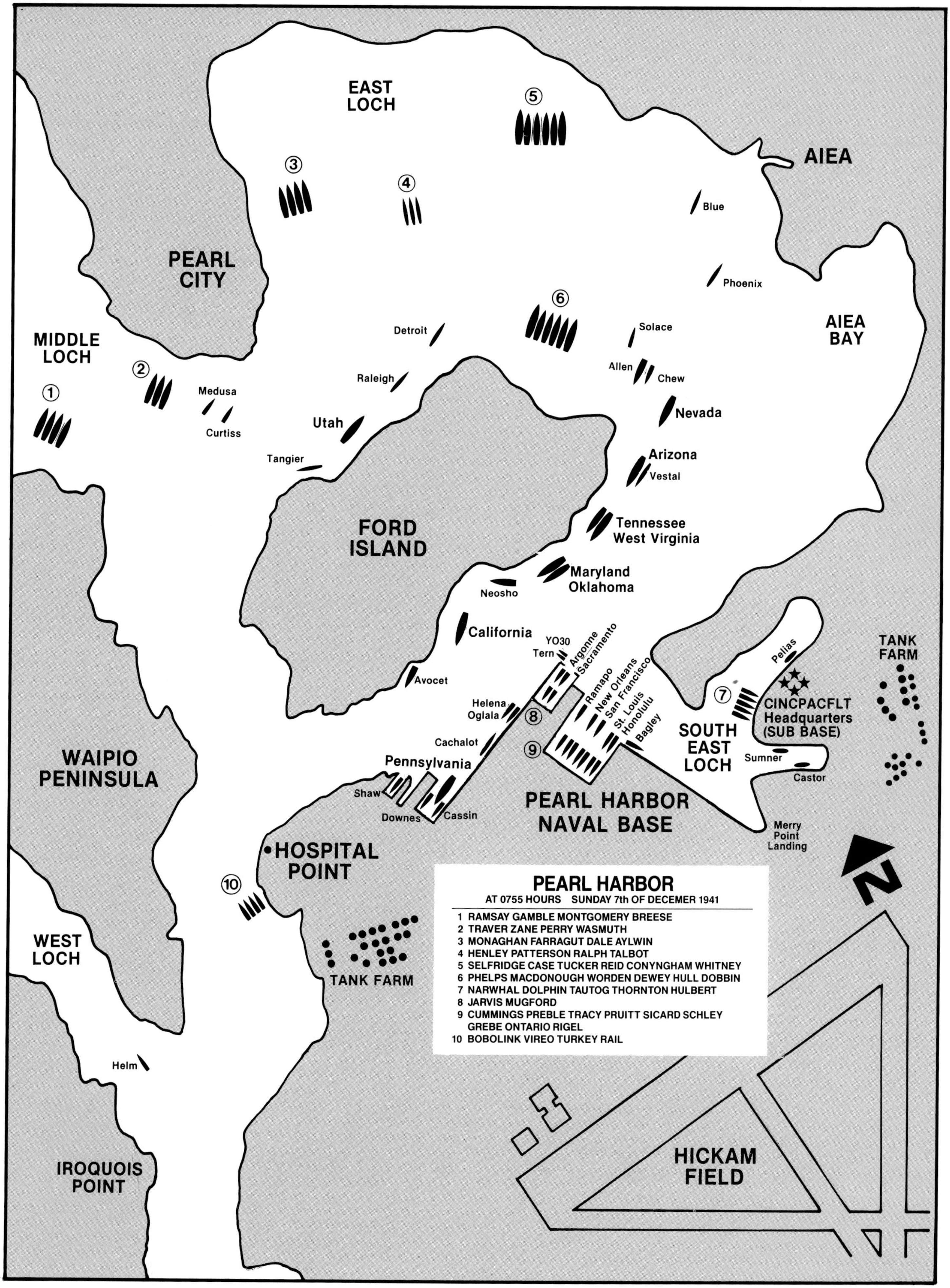

EAST LOCH
AIEA
PEARL CITY
MIDDLE LOCH
AIEA BAY
Blue
Phoenix
Detroit
Solace
Raleigh
Allen
Chew
Medusa
Curtiss
Utah
Nevada
Tangier
Arizona
Vestal
FORD ISLAND
Tennessee
West Virginia
Maryland
Oklahoma
Neosho
California
YO30
Tern
Argonne
Sacramento
Avocet
Ramapo
New Orleans
San Francisco
St. Louis
Honolulu
Bagley
Pelias
TANK FARM
CINCPACFLT Headquarters (SUB BASE)
Helena
Oglala
Cachalot
SOUTH EAST LOCH
Sumner
Castor
WAIPIO PENINSULA
Pennsylvania
Shaw
Downes
Cassin
PEARL HARBOR NAVAL BASE
Merry Point Landing
HOSPITAL POINT
N
PEARL HARBOR
AT 0755 HOURS SUNDAY 7th OF DECEMBER 1941
1 RAMSAY GAMBLE MONTGOMERY BREESE
2 TRAVER ZANE PERRY WASMUTH
3 MONAGHAN FARRAGUT DALE AYLWIN
4 HENLEY PATTERSON RALPH TALBOT
5 SELFRIDGE CASE TUCKER REID CONYNGHAM WHITNEY
6 PHELPS MACDONOUGH WORDEN DEWEY HULL DOBBIN
7 NARWHAL DOLPHIN TAUTOG THORNTON HULBERT
8 JARVIS MUGFORD
9 CUMMINGS PREBLE TRACY PRUITT SICARD SCHLEY GREBE ONTARIO RIGEL
10 BOBOLINK VIREO TURKEY RAIL
WEST LOCH
TANK FARM
Helm
HICKAM FIELD
IROQUOIS POINT

First Wave—The Japanese View

BY DAVID AIKEN

The Japanese aerial armada first sighted Kahuku Point at 0740. Comdr. Mitsuo Fuchida, the overall attack leader, shot a single "black dragon" flare into the air to signal that the attack sequence would be for "Surprise." When the high-flying Zeros failed to respond, he loaded another black-tipped, yellow shell in his flare gun and fired directly at them. The lower flying dive bomber leader saw the second black plume of smoke. Two flares meant "surprise lost" and the dive bombers were to attack the airfields prior to the ship attacks. Thus the silent signals went awry.

At 0749, Fuchida telegraphed the signal "TO," meaning "charge," to his aerial unit commanders. Not in the code book, this signal was recognized among the commanders as bravado. Each unit leader then banked his wing sharply to signal the course changes.

About 0751, 25 *Zuikaku* dive bombers, escorted by eight Zeros, hit Wheeler Field. The formation split with some attacking from the west and the east. To those on the ground, the western formation appeared to have come through Kolekole Pass. Viewing the preemptive strike upon Wheeler, at 0752 Comdr. Fuchida telegraphed the code "Tora" for "surprise achieved." Codes in the book were to be sent three times. Even this did not slow the rest of the dive bombers. Twenty-six *Shokaku* dive bombers, escorted by nine *Akagi* fighters continued down the east side of the valley.

Eleven *Shokaku* and *Zuikaku* fighters dived for lower altitude in preparation for the strafing of Kaneohe Naval Air Station. Also about 0751, two of those *Shokaku* Zeros gave a burst of machine gun fire into a civilian aircraft trainer above the Mormon Temple on Oahu's northeast coast. The *Shokaku* and *Zuikaku* Zeros hit Kaneohe at about 0753.

About 0754, the *Shokaku* dive bomber fighter escort lead unit attacked two Piper Cubs near the Nuuanu Pali Pass. One Cub's engine was torn from its motor mount and the pilot had his first parachute jump. *Akagi* Zero pilot PO1c Takeshi Hirano in AI-154 shared with PO1c Shinaji Iwama in the kill. (Iwama was killed in action in his crash on Eastern Island, Battle of Midway). On the west side of the Waianae Mountain range flew the strike force of 89 attack bombers. Forty with torpedoes were lowering their altitude while they spotted targets. Six *Hiryu* Zeros, led by Buntaicho Lt. Kiyokuma Okajima in BII-101, escorted until they arrived to strafe Ewa Field about 0753. A1c Tetsuo Sento in BII-117 and future ace Kazuo Muranaka participated in this strafing.

The other 49 were loaded with specially converted naval artillery shells and maintained altitude. Nine *Kaga* Zeros were top cover. They had to mark time as only just so many aircraft could be in the air space above Pearl Harbor at a time.

The *Shokaku* dive bombers split up. Nine, led by Lt Comdr. Kakuichi Takahashi in EI-238, dived for Ford Island NAS, nine went for an easterly approach against Hickam Field with A1c Kunio Iwatsuki in EI-239 in the rear. Eight went for the west end led by Buntaicho Lt. Masao Yamaguchi in EI-201 and Shotaicho Lt. (JG) Iwakichi Mifukuin EI-204. The first bombs hit Ford Island at 0755 with Hickam Field within the same minute.

Sweeping from the south *Akagi* Zeros found John Rodgers Field (now Honolulu International Airport) about 0757. Quickly strafing, the first units flew above and below a civilian trainer doing a landing approach, then hit a Hawaiian Airlines DC-3 causing a fire. The following units also strafed the plane, hitting the fire extinguisher which put out the fire! They rapidly went on to Hickam Field.

Eight *Soryu* and eight *Hiryu* torpedo planes were to attack the carrier moorings on the north side of Ford Island. The lead commanders in both units noted the carriers missing, six *Soryu* planes broke away from their leader to attack the ships moored there anyway. These dropped torpedoes at about 0756.

Hiryu Buntaicho Hirata Matsumura, in BII-320, had similar luck with half of his unit straying from him, including BII-314 and BII-322. These attacked the paired *Helena* and *Oglala* which looked like a single battleship at the altitude the planes were flying.

The *Soryu* leader was similarly fooled and followed the *Hiryu* strays. His wingman noted the error and sought a battleship target.

The dozen *Akagi* torpedo planes came across Hickam Field as the dive bombers were smashing the field. They did a quick left turn across Southeast Loch and began to drop torpedoes at 0757. They first hit the *West Virginia*, an instant later the second, dropped by Lt. (JG) Jinichi Goto in AI-308, hit the *Oklahoma*.

The solo *Soryu* and the four *Hiryu* torpedo planes broke into the *Akagi* formation but only a *Hiryu* bomber could get a clear drop.

The dozen *Kaga* torpedo planes had slowed down to allow the earlier aircraft good clearance. They paid for this in blood.

Leading the *Kaga* planes were the three *Hiryu* bombers, including BII-320, which couldn't get into the *Akagi* run. The second *Kaga* plane was AII-312. The small caliber AA fire was getting thick. The sixth *Kaga* plane crashed at the US Navy hospital. The torpedo on the next plane, Buntaicho Lt. Mimori Suzuki in AII-356, exploded.

That single *Soryu* plane finally got into the formation to

launch against the *California*. This gave the ninth *Kaga* plane time to see and drop at a different target, the *Nevada*. He crashed just aft of that ship. The final two were badly hit, one went into the harbor while the other crashed south of Oahu.

The torpedo planes wasted too much ordnance on easy targets such as *Oklahoma*, leaving the *Nevada* almost unscathed, and on incorrectly identified targets like the *Utah* and *Helena*.

The *Shokaku* and *Zuikaku* Zero attacks at Kaneohe NAS initially hit three PBY flying boats moored in the bay. More planes were strafed just outside of the hangers. The Zeros claimed 32 burning on the ground.

Two of the *Shokaku*'s units flew south to check on Bellows Field. One went down to strafe, wounding one medic and claiming three damaged aircraft on the ground.

At Hickam, *Shokaku* dive bombers laid waste. The first of a dozen B-17s attempted a landing. The *Akagi* Zero unit pounced. With wounded aboard, this B-17 went around to Bellows, but it was attacked again by the top cover *Shokaku* Zero which hovered above. When it finally landed, the B-17 was too high. It touched down in mid-runway and wiped out its landing gear across a ditch at the end of the runway.

The second B-17 coming in to Hickam was attacked in the air by the *Akagi* unit. Setting of the port tail of the B-17, Lt Comdr. Shigeru Itaya poured 7.7-mm bullets through the fuselage. Several were wounded, one died later. Magnesium flares caught fire in the radio compartment. The B-17 was able to land but burned in two on the runway.

Strafing at Hickam continued from the *Akagi* Zeros. Future ace PO2c Masao Taniguchi was in on these attacks. Ground fire converged with that coming from ships along the channel with one success, *Akagi* Zero AI-154, PO1c Takeshi Hirano, wingman to the leader of first wave Zeros. Lt. Comdr. Itaya, was hit and, as he crashed, took out some palm trees, then rammed into the entrance of a building. Both the pilot and the observers standing in the entrance were killed. The first look at the mystery plane was of this crashed example.

Freed of the escort duty, the *Kaga* Zeros were late to the fray. Coming low toward John Rodgers Field, they passed a civilian trainer trying to approach the field. This was too much temptation to future ace PO1c Akira Yamamoto, in AII-168, who shot it down. The two enlisted US Army crewmen are still missing. Yamamoto was credited by Japan with the first aerial victory in the attack.

Headed for Ewa Field, two *Shokaku* Vals made a strafing run onto a B-17, just as a *Kaga* Zero, damaged over Hickam, crashed south of the field. The Zero had crushed its belly tank and chipped its propeller on the Hickam runway as it came in too low during strafing.

Ewa Field and Camp Malakole near Barbers Point both put in claims for the *Kaga* Zero which came down into the ocean just west of the camp. *Soryu* Zeros, led by Buntaicho Lt. Masaji Suganami in BI-185, coming from Wheeler also headed for Ewa. They arrived just in time to attack the flight of SBD dive bombers coming from the *Enterprise*.

Suganami pounced upon two of the SBDs. Return fire from one of the SBD wounded the #2 wingman who left immediately for the *Soryu*. The #3 wingman was able to shoot down both SBDs over land, yet one of the SBD crew is still listed as missing in action.

A single *Soryu* Zero flying top cover pounced on several unsuspecting SBDs. He shot down two. One of these planes is still missing. He also approached a third SBD when ground fire from Fort Weaver shot it down.

A civilian plane trying to approach John Rodgers Field was also shot down in the area, whether by ground fire from Fort Weaver or by this *Soryu* pilot is unclear. The Piper Cub was swept ashore weeks later, the crew is still missing.

Early returning *Shokaku* dive bombers from the attack on Hickam Field arrived at the rendezvous point some 20 miles northwest of Kaena Point. An approaching SBD was attacked by three of these *Shokaku* bombers and shot down. The SBD crew is still missing in action.

The large calibre AA guns, ineffective against the torpedo planes, opened up on the approach of Fuchida's high-level attack bombers. These special five plane formations were to hit the inboard American battleships which the torpedo bombers could not.

Immediately, Fuchida's own formation got the brunt of the initial flak. The #5 plane was hit in the bomb shackle. The premature drop hit in the channel to the sea. Ground witnesses thought that mines were being dropped! Fuchida's own plane, AI-301, was also hit.

The approach angle to the target was extremely difficult at best. The highly trained bombardier wasn't able to call course corrections to his pilot quickly enough, so they held the unit's ordnance for a second approach. The following two *Akagi* units were able to make the corrections based on the initial unit's error. They dropped onto the *Tennessee*, with some hitting the *West Virginia* moored outboard.

Following of the heels of the *Akagi* units, the three *Kaga* units were also aiming at the paired *Tennessee*/*West Virginia*, but the second *Kaga* unit noted the undamaged *Arizona* and hit the aft end of the ship just as the final torpedo of that attack struck the *Oklahoma*. The third unit was led by AII-316.

Fuchida still couldn't get into the string of five plane formations when the *Hiryu* units struck. The first set of five also dropped onto the *Arizona*. The smoke from the *Arizona* blocked the second *Hiryu* formation, led by BII-310, from viewing their target, the *California*, and they overshot and missed.

The first *Soryu* unit was able to see through some of the smoke to hit, one each on the paired *Tennessee/West Virginia*. The second *Soryu* unit couldn't see their target, the *Nevada*, and came around again.

Fuchida finally came in and chose the undamaged *Maryland*, inboard of the overturned *Oklahoma*. He claimed two hits. The second *Soryu* unit finally got turned for their run but the bombardier, in BI-312, still missed the *Nevada*.

The high-level units, loaded with the armor-piercing shell, designed specifically for penetration of thick battleship's decks, wasted too much ordnance on the *Tennessee*. They failed in their attempts on the *California* and *Nevada* and missed an obvious target, the *Pennsylvania*, in drydock. Damage assessment studies suggest that they even missed the *Maryland*.

The first attack wave began to leave for the carriers just before 0830 and the most of the stragglers left by 0930. One late plane finally landed aboard the *Shokaku* at 1220, as overall attack leader, Comdr. Fuchida returned after the second attack.

One *Shokaku* dive bomber, EI-239, with problems on board was still flying and radioed requests for position. American radio direction-finders plotted bearings on the plane. The Japanese did the same, but stayed on radio silence. The plane finally radioed its intent to crash into the ocean at 1313 hours. It was the sole dive bomber loss in the first wave.

The foremast and the bridge collapsed forward to an eerie 45-degree angle when the forward section of the ship was destroyed by the magazine explosion. This forlorn yet still-defiant look of the *Arizona* in her death throes is one of the most memorable images of the war. Three of her crew members would earn the Medal of Honor for their actions that day. NA

The *Vestal* (AR-4) a repair ship, was moored at Berth Fox-7, Battleship Row, alongside of the *Arizona.* At 0806 she was hit by a bomb meant for *Arizona.* At 0808 a tremendous explosion occurred on the *Arizona*, the force of which blew many of *Vestal*'s crew overboard, including the skipper, Cmdr. Cassin Young. Commander Young, who would earn the Medal of Honor for his valor, swam back to his ship and rallied the crew to fight and save her. By 0830 *Vestal* began moving away from the dying *Arizona* and was beached off Aica Shoals to prevent her sinking. NA 80-G-32607

Capt. Franklin Van Valkenburgh of Minneapolis, Minn., was the Commanding Officer of the *Arizona.* He received the Medal of Honor posthumously for extraordinary courage in the tragically short time allotted him on the morning of Dec. 7, 1941. USN

When the magazines of the *Arizona* blew up in a volcanic explosion, the forward two-thirds of the ship, from the mainmast to the bow, was engulfed in flames. Nearly all those who survived were stationed in the after part of the ship. The fires would not be extinguished until Tuesday afternoon, Dec. 9. USN

Left, the yard tug *Hoga* (YT-146) commanded by Chief Boatswain's Mate J.B. McManus and the garbage lighter, YG-17, commanded by Chief Boatswain's Mate L.M. Jansen, fighting fires on the wrecked battleship *Arizona*. Both vessels would stay alongside *Arizona* until all fires were finally out on Dec. 9. USN

View from Ford Island showing *Arizona* burning on the afternoon of Dec. 7. USN

On Monday afternoon of the 8th, the *Tern* (AM-31) came alongside the still-burning *Arizona* to assist in fighting fires and stayed until the fires were out on Tuesday afternoon. The superstructure of the fleet tug *Navajo* (AT-64) can be seen aft of the *Tern*'s smokestack. NA 80-G-32610

The forward half of the *Arizona* was totally destroyed. There was no thought of raising the ship and returning her to service, although at one time it was believed the after section could be salvaged. One hundred and five bodies had been recovered during salvage operations. The remaining bodies could not be recovered as the ship was never raised. By October 1943 all salvage work had ceased. USN

The fleet oiler *Neosho* (AO-23), moored at the gasoline wharf on the east side of Ford Island, had just finished discharging most of her cargo of aviation fuel five minutes before the first bombs fell. Cmdr. John S. Phillips got his ship underway by 0842 and moved the ship, and the remainder of its highly volatile cargo, to a safer berth at Merry Point. The *California* is listing to port from torpedo damage. EA

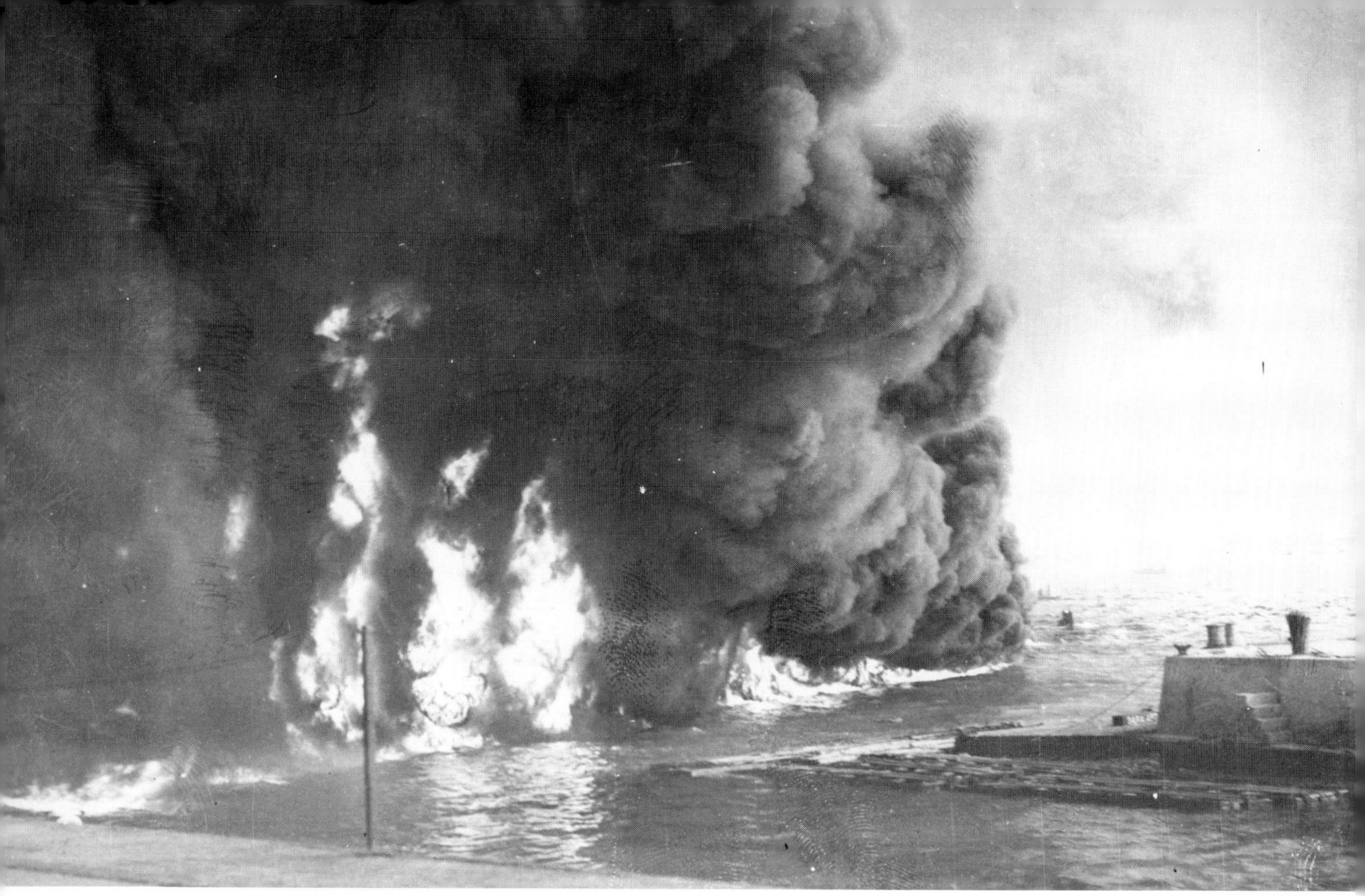

The *California* is completely engulfed by smoke and flames from burning fuel oil drifting from the stricken battleships, *West Virginia* and *Arizona*, and her own fuel escaping from her damaged hull. USN

Looking up Battleship Row before 0900. The towering column of smoke is from the inferno of the battleships *Arizona* and *West Virginia*. The oiler *Neosho* (right) has backed up the channel away from the gasoline pier and will move to Merry Point. Many of the officers and enlisted men were on weekend leave and their struggles to get back to their ships became stories of heroism, ingenuity and individual accomplishment. NA 80-G-32640

California listing to port and smoking profusely about 1000 hours as men in the foreground are watching from the Ford Island Headquarters Building for hostile planes. The order to abandon ship has already been given as drifting fuel oil from the *Arizona* and *West Virginia* burns on the water. By the evening of Dec. 9, the *California* will sink on an even keel and settle on the bottom. Her watertight integrity was lessened because of an impending hull inspection that required many of her hatches and manhole covers to be open for thorough venting of tanks and voids. NA

The stricken *California* is surrounded by many rescue vessels in a valiant effort to keep her afloat and from capsizing. She would finally come to rest in the mud on an even keel after three days. She was raised on March 24, 1942, and placed in Drydock #2 on April 9, 1942.USN

Stern view of the burning *California*, smoking and listing to port from torpedo and bomb damage. About 20 minutes after the abandon ship order had been given Capt. J.W. Bunkley, commanding officer of the *California*, saw that the ship was no longer endangered, and ordered his crew back on board to fight fires. The heavy pall of smoke from the burning ships rose thousands of feet, turning daylight to twilight. USNI

General Quarters is sounded along Battleship Row as the U.S.S. *Oklahoma* is struck by torpedoes dropped from low flying Type 97 "Kate" torpedo bombers. PAUL BENDER

The *Maryland* escaped serious damage as it was berthed at Fox-5 inboard of the *Oklahoma* whose capsized hull is on the right. *Maryland* was protected from torpedoes but was hit by two 15-inch armor piercing bombs that caused minor damage to the ship and killed four men. On Dec. 11, she was moved from behind the sunken *Oklahoma* to the Navy Yard for temporary repairs. She departed Pearl Harbor on Dec. 20, 1941, for Bremerton, Wash., in company with the *Pennsylvania* and the *Tennessee* for permanent repairs and upgrading of anti-aircraft weapon systems. USN

The *Maryland* was protected from the torpedo attack by the *Oklahoma* which was moored outboard. The *Oklahoma* was repeatedly struck by as many as nine torpedoes in just a few minutes. Less than 15 minutes after the first torpedo hit, the *Oklahoma* rolled over with the loss of 429 officers and men. NA 80-G-33138

Raleigh, moored at Fox-12 on the east side of Ford Island, was struck by a torpedo at 0756. With the forward engine and fire room compartments completely flooded, the ship listed heavily to port. Fearing his ship might capsize, Capt. R. Bentham Simons, ordered the crew to jettison equipment to reduce topside weight. That afternoon, the tug *Sunnadin* (AT-28) received orders to assist the cruiser in her struggle to stay afloat. *Sunnadin* stood by *Raleigh* until Dec. 9, pumping, and supplying electricity and fresh water. The overturned hull of the *Utah* is on the right. NA 80-G-32742

Framed by plumes of smoke are the sunken *West Virginia* and the *Tennessee. West Virginia* was hit by two armor piercing 15-inch projectiles and by at least seven torpedoes (possibly as many as nine) that literally blew open the whole port side of the vessel. Note the early type SC radar atop the foremast of *West Virginia*. NA 80-G-32414

The devastation at Battleship Row as viewed from the deck of the *Argonne* (AG-31) berthed at B-4 on TenTen Dock shortly after the attack had ended. The *Maryland*, inboard of the capsized *Oklahoma* (left), the sunken *West Virginia* and *Tennessee* (center), and the shattered *Arizona* are draped by a mantle of black smoke that rises over the death and destruction. NA 80-G-32691

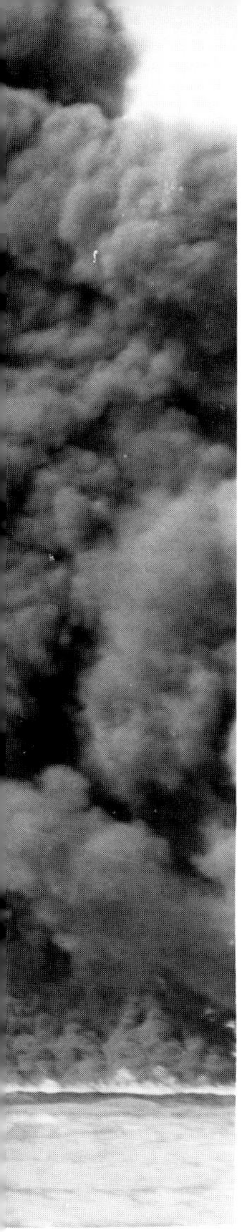

Gallantly, against a background of black oily smoke, the national ensign of the sunken *West Virginia* flies proudly as an inspiration for all, as rescue operations continue on the fantail. NA 80-G-32677

Late in the afternoon of Dec. 7, *West Virginia*, *Tennessee* and *Arizona* (left to right) burn on Battleship Row. The heat from the *Arizona*'s fires were so intense, the endangered *Tennessee* had to flood her aft magazines and keep her screws turning to prevent the ship from being engulfed by the burning fuel oil on the water. NA 80-G-32424

While conducting the defense of his ship the *West Virginia* from the flag bridge, Capt. Mervyn Sharp Bennion was fatally wounded. He would die later in the day from his wounds and was posthumously awarded the Medal of Honor for his gallant actions. A destoyer, the USS *Bennion* was named in his honor, christened by his wife, Mrs. Louis Clark Bennion on July 4, 1943.
UTAH STATE HISTORICAL SOCIETY

The garbage lighter YG-17 sends streams of water onto the burning *West Virginia*. Quick counterflooding by her crew saved her from capsizing and she would settle on the shallow bottom of the harbor. She lost 105 men including her commanding officer Capt. Mervyn S. Bennion, who, though mortally wounded, refused to leave the bridge and continued to inquire of his officers the conditions of the ship. NA 80-G-11947

Second Wave Attack and the American Reply

BY DAVID AIKEN

Leaving the carriers one hour later than the first wave, the Japanese force arrived in the vicinity of Oahu one hour later at 0840. *Zuikaku Hikotaicho* Lt. Cmdr. Shigekazu Shimazaki sighted Kahuku Point off to his far right. He shot the flare to assemble into attack formation.

The main strike force of 78 dive bombers broke right to cross above the Koolau mountain range escorted by nine *Kaga* Zeros. Twenty-seven *Zuikaku* high-level bombers broke left to head farther south escorted by nine *Akagi* Zeros.

Traveling south off of the east shore, he signaled the attack at 0854 as they came upon their first target, Kaneohe NAS. The 27 *Shokaku* high-level bomber unit split as 18 hit Kaneohe at 0855. The other nine headed over the mountains to hit Ford Island.

The dive bomber approach to Pearl Harbor was met with heavy flak from the ships. Leader of all dive bombers, *Soryu* Hikotaicho Lt. Cmdr. Takashige Egusa pointed out the undamaged battleship *Pennsylvania* in drydock to his *Soryu* wingmen.

He personally began the dive bombing of the harbor with the *New Orleans* at 0902. In the dive bombing, Egusa lost one of his wingmen. Both overshot to hit the destroyers in the drydock and flak got one.

Each flight of three planes followed the leader after select targets. Some made isolated runs on widely separated targets.

One *Soryu* leader went after the *Neosho* as she left her berth to avoid the approaching oil fire on the water. Awaiting their turn, other units hovering above pinpointed the *Neosho* as a possible target.

While waiting, two *Hiryu* bombers saw the *Helm* outside the harbor. The near miss caused some minor damage. It didn't prevent completion of her mission.

Following the *Soryu*'s guide, the *Hiryu* unit hit the *Pennsylvania*, but the majority went after the *Maryland*, the *West Virginia* and the seemingly undamaged *California*. Some tried the repair ship *Rigel*.

The *Akagi* unit had three chances against the *Neosho* during her short sortie and came close. Three dive bombers went after the floating drydock and succeeded in starting a fire aboard the *Shaw* in drydock.

Watching the previous *Hiryu* bombing of the *Maryland*, six bombers tried, but smoke from the *Arizona* obscured the ship. Although the *Raleigh* was sinking from a torpedo hit, one leader still went after her. His wingmen bombed the *Curtiss*, recognized as a seaplane tender. One unit bombed the *Pyro* moored away from the rest in West Loch. They put holes in the dock instead.

The *Kaga* dive bombers had the biggest unit, an extra nine planes. They were beginning to make their runs against Battleship Row when the *Nevada* surprised all participants in making a sortie. This target of opportunity was too good.

If they could sink her in the channel, the harbor could

At 0905 an Aichi D3A1 dive bomber was hit by anti-aircraft fire from several ships, killing the pilot. The crippled plane crashed into the *Curtiss*, hitting the starboard side boat crane and exploding. Seven minutes later *Curtiss* was hit by a bomb and straddled by three near misses, killing 20 men. Fully repaired by January 1942, the *Curtiss* would serve the U.S. fleet until she was decommissioned on Sept. 24, 1957.
NA 80-G-32614

be blocked for months. Twenty-three bombers converged upon the *Nevada* and the rest of the harbor threw up heavier fire to give her cover. Damaged by this fire, one of the crashing planes hit the *Curtiss* in a suicide attack, a projection of future Kamikaze attacks.

The *Nevada* beached near the *Shaw* to prevent the Japanese from having their way to block the channel. Just, as the current turned the ship toward the way she had come, the *Shaw* exploded which signaled the final action in the harbor.

With less fighters than the first wave, *Akagi* Zeros hit Ewa, *Kaga* hit Wheeler, *Soryu* hit Kaneohe and *Hiryu* hit Bellows Field.

The first armed and angry American aircraft to climb for the sky came from Haliewa. Essentially a beach with enough room to have fighter operations, most of the fighter units held gunnery school here.

Their P-40s armed only with .30 caliber ammunition, 2nd Lt. George Welch and 2nd Lt. Ken Taylor headed for Ewa Field.

2nd Lt. Harry W. Brown drove his roommate, 2nd Lt. John Dains, and the executive officer, 1st Lt. Robert J. Rogers, to Haliewa. Dains grabbed the next P-40 readied.

Rogers had a P-36 set out at the end of the runway so another pilot could get immediately airborne. Just as it was positioned, a second wave dive bomber headed for the rendezvous was attracted and strafed the P-36.

Two B-17s from California picked Haliewa to land. Crewmen aboard each had been stationed in Hawaii and thus knew of this alternate field.

Brown got up in a P-36 soon after the B-17s landed. Rogers followed. 1st Lt. John J. Webster got airborne next.

One of the intermediate rally points for the Japanese aircraft was just west of Barbers Point. *Akagi* Zeros hit Ewa to keep Marine fighter response stifled. After three passes, the *Akagi* unit went on to Hickam Field.

Akagi and *Kaga* dive bombers picked up the suppressive fire at Ewa. An *Akagi* unit was pounced by Welch and Taylor's P-40s. One *Akagi* dive bomber was immediately shot down. A *Kaga* bomber held its course but lost its bid to fly to the Niihau area. Near there a submarine was to pick up crews from damaged planes.

Covered by smoke, a host of ground crews shoved planes from the burning caldron at Wheeler Field. The first four salvaged were readied for combat.

One of these four was 2nd Lt. Henry Lawrence's P-36, the sole surviving 45th PS plane. He went to his commander for orders. During his absence, 1st Lt. Lewis Sanders, the 46th PS Squadron Commander assigned 2nd Lt. John Thacker, 2nd Lt. Phillip Rasmussen, 2nd Lt. Othneil Norris and himself to the planes.

Norris got out of Lawrence's P-36 and rushed back to the truck for a different parachute harness. Operations Officer 2nd Lt. Gordon Sterling saw the other P-36s taxi out. He jumped into the remaining plane and followed. Norris got into the air in a later flight.

1st Lt. Malcolm A. Moore, born in Hawaii, was next in the air. Lawrence and 2nd Lt. William F. Haney, in P-36s, and 1st Lt. Woodrow B. Wilmot and 2nd Lt. Fred B. Shifflet, in P-40s, were right behind.

The *Kaga* fighters assured one return path for many of the dive bombers by hitting Wheeler. *Kaga* made a run across Ford Island NAS before coming on to Hickam.

Kaga dive bombers approached Wheeler as Welch and Taylor halted the refueling/rearming process and clawed for altitude. Taylor was immediately pounced by one on takeoff and wounded. Welch got on its tail and shot it down. Taylor continued after another and got it. Ground fire got a third.

The eight *Hiryu* Zeros made a strafing pass at Kaneohe about 0855 in route to Bellows Field. There they caught the American aircrews preparing to launch fighters.

The first P-40, piloted by 2nd Lt. George A. Whiteman, was hit on takeoff and crashed at the end of the runway. Whiteman AFB, Mo., is named in his memory. The second, flown by 2nd Lt. Samuel M. Bishop, was able to get into the air but was followed by the same Zero pilot who got Whiteman. After splashing Bishop, this victor and his wingman flew north to Kaneohe NAS. With a leg wound, Bishop swam ashore.

Bellows Field personnel noted with satisfaction that one fighter left early streaming fuel. The *Hiryu* unit noted the absence upon reforming.

The *Zuikaku* high-level bombers came around the south end of Oahu to attack Hickam Field at about 0905.

While the Shokaku bombers hit Ford Island NAS, the escorting *Kaga* fighters hit Wheeler Field. They went on to Ford Island NAS and then to Hickam. *Akagi* Zeros arrived from Ewa to Hickam to prevent any U.S. aircraft following.

The nine *Soryu* Zeros waited until a pause in the *Shokaku* bombing, then strafed until the bombing began again. The last strafing run caught Lt. Fusata Iida in the main fuel tank. He gave leadership over to the second in command, Lt. (jg) Iyozo Fujita and sought an honorable death by crashing into a target. The last flight of three went down to cover him. They were still strafing Kaneohe when the two *Hiryu* fighters joined the six *Soryu* aircraft.

As Fujita noted the arrival of the new *Hiryu* aircraft, they were hit from above by a flight of P-36 fighters. Fujita was hit in the initial pass by 1st Lt. Lewis Sanders, but was able to outmaneuver him.

His #3 wingman was also attacked and Fujita got on the tail of Gordon Sterling, Sanders' wingman. This interruption wavered the concentration and that #3 wingman escaped and Sterling was shot down. Yet, Fujita had not shaken Sanders who damaged his plane so badly that he just barely made it back to the *Soryu*.

In the bounce, Thacker's guns jammed and Rasmussen had a gun that continued to fire. One plane ran through Rasmussen's stream of bullets. He claimed an "uncertain" which was later "confirmed."

Having good hunting at Ewa Field, George Welch returned to claim another of Barbers Point. Lightly wounded, Taylor fired on a dive bomber off the north shore.

The pathway between the Koolau and Waianae mountain ranges ended at the north end of Oahu at Haliewa Field. Those P-40 and P-36s blocked that exit.

As the harbor battle concluded, Harry Brown and Robert Rogers joined up to make a pass onto a dive bomber headed along the north shore. Brown fired into another dive bomber until he broke contact at Kaena Point.

Malcolm A. Moore and Harry Brown joined up warily, each thinking that the other was Japanese. The *Soryu* Zero unit flew to the north shore where they turned west toward the rendezvous point. They were attacked this time by Brown and Moore. Both Brown and Iyozo Fujita saw one Zero afire, while the other was last seen headed west.

John Webster, in a P-36, and John Dains picked on dive bombers coming across the Haliewa area. A tail gunner put holes into both Webster and his plane. Dains chased his until he got to the east shore while the tail gunner kept peppering his P-40. The dive bomber went down.

"Hank" Lawrence joined up with Wilmot and Haney and went near Pearl Harbor to find their quarry. Alas, they found that they were the target instead. Haney's plane lost power and he glided to Wheeler.

Fred Shifflet also went near Pearl Harbor to Hickam Field. Those on the ground had cried, "Where are our fighters?" In answer to this, he flew low over Hickam. Filled with ground fire, he landed at Wheeler with two flat tires.

The one fuel tank punctured *Hiryu* Zero hit above Bellows Field arrived near Niihau. The expected submarine was not on the surface for rescue duty. The Zero pilot finally tried to land on the remote island only to wipe out his landing gear on a fence and rock wall.

After the attack one of the VP-14 PBYs flew across the Japanese rendezvous point 20 miles northwest of Kaena Point. They had a running battle with *Akagi* dive bombers. Little damage occurred. The PBY briefly radioed the encounter and Ford Island NAS thought the plane was shot down. They diverted another PBY to cover that sector.

The *Enterprise* task force launched six SOC seaplanes from the *Chester, Salt Lake City* and the *Northampton*. The two from the *Northampton* were north of Niihau when they were attacked by an *Akagi* Zero. It was one of two in the Combat Air Patrol above the Kido Butai defensive area. The action was between 1135 and 1155. Little damage happened to the SOCs. The Zero left streaming smoke and returned to the *Akagi*.

Of the many reconnaissance aircraft that took to the air after the attack, two JRS flying boats were assigned a flight due north. Armed with Browning automatic rifles and Springfield 1903 bolt-action rifles, they were flying 75 miles apart. Each made the turn to the right at the 200 mile distance for 50 miles then began their return. At 1:10 p.m. the plane to the west was briefly attacked by a *Shokaku* fighter. This plane is now at the National Air/Space Museum awaiting restoration.

The plane on the eastern course passed the Japanese fleet by 35 miles. At the altitude flown the distance they could see was about 25 miles.

Phoenix was anchored between Ford Island and the Aiea boat landing at the opening of hostilities. She was not damaged in the attack and was able to get underway clearing the harbor at 1144 for the open sea. Here she joined the cruisers *St. Louis, Detroit* and several destroyers as a temporary Task Group. This photo shows *Phoenix* moving down the south channel past the burning *Arizona* at about 1100. USN

"A Gallant Sortie"
U.S.S. *Nevada* BB-36

As a young 18-year-old Marine PFC, I reported aboard the USS *Nevada* in March 1941. I was assigned to Battle Station on the 5" secondary battery directors located near the top of the main mast.

On Dec. 7, 1941 at about 0750, I was part of the Marine Color Guard that mustered on the ship's fantail in preparation for colors at 0800. Prior to and during colors we observed aircraft, which we believed to be our own, making runs on the ships in the harbor. We took a near miss on our port quarter at about the same time the ships went to general quarters.

We were taking hits from Japanese dive bombers and one from a torpedo bomber. One very large bomb hit us on the forecastle and went down through the ship without exploding. Due to these hits we lost our electrical power on the directors and communication to the 5" guns. We broke out the Lewis machine guns and were able to bring the Japanese planes under fire as they were making runs on us.

As I look back to that fateful day, three events stand out vividly in my recollection. They were 1.) seeing the *Arizona* explode about 50 yards ahead of us and feeling the tremendous concussion. 2.) Watching the *Oklahoma* capsize onto her port side. And 3.) I felt the greatest excitement of the entire action was moving out from our mooring, aft of the *Arizona*, without tug assistance and sailing the channel in our dash for the open sea. It seemed like the skies were filled with enemy aircraft, all swarming over us in an attempt to sink us in mid-channel. Due to fire and torpedo damage, the *Nevada* was beached away from mid-channel. In the days and weeks following the attack the surviving Marines and sailors worked to clean up and refloat the ship in order to get her into drydock. This was accomplished on Feb. 14, 1942.

COL. JACK EPPERSON, RET.
Hunning Beach, Calif.

The torpedo damaged *Nevada* passes close by the Navy Yard's TenTen Dock on her epic sortie. In the foreground is the Naval Air Station's Headquarters Building and the *Avocet* at the pier. This view is from the signal tower on Ford Island. USN NH 32559

At 0910, looking across the superstructure of the small seaplane tender *Avocet*, her gun crews at battle stations. The heavily damaged and smoking *Nevada* at the end of her gallant sortie, has just run aground off Hospital Point. *Nevada* was the only battleship to get underway during the attack. USN

The *Nevada* became a prime target of attack when a flight of Japanese dive bombers saw the ship underway at 0850 attempting to move out of the harbor. They tried to sink her in the main channel but the *Nevada* was intentionally grounded off Hospital Point at 0910 when she received orders not to leave the harbor because of reported submarines in the channel. USN

The damaged *Nevada* was able to get underway from her berth on Battleship Row at 0840. As she headed down the channel, she became the target of a flight of Japanese dive bombers from the carrier *Kaga*, hoping to sink her and block the harbor. After first running aground off Hospital Point, she was eventually beached stern first on Waipio Peninsula by two yard tugs. The tug *Hoga* fights the raging fires on *Nevada*'s bow. This area has since been known as Nevada Point. NA 80-G-19940

Looking from Ford Island, the destroyers *Cassin* and *Downes* burn furiously in Drydock #1. The *Pennsylvania* is smoking from a hit amidships. In midstream is the civilian dredge *Turbine*. NA 80-G-32580

The severely damaged destroyers *Cassin* and *Downes* are forward of the battleship *Pennsylvania* in Drydock #1. The hulls of the two destroyers were scrapped in 1942. Both ships would sail again in name and new hulls built by the Mare Island Navy Yard in 1943 when the main propulsion systems, various machinery and hull fittings of the two ships were salvaged and installed in the new hulls. USN

The *Shaw* was in the floating drydock for overhaul. She burned furiously from three 250kg aerial bomb hits. This photo was taken before 0930, only minutes before her forward magazines blew up in a fiery explosion. USN

One of the most dramatic photos of World War II is the explosion of the U.S.S. *Shaw* in the floating drydock YFD #2. The *Shaw* was hit by three 250-kg. bombs that were meant for *Nevada*. One passed through the bridge, igniting fires and rupturing fuel tanks. The blazing oil fires caused the forward magazine to explode in a fiery blast that tore the ship's bow off. The *Nevada* with the tug *Hoga* is on the right. USN

The *Shaw*'s forward magazines erupt in a fiery blast, sending smoke and flame hundreds of feet into the air. The *Nevada* had swung around (right) after running aground at Hospital Point. At the left, the garbage lighter YG-21 pulls in behind the *Avocet* at the NAS Pier on Ford Island. USN

At 1010 dock men from the capsized *Oglala* set up a first aid station and mounted four .30-caliber machine guns on the dock that were saved from their ship before she rolled over. The *Helena* is just ahead of *Oglala*. To the left is the burning *Shaw* in the floating drydock YFD-2. NA 80-G-464887

Late on the morning of Dec. 7, with her bow and bridge area completely destroyed by the explosion of the forward 5-inch ammunition magazine, the *Shaw* lies in the sunken floating drydock, YFD-2. On the right is the listing battleship *California* and the civilian dredge *Turbine*. The port side of the sinking yard tug *Sotoyomo* YT-9 can be seen in the lower left of the drydock. NA 80-G-19939

Looking southwest toward Ford Island and the Navy base, across the cane fields of Aiea. In the aftermath, smoke billows from the devastation wrought by the Japanese Air Armada. USN

This view, taken around 0926, shows two nests of destroyers alongside their tenders. In the center of the photo are (left to right), *Dobbin* (AD-3), with *Hull* (DD-350), *Dewey* (DD-349), *Worden* (DD-352) and *MacDonough* (DD-351) alongside. The ship to the left of the nest is *Phelps* (DD-360), which got underway on two boilers around 0926. The other nest consists of (left to right), *Whitney* (AD-4), *Conyngham* (DD-371), *Reid* (DD-369), *Tucker* (DD-374), *Case* (DD-370) and *Selfridge* (DD-357). *Solace* is barely visible at far left. NA 80-G-33045

Pearl Harbor as seen from Aiea shortly after the last planes of the Japanese First Air Fleet left the scene of their shattering victory. Columns of smoke rise thousands of feet into the late morning skies from the havoc wrought by the attackers. In the foreground are a pineapple processing plant and surrounding pineapple fields. The *Vestal* (AR-4) is aground on Aiea Shoals (right). NA 80-G-32893

PSNY 8-7-41 26M
Original

U.S. NAVAL AIR STATION, KODIAK ALASKA
NAVAL COMMUNICATIONS

Heading: NPC NR 63 F L Z F5L 071830 CBQ TART 0 BT

Date: 7 DEC 41

From: CINCPAC

To: ALL SHIPS PRESENT AT HAWAIIN AREA.

Info: - U R G E N T -

DEFERRED unless otherwise checked | ROUTINE | PRIORITY | AIRMAIL | MAILGRAM

AIRRAID ON PEARLHARBOR X THIS IS NO DRILL

07014

RM 58 1910 7DEC

Comdg Off	Exec	Comm	Oper	Supply	Disb	Med'l	Aerog	Pers	Pub Wks	Mar Det	A & R	Files	FAD	NRAB	OOD	WDO

A–Denotes action I–Denotes information X–Denotes copy only

PSNY 8-7-41 26M
Original

U.S. NAVAL AIR STATION, KODIAK ALASKA
NAVAL COMMUNICATIONS

Heading: NPC NR93F// L Z PARD Ø72334 SNAG P GR36 BT

From: COMDT 13TH NAVDIST

To: ASTA, 13TH NAVDIST

Date: 7 DEC 1941 GCT

DEFERRED unless otherwise checked | ROUTINE | PRIORITY XXX | AIRMAIL | MAILGRAM

UNTIL FURTHER INSTRUCTIONS ARE ISSUED ALL PLANES FLYING OVER NAVAL STATIONS OTHER THAN AIR STATIONS WILL BE REGARDED AS HOSTILE AND WILL BE FIRED ON WITHOUT WARNING X GIVE WIDE-PUBLICITY X THIS IS SNAG FOUR

08001

58 KCS HB AT 0015/8TH

Supply	Disb	Med'l	Aerog	Pers	Pub Wks	Mar Det	A & R	Files	FAD	NRAB	OOD	WDO

I–Denotes information X–Denotes copy only

Naval stations around the world were notified of the Pearl Harbor attack.

On the left, beyond 1010 Dock, the thick oily smoke is from burning destroyers in Drydock #1. The heavy smoke blackening the morning sky farther to the right is from the *Shaw* and the *Nevada. Argonne* is at the extreme left. To the far right one of the yard tugs heads toward Battleship Row to assist in fighting fires. USN

A low-flying Japanese plane passes over the Sub Base headed for Hickam Field. The crew of the submarine *Narwahl* (SS-167) man the antiaircraft guns to defend the ship (left). Across the channel, the destroyer *Bagley* (DD-386) moored at the Navy Yard (right), assisted in shooting down several of the attackers. NA 80-G-37737

From Pier One of the Sub Base approximately 0915. The gun crews of the sub, *Narwahl* watch the skies for attacking aircraft. The oiler *Neosho* having left her exposed position at the Gasoline Pier, Ford Island, moves past the Navy Yard to a berth at Merry Point (right). The sub *Dolphin* (SS-169) is on the left. USN

The starboard 3″/50 gun crew of the *Avocet* (foreground) claimed a hit on a Japanese torpedo bomber with their first salvo. The plane bursts into flames and crashed in the vicinity of the Naval Hospital. Seen above *Avocet*'s bow, a Boeing B-17E of the flight that arrived from the West Coast during the height of the attack passes over Aiea looking for a place to land. NA 80-G-32458

Set up amongst the scattered debris near the seaplane hangar, an impromptu gun emplacement, manned by two servicemen, awaits the follow-up raid which never came. The servicemen man a .30-caliber air-cooled machine gun and don World War I vintage "tin" helmets. NA 80-G-32546

The heavy cruiser *Northampton* enters Pearl Harbor on the morning of Dec. 8, 1941, her men observing the devastation wreaked by the Japanese planes the previous day. From her bridge, Rear Adm. Raymond A. Spruance silently looked on. His reading and studying about war had not prepared him for the awful sight that lay before him. That evening, he emotionally and tearfully related his feelings to his wife and daughter. Apparently, though, he never spoke of it again.
NA 80-G-32548

Looking across to Sand Island are the submarine nets guarding Honolulu Harbor. It was these same type of nets at the entrance to Pearl Harbor on Dec. 7 that the five midget submarines of the Japanese Special Attack Unit would attempt to breach. At least one sub was known to have successfully gained entry into the harbor.
USA

Marine barracks at Pearl Harbor as seen from across the parade grounds. Smoke from the harbor rises behind the barracks. AMC

Looking toward the Navy Yard area from the north end of the Marine Barracks Parade Grounds. The late morning skies are filled with towering clouds of smoke from the carnage wrought at Battleship Row. A 3-inch antiaircraft gun is being set up in the foreground expecting the attackers to return. The center water tower is the Pearl Harbor signal tower. It was from here at 0755 that the blue signal flag for "prep" was raised prior to the raising of morning colors at 0800 on all ships and stations in the harbor. USN

View of the Marine Barracks Parade Grounds at the Pearl Harbor Navy Yard between 0930 and 1030. The skies have been darkened by billowing clouds of black oily smoke from the crippled ships of Battleship Row. USN

Destruction

The Enemy Achieved Complete Surprise

Aerial view of Battleship Row on Dec. 10, 1941. The sunken *California* is at upper left. In the center is the capsized *Oklahoma* with *Maryland* inboard, followed by the sunken *West Virginia* alongside *Tennessee*. The *Arizona* is at lower right. Fuel oil is still leaking from the shattered hulls. NA 80-G-387565

Aerial view of the drydocks at the Navy Yard on Dec. 10, 1941. *Pennsylvania* with the wrecked destroyers is in Drydock #1 at the bottom. The torpedo-damaged cruiser *Helena* is in Drydock #2. The bowless destroyer *Shaw* is in the floating drydock (top). USN

The damaged *Curtiss* (AV-4) at left and the undamaged *Medusa* (AR-1) at right. NA 80-G-32733

View looking southwest from Ford Island, about one hour after the last of the attacking Japanese planes had left the area. The *Raleigh* is listing heavily to port. Her crew is jettisoning topside equipment in the fight to save their ship. Astern is the capsized *Utah* and the seaplane tender *Tangier* (left). NA 80-G-32650

The torpedoed *Raleigh* was listing dangerously to port. The fleet tug *Sunnadin* brought a barge with four salvage pontoons alongside. The barge was lashed to the cruiser's side to prevent her from capsizing. USN NH 50769

The *Shaw* in the half-sunken floating drydock after the attack. Earlier, the ship had been hit by three bombs from the group of divebombers that were attacking the *Nevada* as it passed by the drydocks. The entire forward section, including the bridge, was completely destroyed. The dock was flooded intentionally to help put out fires on the burning *Shaw.* NA 80-G-32531

The *Shaw* still burning and smoking after the explosion of her forward magazine. The crew of the *Sotoyomo* (left), a small yard tug, is fighting to keep their damaged ship afloat. NA 80-G-32753

Bridge structure of the *Shaw* showing damage caused by the explosion of her forward magazines. The superstructure of the half sunken drydock is in the foreground. NA 80-G-32771

The *Cassin* shifted from her graving blocks and rolled onto the *Downes* when the drydock was flooded in an attempt to put out raging fuel oil fires from damage done by *Soryu*'s dive bombers. USN

The *Cassin* rolled off her blocks onto the *Downes* about 0915 when the dock was flooded. This was done to aid in putting out fuel oil fires. The operator of the large dockside crane attempted to ward off attacking aircraft by running the crane along the dock as bombers approached. Note damage to the bow of *Pennsylvania*. NA 80-G-32509

1010 Dock as it appears on Dec. 8 with *Argonne*, the base force flagship, still at her berth at B-4. The 150-ton floating gantry crane (YD-25) would play a major role in the salvage operations to follow. Target sleds at far left were hurriedly set in place to discourage any sabotage attempts. USN NH 83066

View looking northwest from Ford Island about one hour after the attack had ended. The hospital ship *Solace* (center) had moved earlier to berth X-13 in East Loch. The capsized *Utah* is at left. The *Raleigh* (right), listing heavily to port, is fighting to keep afloat from torpedo and bomb damage. NA 80-G-32672

About one hour later, after the last bombs had fallen, the *Raleigh* (right) is listing to port from torpedo and bomb damage as her crew jettisons heavy topside equipment in an effort to save the ship. The damaged *Curtiss* is seen beyond the overturned hull of the *Utah* (center) where a rescue crew can be seen on her hull. The *Tangier* escaped serious damage. NA 80-G-32673

In this view from Ford Island, looking towards Pearl City, rescue workers are cutting a hole in the capsized hull of *Utah*. Fireman John B. Vaessen escaped a watery grave when he was pulled through the 18-inch hole. Fifty-four men are still entombed in the ship as the *Utah* was never salvaged. A memorial was built near the ship and dedicated on May 27, 1972, to all the men who served and died on the ship. USN

The capsized *Utah*, a mobile target and anti-aircraft gunnery training ship, lies at berth Fox-11 on the northwest side of Ford Island, a berth usually occupied by an aircraft carrier. Torpedo planes of the first wave from the Japanese carrier *Soryu* had hoped to find one there on the morning of Dec. 7. But the *Lexington* had sailed on Dec. 5 and the *Enterprise* had left earlier on Nov. 28 for their assigned missions. The seaplane tender *Tangier* is to the right. USN

The *Nevada* beached at Hospital Point. USN

Shortly after the attack, salvage work on the beached *Nevada* is underway. The *Widgeon* (ASR-1), a salvage vessel, is alongside, right. The divers and crew of *Widgeon* would earn a commendation from Admiral Nimitz for their successful efforts in helping to refloat the *Nevada*. NA 80-G-32452

The *Vestal* was beached off Aiea landing. Note paint after where she was scorched by the burning *Arizona*. USN NH 50273

The *Arizona* on the morning of Dec. 9, with her main decks awash, fires are still smoldering amidships. Entombed forever within her shattered remains are the bodies of over 1,000 of her crew. USN

A work party had just finished rigging awnings on the *Arizona*'s quarterdeck for morning church services before the first bombs fell and mortally wounded the ship. Lt. Cmdr. Samuel G. Fuqua was the senior surviving officer and from his station on the quarterdeck he directed firefighting and the removal of wounded. When he realized the ship could not be saved, he gave the order to abandon ship. His coolness and bravery under such extraordinary conditions earned him the Medal of Honor. USN

Several days after the attack, fires are out on the sunken *West Virginia* and just aft, the *Arizona*. When the *West Virginia* settled on the bottom, the inboard *Tennessee* was wedged against the quays which had to be partially dismantled to free her. The *Tennessee* was finally freed on Dec. 16 and sailed for the West Coast on Dec. 20, 1941. USN

Several days after the attack, two yard oilers are tied up (photo, left) alongside the sunken *West Virginia* to recover fuel oil still remaining in her bunkers prior to the start of salvage work. When the *West Virginia* settled on the bottom, the inboard *Tennessee* (photo, lower left) was wedged against the quays, which had to be partially dismantled to free the ship. The *Tennessee* was finally freed on Dec. 16, 1942, and the *West Virginia* was refloated and put in drydock on June 9, 1942 for repairs. USN

On the overcast morning of Dec. 8, the minesweepers *Bobolink* (left) and *Vireo* (right), along with the water barge YW-10, are moored to the stern of the sinking battleship *California*. USN

The crew of the *California* and the rescue craft, alongside, are pumping out water-filled compartments and removing fuel oil in an attempt to lighten the ship and prevent it from settling on the bottom. The salvage vessel to the right is the *Widgeon*. USN

The *Arizona*, as she looked on Dec. 10. USN

On Dec. 10, a crashed Aichi D3A1 dive bomber from the *Kaga* was recovered by the seaplane wrecking derrick, YSD-19, from the waters in Middle Loch. The tailless Val was brought over to the Navy Air Station on Ford Island for investigation. Salvage work on Battleship Row is in full effect. USN

The *Oglala*, a minelayer, was tied up outboard of the light cruiser *Helena* berthed at 1010 Dock. At 0758, a torpedo launched by Lt. Tsuyoshi Nagai, flying a Nakajima B5N2 from the carrier *Soryu* passed under the *Oglala* and exploded against the *Helena*. This explosion and one from a bomb that fell between the two ships weakened *Oglala*'s 35-year-old hull causing severe flooding. She was moved at 0900 to a berth aft of *Helena* by two small tugs where she capsized an hour later. The vessel with the checkerboard paint scheme is the ferry *Nihoa*. NA

The capsized *Oklahoma* with the *Maryland* in the background. The *Oklahoma* lost 395 enlisted men and 20 officers. Thirty-two sailors were rescued in the next 30 hours after tapping sounds were heard coming from within. Julio De Castro, a civilian employee of the Navy Yard, organized and led a rescue team to cut through the hull of the ship. He was commended by Ad. Claude C. Bloch for his heroic actions and complete disregard for his own personal safety. Note one of the rescue holes at the stern of the *Oklahoma*. NA

Honolulu Star-Bulletin 1st EXTRA

WAR!

(Associated Press by Transpacific Telephone) SAN FRANCISCO, Dec. 7.—President Roosevelt announced this morning that Japanese planes had attacked Manila and Pearl Harbor.

OAHU BOMBED BY JAPANESE PLANES

SIX KNOWN DEAD, 21 INJURED, AT EMERGENCY HOSP

Attack Made On Island's Defense Areas

Honolulu Star-Bulletin 2nd EXTRA

DEATHS OVER 400 ON OAHU, LATEST REPORT

TOKYO ANNOUNCES "STATE OF WAR" WITH U. S.

Japanese Raids On Guam, Panama Are Reported

Oahu Blackout Tonight; Fleet Here Moves Out to Sea

Four Waves, Start At 7:55, Oahu Hit In Many Places

Governor Proclaims National Emergency

Honolulu Star-Bulletin 3rd EXTRA

MARTIAL LAW DECLARED DEATHS ARE MOUNTIN

OVER 400 KILLED HERE; JAPAN ANNOUNCES "WA

Japanese Raids On Guam, Panama Are Reporte

Oahu Blackout Tonight; Fleet Here Moves Out to S

Four Waves, Start At 7:55, Oahu Hit In Many Places

Governor Proclaims National Emergency

MARTIAL LAW

Civilian Casualties

BULLETINS

Mrs. M. D. White Killed in Raid

Editorial

Blackout Fo Isles Ordere

Honolulu Star-Bulletin 1st EXT

ROOSEVELT DENOUNCES 'TREACHERY'; CALLS FOR KNOCKOUT OF JAPAN

United States Congress Declares War On Japan

49 Civilians Dead, 83 Hurt; Service Men Unknown

Congress Called In Extraordinary Session For War

BULLETINS

3,000 Casualties Are Indicated on Oahu

War Declaration Before Congress

U. S. Has Begun Counter Attack

No Raids on Oahu Since Sunday Night

Attacks on Wide Scale

Germans Quit Effort To Capture Moscow

Business To Continue As Usual, Doty Announces

Blackouts To Continue

DEAD, INJURED

On the morning of Dec. 7, the editor of the *Honolulu Star-Bulletin*, Riley N. Allen, found himself with the most momentous story in local history and the greatest exclusive of his life, owing to a press breakdown at the *Honolulu Advertiser*, the *Star*'s competitor and the city's only Sunday newspaper. Allen's hastily recruited staff issued three extras that day. The first was printed fewer than two hours after the attack. HA

Japanese Photos

Great Propaganda Value

This is the only known photo showing all six Japanese attack force carriers, taken from the deck of the *Akagi* in Hitokappu Bay in November 1941. Aircraft on board are four TYPE 99, Model 11 "Val" bombers. Large carrier to the left is the *Kaga*, the two distant ones are the *Shokaku* and *Zuikaku*. To their right is the *Hiryu* and out of sight to the right is the *Soryu*.

The *Akagi* (top) and *Kaga* (bottom), Japanese carriers of the First Carrier Division. USN NH 73059, 73060

The *Hiryu* (top) and *Soryu* (bottom), Japanese carriers of the Second Carrier Division. USN NH 73063, 73061

The *Zuikaku* (pictured) and the *Shokaku* made up the Fifth Carrier Division. USN NH 73069

Capt. Koji Shiroshime of *Shokaku* stands before a blackboard which stated: "Japanese Imperial Fleet! You must obey and die for your country, Japan! Whether you win or lose, you must fight and die for your country!" NA 80-G-182248

Airmen prepare for their epic flight. USN

One of the eight fleet oilers that made up the support force.

View of the *Akagi* shipping water over the bow en route to Hawaii. Photo taken from above the starboard boat stowage deck (forward).

View of the *Akagi* (left), *Kaga* (center) and *Hiryu* (right) en route to Hawaii.

View from the *Akagi*'s stern. Directly behind is *Kaga* and to her rear is *Hiryu*.

Flight deck of the *Akagi*. Visible are two A6M2 "Zeros" (one is AI-110) and three B5N2 "Kate" bombers with green upper surface camouflage paint.

Flight crews rush to their planes on the *Shokaku*.

AA gun practice aboard *Akagi* at Hitokappu Bay (Kurile Islands) in November 1941 before departing for Hawaii. Gun in the foreground is an aircraft Type 92. 7.7 mm (copy of the Lewis) used in the rear position of the "Val" and "Kate" aircraft. Some flight crew members look on.

This remarkable series of Japanese photos is courtesy of the University of Hawaii via the U.S. Army Museum in Honolulu.

Attaching bomb splinter padding to *Akagi*'s island bridge. Aircraft is an A6M2 "Zero" with quilted engine cover.

On board the *Agaki*. The aircraft is a A6M2 Model 21, Type O Carrier fighter (Zero). Note the splinter padding on the island and an AA machine gun fitted on top. The rope coil by the range finder provided splinter protection but also could be played out for abandoning ship. The crew is being briefed in the background for the second wave attack. The Zero shown is AI-101 piloted by Petty Officer 1st Class Tadao Kimura. It was the second plane launched in the second wave.

The *Kaga* and *Zuikaku* underway in heavy seas.
USN NH 75483

Aircraft take off for their destiny at Pearl Harbor. AM

An *Akagi* Kate landing after its attack on Pearl Harbor. AM

Akagi's island was protected by bomb splinter padding. AM

Gun crews man a twin 120mm, .45-caliber AA mount on *Akagi*. AM

Zuikaku in the foreground, *Kaga* in the background. AM

Shokaku crews receive instructions.

The Type 91 modification torpedo.

Photo taken aboard *Akagi* in May 1942 during filming with training unit of B5N1 Kates for the Japanese movie *Hawai Marei Oki Kaisen*. NA 80-G-182245

Air group leader Cmdr. Mitsuo Fuchida was navigator on this Kate high-level bomber. March 1942.

A Val taking off from the *Zuikaku* by a Shotaicho (flight leader). The plane is the 58th gift from Japanese people as noted by the inscription on the fuselage side. AM

Blackboard on *Akagi* lists orders for the impending battle. AM

Blackboard on *Akagi* displays a map of the Pearl Harbor area. AM

P01c. Tadao Kimura warms up for takeoff to the left in A1-101. Type 99 dive bomber, Vals warmup in the background. AMI

Shokaku airmen pose on board before their day of destiny. AM

Battle flags waved in the breeze as the fleet left Hitokappu Bay. AM

Lt. Comdr. Tadashi Kusumi, leader of *Hiryu*'s Horizontal bombers. His own flight caused the destruction of the *Arizona*. USN

A "fleet defense" (Combat Air Patrol) Mitsubishi Zero (A6M2) fighter prepares to launch before the Nakajima B5N2 high-level bombers warm up on the flight deck of the carrier *Shokaku*. They are preparing to take off to launch the second attack wave. USN

Flight deck, possibly on the *Hiryu*, showing planes ready for takeoff for the second wave. The Zero in the foreground may be the last of the nine Zeros to launch from the *Hiryu* (it had engine trouble and had to land back on the carrier). The planes in the background are Type 99 dive bombers. USN

The 183 aircraft of the First Attack Group began launching in the gray light of predawn with the first plane lifting off at 0615. Sunrise that morning was 0626 Honolulu time. A torpedo bomber is given the "Banzai" salute by the flight crew of the carrier *Soryu* as it readies for takeoff on the second wave attack. USN

This aerial view of Ford Island, looking northeast, early in the opening phase of the attack at approximately 0800, shows seaplane Hangar 6 smoking heavily (extreme right), the *Utah* listing from repeated torpedo hits (lower left of Ford Island) and a torpedo explosion on the *Oklahoma* at Battleship Row. One attacking plane can be seen over the *Neosho* and another over the Navy Yard. USN

A view looking northeast during the initial minutes of the first wave showing torpedo hits on the *West Virginia* and *Oklahoma* in the background. Ford Island's PBY hangars to the far right have also been hit. Several destroyers (*Ramsay, Gamble, Montgomery*) are in the foreground along with the tenders *Medusa* and *Curtiss* at the entrance to the middle lock. USN NH 50929

Smoke bellows from Hickam Field at about 0800 in this early Japanese attack photo. Torpedo wakes can be seen streaking toward the battleships. USN

This aerial view of Battleship Row was taken at 0806 by a *Kaga* bomber. It shows the *Oklahoma* and the *West Virginia*, both listing heavily and leaking fuel oil from repeated torpedo hits. The *Arizona* on the right is hit aft by *Kaga* high-level Kates. The *Oklahoma* is receiving its final torpedo. EA

This Japanese photo was taken about 0809 from a *Soryu* horizontal bomber after the *Arizona* exploded, obscuring the battleships in front of her. The *Nevada* is the first ship to the left. USN NH 30552

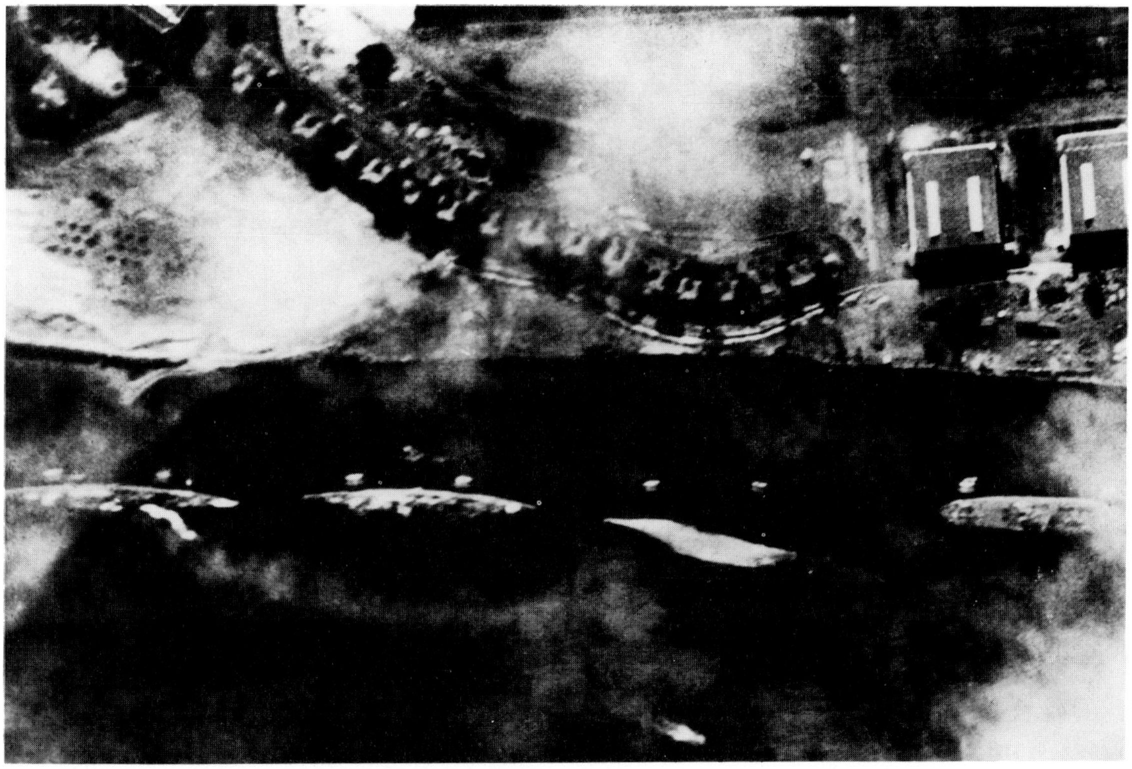

This photo was taken of the west side of Ford Island by a Japanese Aircraft between 0820 and 0840. It shows, from left to right, the light cruiser *Detroit*, her sister *Raleigh* listing from a torpedo hit, the capsized target ship *Utah* and the seaplane tender *Tangier.* This is where the torpedo planes of the first wave expected to find the American carriers berthed. USN

This painting, in color by Tsuguji Fujita, was done in 1942 and shows strikes around Ford Island. USN 86637-KN

This remarkable photo shows four "Vals" over the burning Wheeler Field with the Schofield Barracks in the center.
FROM COLLECTION OF HARUZO YAEGASHI, *ZUIKAKU* HIGH-LEVEL KATE PILOT

Rows of P-36s and P-40s are parked undamaged at Wheeler Field during the initial phase of the attack. The untouched Schofield Barracks is in the foreground. "Gabby" Gabreski, later America's top living ace, received a citation for saving some of the aircraft by taxiing them to safety. He later got into the air after the attack. USN NH 50473

A "Kate" from the *Zuikaku* flies over Hickam Field. The smoke directly underneath the bomber is from the burning *Nevada* and the destroyers *Casssin*, *Downes* and *Shaw*. On the right the *Neosho* has moved past the column of smoke from the *Arizona* to Merry Loch. USN 80-G-21218

Two Nakajima B5N2 torpedo bombers from the carrier *Kaga*, having completed their attack mission, are flying over Waipio Peninsula (white tip, right) and West Loch. They will rendezvous 20 miles northwest of Kaena Point with other aircraft and fly back to the carriers in groups. EA

This unusual photo is actually taken from a Japanese movie for the Dec. 7, 1942, release of *Hawai & Malaysia Sea Battle* (note the Japanese spell Hawaii with only one "i"). The Japanese placed small houses in the shipyard area and built mountains where Ford Island is located. The overturned battleship is where the *West Virginia* was located. Obviously the movie director has his facts and geography mixed up.
USN NR&L(M) 37246

This captured Japanese photo shows a mock-up of Pearl Harbor. This was a movie set made up after the attack to produce a film for propaganda purposes. (Japanese title: *Hawai Marei Oki Kaisen*). It was first shown on Dec. 7, 1942.
USN

Hickam Field

Flying Fortresses Were Sitting Ducks

A burned B-17C rests near Hangar #5 at Hickam Field following the attack. USAF

Hawaii's first military aviation preserve was established in 1917, with the arrival on Oahu of three N-9 seaplanes of the Sixth Aero Squadron. Later in the year the government bought Ford Island in Pearl Harbor and named the new airstrip Luke Field.

Wheeler Field was completed in 1923, but by 1934 the Army Air Corps wanted a bomber base and started construction of Hickam Field next to Pearl Harbor. The job was handed to the Army's Quartermaster Corps, which devoted nearly four years to the job of hacking a modern air base out of the brush and cane fields. Hickam was the Corps' largest peacetime construction job.

Completed in 1938, the field was named in honor of Lt. Col. Horace M. Hickam, who was killed in a 1934 aircraft accident in Texas.

The first airmen arrived in August 1937, while construction was still going on. The first mass flight of bombers, twenty-one B-17s, arrived at Hickam on May 13, 1941, from Hamilton Field, California. Nine went on to the Philippines in September 1941, leaving 12 at Hickam.

In late 1940, the Hawaiian Air Force was organized as an integrated command of fighters, bombers and observation planes. It consisted of 754 officers, 6,706 enlisted men and 231 aircraft stationed at Hickam, Wheeler, the auxiliary fields of Haleiwa, Bellows and elsewhere.

Japanese strategy was to knock out the Hawaiian Air Force on the ground, and the surprise attack worked so well that the Nipponese pilots were virtually unchallenged by American interceptor aircraft. At Hickam, planes of the 18th Bombardment Wing were lined up on the warm up aprons, three or four rows deep with wingtips only 10 feet apart. About 130 feet separated one row of planes from the next.

The first attack, at 7:55 a.m., lasted 10 minutes. Seventeen dive bombers attacked buildings and hangars. Several minutes later, nine Zeros swept over the field from the southeast and strafed the hangar line. Nine more Zeros came in from the southwest.

About 9:05 a.m., a second attack brought 27 planes, which bombed the parked bombers, the base service buildings and the large barracks. The baseball diamond was pounded from a high altitude, perhaps in the belief that it covered a gasoline storage system.

The second wave attack lasted about eight minutes. Eighteen Zeros swooped down to hit individual aircraft that had been dispersed and to renew their attacks on service buildings, barracks and the post exchange.

Most of the B-17 and B-18 bombers of the Hawaiian Air Force were lost. The Hawaiian Air Depot, which included engineering, administrative and drafting offices, was knocked out, as was the base parachute unit. Mostly destroyed were the aero repair facilities, as well as aircraft undergoing repairs. More than half of the aircraft maintenance supply stock was wiped out. Bombs landed on the guardhouse and the ordnance building, delaying access to ammunition.

Damage was done to the main barracks (Hale Makai), the base's water system, hangars, technical buildings and the Hawaiian Air Defense buildings.

There were many acts of heroism that day. One soldier set up a machine gun in the nose of a parked bomber and kept firing until his plane was engulfed in flames from an attacking Zero. Others shot at the attacking planes with pistols, rifles and hand-held machine guns.

Two B-17s, two B-18s and four A-20s managed to get into the air in the morning after the attack was over. The

The main gate to Hickam Field in the late 1930s. HA

planes had been locked and the keys were in the armament section, which took a direct bomb hit. Airmen had to shoot off the locks and load bombs by hand with the help of ropes as the bomb-loading equipment had been damaged. Some arriving back at Hickam about 6 p.m., were shot at by soldiers who mistook them for the enemy, but managed to land safely.

Casualties included 121 killed, 37 missing and 274 wounded. Many occurred at the barracks complex.

It was a devastating attack on the Hawaiian Air Force, and Hickam's air defense facilities.

Aerial view of Hickam Field during construction in 1938. USAF

Douglas B-18 bombers at Hickam, 1940.
CAMERA HAWAII/WERNER STOY

Hale Makai barracks, Feb. 15, 1940. USAF

A Day to Remember

I was alerted at about 1600 hours on Sat., Dec 6, 1941, to draw all battle gear and remain in the radio transmission building at Hickam Field for the complete night shift. This was an unusual request which I later found out was the result of the programmed flight of B17's from Hamilton Field en route to the Philippines with a Hickam Field stopover for refueling early in the morning of Sun., Dec. 7. I had returned to my barracks for cleanup at about 0745 when all hell broke loose with the strafing of the wooden barracks by Zeros as they made their run against Ford Island and Pearl Harbor targets.

I commandeered a weapons carrier with a mounted .50-caliber gun and raced down Hangar Ave. toward my radio transmitter building on the ball field. The hangar line was ablaze with aircraft and fuel trucks and smoke was belching from the hangars. I remember seeing bodies and walking wounded as I raced up the street and also briefly firing the machine gun with questionable results.

As NCOIO of the transmitters I checked all operating equipment and was concerned some of the rhombic antennas had been destroyed. However, the B17's were already over Hickam Field and it was apparent that the navigation to Hickam and the air-to-ground support by my radio transmitters had performed their mission.

The second wave was more disconcerting as rumors were rampant that all water had been poisoned, invasion of Nuuani Pali had taken place, the "fifth column" Japanese on the island were infiltrating military installations and poison gas had been dropped. In addition, the chaos and pandemonium of the first wave created an open season on all targets with constant low-level strafing and bombing. It was a day to remember!

Nick Gaynos
Sgt. 328th Sig Avn. Co.
Hickam Field, T.H.
Hdqs Hawaiian Air Force

Wreckage of the barracks as seen from the parade ground off Hangar Field at 1045 on Dec 7. USAF

Today the old barracks is headquarters for the Pacific Air Forces.

The same area today.

Courtyard of the Hale Makai at 11:00 a.m. USA

Outside walls of the old barracks still show signs of the Japanese attack.

Bomb damage to the sanitation facility on Cornet Avenue. AMC

Looking out toward Hangar Avenue and the flight line from between two heavily damaged wings of the Hale Makai. 1st Lt. Raymond Swenson's destroyed B-17C in the background. USAF

This photo of a bomb crater in front of Hale Makai Barracks was taken the night of Dec. 7. Another bomb, hitting the mess hall adjacent to the barracks, took the lives of 40 airmen. AMC

Close-up view of one of the most severely damaged wings of the Hale Makai.
USAF

Hickam Field's old post exchange, which now houses offices and a food service. The building was badly damaged in the attack.

Rubble covered the parking lot at Hickam's bomb-damaged post exchange.
USAF

1st Lt. Raymond Swenson's B-17C was hit in the air, landed on fire and burned in half on the tarmac. The tail was pulled out of the landing path. AMC

A 5th Bombardment Group B-18 bomber sits damaged in the wrecked hangar. USAF

Wreckage of barracks from the parade ground off of Hangar Avenue. USAF

Flight line personnel examine a bomb crater between Hangers 11-13 and 15-17. AMC

Bombed and burned out hangers, shops and other facilities. AMC

Damage at Hangar #11. Note the effect of concussion and bomb fragments on the hangar door. AMC

The hangar area today.

Rear view of damage to Hangar #11. The plane is a B-18 of the Headquarters Squadron, 18th Bomb Wing. AMC

Railroad tracks twisted and smashed in front of the firehouse. AMC

A worker stands in a bomb crater in front of Hangar #15. AMC

The hangar area today.

Bulged doors and blown-out windows indicate that a bomb blew up inside Hangar #7. AMC

A Fearful Scene

On the morning of Dec. 7, 1941, during the time of the attack on Pearl Harbor, I was flying my J3 Piper Cub out of the Anaheim Airport just back of Knotts Berry Farm.

Upon landing and going into the Airport office, the radio was giving the bad news—Pearl Harbor was being bombed. It was hard to realize where this was and to believe what was being told. I went back to the J3 and took off again, trying to visualize what I had heard. Within less than 10 minutes the airport manager's plane, a red beechcraft, was on my tail, giving me the sign to land. After landing I was told the President had grounded all flying in the U.S.A.

Within a short time I was notified to be at the Douglas plant that afternoon for a flight with the Air Corp.

My background and knowledge in aviation had placed me in the position with Civil Air and Airforce (called Air Corp at the time of Pearl Harbor) as one of the most experienced in building and assembling airplanes, one being the B17, which I had been assigned to at Douglas, Long Beach. The plane was completely built, assembled and test flown at the Long Beach plant. At the time of Pearl Harbor, Douglas was just getting started in Long Beach.

Three other men and I were picked to make the flight crews of 10. The B17's first overseas flight was in this group to the islands. We left the States the night after Pearl Harbor and arrived the following morning at Hickam. (Time seems 13 hours overall). Fear was the strongest thing on one's mind. We were the first over water by land planes in a group. If the Japanese took you out of the water you would be considered a spy. Looking for land, I could not believe the small objects sticking up were islands. As we came in, it looked very much like a battle scene—fire, storm, lots of smoke, and staunch odor in the air, which sometimes comes back to one at the smell of a bad fire. Questions in our minds concerned what happened? and what will I do when I get on land again? One could almost feel that you could smell death itself.

James "Robbie" Robertson

Hangar #7, shattered by a direct bomb hit, is documented by a cameraman. USAF

Workmen at a bomb crater by a hangar on C Street. Note damage to adjacent areas. AMC

Hickam's fire station pockmarked with Japanese machine gun fire. The building now houses the 15th Security Police Squadron's Law Enforcement Unit. USAF

Wrecked passenger cars and burned bodies on F Street. USAF

A truck burns four hours after the attack. USAF

The oil storage area behind the barracks was destroyed. AMC

A postattack view of the fires burning at the hangars and barracks area. AMC

Fires burning at Pearl Harbor could be seen over the Officers' Quarters at Hickam. AMC

Broken water main on 6th Avenue between Worthington and Signer Avenue at 1610 on Dec. 7. USAF

Looking down Hangar Avenue shows the extent of damage to the hangars. USAF

A fire truck stands by while workmen frantically attempt to repair a bomb-ruptured water main. AMC

Workmen repair a bomb crater in a road near the firehouse. AMC

The body of an airman lies in front of the Post Exchange building on F Street next to Hangar #2. AMC

Dead bodies lie in the courtyard of the Hale Makai barracks. USAF

The wing operations building at Hickam in May 1940. USAF

A modern-day view of the old wing operations building at Hickam Field, built in 1937. At that time the runway extended into the background where base housing can be seen.

The water tower at Hickam Field, built in 1937, was, and still is, the focal point of the air base. The prominent landmark was not hit during the attack, perhaps – one theory suggests – because the Japanese thought it was a church.

The following photos courtesy Lee Embree, Port Angeles, Wash.

During final approach for landing at Hickam Field, we were attacked by two Japanese aircraft shown here. One aircraft, a *Kaga* Zero, had crashed (I saw it go down) and was burning. The two Japanese aircraft then circled in on our tail and attacked, but made only three or four hits. In foreground is the shoreline on the left side of an approach to the entrance of Pearl Harbor, or aircraft landing at Hickam Field. USAF

The same two Japanese aircraft, as shown in top photo, after strafing our aircraft from the rear, pass on toward Pearl Harbor or Hickam Field. This was our third attempt to land at Hickam Field and was our last, because we were very low on fuel. These two photos are said to be the first aerial photographs by the United States at the start of our involvement in World War II. USAF

B-17E in foreground from 38th Reconnaissance Squadron, after arrival from Hamilton Field, Calif. Smoke billowing in right background is from the *Arizona*. B-17D in background is from the 5th Bomb Group. This photograph appeared on the front page of the December 27, 1941, issue of *Life* magazine. USAF

After landing at Hickam Field, we taxied to a dispersement area and unloaded all available combustible material in case of an incendiary attack by the Japanese aircraft during strafing. The *Arizona* is burning in background. Left to right in photo, assistant crew chief, Sgt. Vance H. Spears and crew chief, T/Sgt. Roy H. Coulter. USAF

Hickam Field hangars were badly damaged by Japanese bombs and machine gun fire, which left the buildings and aircraft burning. On right is a badly damaged B-18 airplane. USAF

S/Sgt. Lee R. Embree, at camp site on the edge of Hickam Field. Air crews of the 38th Reconnaissance Squadron were forced to spend the night of December 7 at this site, because the Hickam Field barracks were destroyed. It rained most of the night and there was heavy antiaircraft firing around midnight. USAF

Schofield Barracks & Wheeler Field

Deadly Visitors Wreak Havoc on the Ground

One of the many destroyed fighter planes at Wheeler Field. USA

Situated on the Leilehua Plain almost in the center of Oahu are Schofield Barracks and Wheeler Air Force Base. Both were targets for Japanese planes in the opening minutes of the Pearl Harbor attack.

Schofield Barracks was named after Maj. Gen. John M. Schofield, the prominent U.S. Army officer who helped establish the post. He won the Congressional Medal of Honor during the Civil War, was superintendent at West Point and served as Secretary of War. In 1872, he led a survey party to Oahu and initiated the agreement that gave the U.S. use of Pearl Harbor as a naval base. He was influential in the eventual annexation of Hawaii as a territory in 1898.

The first unit, the 5th Cavalry, arrived at Schofield in 1909, but the construction of the principal barracks and buildings did not begin until 1916. The Hawaiian Division was organized on March 1, 1921, and was stationed at Schofield.

At the outset of World War II, Schofield Barracks was the largest post in the U.S. Army.

Wheeler Field was named on Nov. 11, 1922, in honor of Maj. Sheldon H. Wheeler. He was the commander of Luke Field, on Ford Island, from 1919 until his death in an airplane crash on July 12, 1921.

Construction of the field, which is situated just south of Schofield Barracks, began on Feb. 6, 1922. At the time of the Pearl Harbor attack, it was the largest fighter base in the Pacific area.

The first nonstop flight from the U.S. mainland to Hawaii terminated at Wheeler Field on June 29, 1927, and famed aviatrix Amelia Earhart used the field as her starting point when she made the first solo flight from Hawaii to the mainland on Jan. 11, 1935. Wheeler officially became a separate permanent military post in 1939.

Auxiliary fields were eventually built at Haleiwa on Oahu's northern coast and Bellows on the eastern coast. At the time of the Pearl Harbor attack, some of Wheeler's Army fighters had been dispersed to these coastal airstrips.

On the morning of December 7, Japanese fighters flew to the west of the bases and pounced on Wheeler in an effort to knock out as many of Oahu's land-based fighter planes as possible.

Wheeler Field, May 14, 1931 with Schofield Barracks in the background. HA

Schofield was not attacked with bombs, but by strafing planes. Building 1492 on the west end of the post was one of the first structures hit. Quad C, one of the main barracks, was strafed as was the post library.

But Wheeler Field was the main target. Planes were parked wingtip to wingtip in long parallel lines in front of the hanger.

At 7:51 a.m. the first wave of 25 *Zuikako* dive bombers bombed and eight *Soryu* Zeros machine-gunned the parked planes for 15 minutes. It was a simple matter for the enemy planes to fly up and down the flight lines, picking off the fighters. The barracks and tent areas and several hangars were just as vulnerable, and were soon in flames.

A second attack, lasting fewer than five minutes, came about 9:10 a.m. Eight *Kaga* Zeros machine-gunned Wheeler fighters as they were taxiing to the runway.

Eleven pilots managed to take off from Wheeler or Haleiwa during two attacks. They claimed 11 enemy planes shot down.

Altogether 83 aircraft of the 153 based at Wheeler were destroyed or damaged; thirty-seven Americans were killed, six were missing and 53 were wounded in two attacks.

Bellows Field on the east coast of Oahu below Kaneohe was established in 1917 as the Waimanalo Military Reservation. It was renamed Bellows Field in 1933, in honor of 2nd Lt. Franklin D. Bellows, an aviator killed in World War I.

An auxiliary base of Wheeler, Bellows had 20 fighter and reconnaissance planes parked in a line at 10- to 15-foot intervals. At 8:30 a.m. a single Japanese fighter machine-gunned the tent area, wounding one. At about 9 a.m. eight *Hiryu* Zeros machine-gunned the parked aircraft, destroying two fighters and one reconnaissance plane. Five airmen* were killed and nine wounded.

Haleiwa Field on Oahu's northern coast was not attacked, although there were a number of planes parked there.

The attacks on Wheeler and Bellows were devastating. Very few fighters were able to get into the air to combat the Japanese fighters, dive bombers and torpedo bombers that were attacking the U.S. fleet at Pearl Harbor. This is exactly what the Japanese had counted on—catching American airpower on the ground.

*2 P-40s shot down on takeoff (1 KIA, 1 WIA), 1 P-40 hit on ground with pilot KIA, 2 P-40s destroyed on ground.

For years, these holes in the wall of Carter Hall, the original post library at Schofield Barracks, were thought to be bullet holes from the attack. This building, however, was not attacked during the raid.

Front view of Funston Gate at the entrance to Schofield Barracks. It was constructed by the 3rd Engineers, Hawaiian Division, in the 1930s. USAMHI

Front view of the south side of Hangar #3 at 1020. Several hangars were badly damaged. USA

The base engineering shops a few days after the attack. It did not take long for military and civilian personnel at all Oahu bases to get back into operation. CAMERA HAWAII/WERNER STOY

A view of the southwest corner of the machine shop, completely destroyed during the attack. AMC

Damage to the gas engineering building. AMC

Interior view of the assembly shop showing damage to windows and frames. AMC

A TIN HAT WITH NO TOP

On Nov. 19, 1941, at Wheeler Field, Hawaii, final preparations were being made by the 6th and 19th fighter squadrons of the Army Air Corps for departure by aircraft carriers for stations at Midway and Wake islands. The date of departure from Pearl Harbor was set at Dec. 1, 1941.

At that time I was a staff sergeant serving as a flight chief in the 19th fighter squadron. Both the 6th and 19th squadrons were full strength in personnel, planes and equipment.

Excitement was high; the men of the other eight squadrons at Wheeler Field envied us. We expected the Japanese to attack the Philippines but not Hawaii, and for some reason not known to us our departure date was changed to Dec. 8, 1941.

The delay was a great disappointment to us as we felt that perhaps our orders would be canceled, thereby depriving us of getting closer to the Philippines and possible battle.

On Saturday, Dec. 6th, Lieut. Ahola, my flight leader, had flown his plane to Pearl Harbor where it was placed aboard a carrier so that he could practice a take-off to determine the degree of flaps to use. When he returned to the field I decided to place his plane in the hangar for final landing gear check prior to departure on Monday morning. The hangar was completely empty so Lt. Ahola's plane was placed facing out towards the field.

During the past few months we had been on continual alert and ready to fight, our planes dispersed around the field; however, our alert status had changed to protect against sabotage. All planes at Wheeler Field, about 300 of all types, were lined up on the ramps, wing-tip to wing-tip and tail to tail, so as to present as small an area as possible to guard against any possible sabotage.

Sunday, Dec. 7, 1941, started out a beautiful and peaceful day for me. Having finished breakfast with a few other sergeants, I went outside to the road in front of my barracks and waited for the arrival of the paper boy, along with Sgt. Moore and several other early birds.

My thoughts were interrupted by the sound of planes coming through Kolekole Pass. There were three two-engined land planes somewhat resembling our own A-20's, an attack bomber. They were painted olive drab color and as they approached opposite our field they cleared their machine guns by firing short bursts and continued toward Pearl Harbor. There were no identifying markings on the planes, and as they came abreast of the field our anti-aircraft protection located around the field opened fire with 50 caliber machine guns. I don't know to this day how they knew the three planes were Japanese or why they opened fire as no attack had as yet taken place.

I felt apprehensive but suggested to the group that we go on the ramp and watch what I thought was practice firing. At this time our attention was attracted above us to a squadron of silver planes which were peeling off singly and diving very slowly towards us. I looked toward Pearl Harbor and could see no planes in the air except the three that had come through Kolekole Pass and had headed in that direction. As I looked back to the planes diving at us, the rising sun painted on the wings became visible.

Several comments were made that the Navy was certainly conducting realistic exercises. When the leading plane released two 100-pound bombs, I could see that they were headed for the dump at the end of the hangar line. I just couldn't believe the Navy would drop practice bombs in that area and my heart beat faster as I watched the bombs drop.

When they hit the engineering hangar, the last on the line, all my doubts vanished. Heart beating furiously, I ran into the barracks, up the second floor stairs, all the while shouting, "It's war, men, get to the hangars," my thought being to get to the hangar as I felt sure some of the pilots would do the same and that should be our rightful place of duty.

Men first sat up in their bunks unbelieving. I then ran into my room off the rear porch which I shared with Staff Sgt M. A. Crawford. Crawford was shaving; I didn't say a word, but reached under my bunk, pulled out my pack with the tin hat attached. I couldn't unfasten the helmet so I ran out of the room carrying the pack and tin hat and attempting to unfasten the hat as I ran.

None of the men had as yet reached the stairway and my plan was to get the tin hat on, crawl to the hangar by using the gutter which was about 12 inches deep and get Lt. Ahola's plane warmed up and open the hangar doors. The plane could take off directly to the front between the parked planes.

As I reached the main floor, I noticed a tin hat lying on the hallway floor; how it got there I never found out. I dropped my pack and put on the tin hat, at the same time I was mentally keeping track of the planes attacking us. They were diving between two rows of barracks with the rear machine gunner spraying the barracks to keep personnel away from the planes. At the time I was picking up the tin hat, three planes had passed us, the first plane dropping two bombs and machine gunning. The second dropped no bombs, but machine-gunned and the third passed machine- gunning. I didn't think the third plane dropped any bombs so figured I could continue running to the street, hit the gutter and crawl along it to the hangar.

As I left the shelter of the porch I was looking to my right front and saw Sgt. Guthrie running in the center of the street about twenty yards from me. I got out about five yards from the porch when a bomb hit just about where Sgt. Guthrie was. I didn't hear it, but saw the tree between the bomb and me turn gray and shake. I thought the bomb hit in the tree.

When I regained consciousness I was lying on my stomach and facing toward the barracks, looking at my tin hat with the top cut off. I remember thinking that I must get under cover and getting up on my hands and knees. I then became unconscious for the second time and it was during this period that Sgt Malakowski pulled me into the porch. I got up from the floor while still unconscious and came to just as I was opening the screen door. I did not know then that I had been unconscious a second time. I went to the stairway where the men were lined up to the top floor. I was covered with blood and several men fainted when they saw me. Sgt. S. M. Rackowski was at the foot of the stairs and I instructed him to get the men down on the ground floor, which he did. After the attack was in progress about 15 minutes we had several men wounded. Sergeants Malakowski, Rackowski, and Morgan cleared a space for the wounded and provided first aid; there was no panic and everyone waited for the attack to subside.

My wounds consisted of bomb fragments in the left forearm and left thigh; cement, sticks, stones and other debris embedded over my entire right side and ruptured blood vessels in my lungs. While Sgt. Malakowski administered first aid to me, I attempted to get the men to go to the hangar, thinking that a pilot might have made it to the hangar and would need help to get a plane into the air.

Staff Sgt. Paul Cipreano restrained the men from going to the hangar at this time, and rightly so, due to the entire attacking force concentrating its efforts on the hangar line. Paul said the hangar line and all planes appeared to be on fire and that the Japanese were using 20- millimeter cannon to do the job. As it turned out later, Capt. Morris and Lt. Ahola did make it to the hangar but couldn't have taken Lt. Ahola's plane up as the hangar was under continual heavy enemy fire.

I wondered if the Japanese had landed on our beaches and where the Navy and Marine planes were; everyone was asking the same questions, hoping and praying for the Navy planes to appear, just as the Navy was asking for the Army planes.

Wheeler Field was under attack three times during a period of about 50 minutes. After the enemy planes completed their mission the wounded were assembled on the ground behind the dispensary awaiting transportation to Schofield Barracks Station Hospital. Due to the large number of casualties the hospital staff worked until well after midnight. In my ward we were taken to the operating table on a porch in the order of our arrival, and as a consequence I waited 14 hours to get my wounds attended to and there were two more men after me.

The casualties suffered were high as was the property damage. Out of all the P-40s at Wheeler Field it took an entire week to assemble seven planes from the salvaged parts of destroyed planes.

Initially when we were under attack, I did not see any planes over Pearl Harbor, which leads me to believe that probably Sgt. Guthrie was the first American killed in World War II, and I the first wounded. I have often wondered what course the war with Japan would have taken if our movement to Wake and Midway islands had proceeded as originally scheduled and we had departed from Pearl Harbor on Dec. 1st. We probably would have run into the attacking fleet. Our fighter planes were equipped with bomb racks; perhaps we would not have inflicted much damage, but the defenses of Hawaii would have been alerted to stop the infamous attack.

Maj. George Sallick, USA Ret.
Pensacola, Florida

Hangar #3 and destroyed fighters at 10:25 a.m. USAF

Interior damage at Hangar #3. AMC

Roof of a hangar riddled by machine gun fire. USAF

By the next morning, destroyed aircraft had been bulldozed into a pile to clear the flight line for operations. AMC

Some airmen were killed in their tents. USA

Charred remains of airmen's personal belongings after their tents were set afire during the attack. USA

The barracks at Wheeler Field suffered heavy damage. USAF

Air Corps personnel record the engine serial number of a destroyed P-40. AMC

A. Brick taking movies of the wreckage at Wheeler Field. USAF

Bomb damage from the attack 50 years ago is still visible today.

Base headquarters at Wheeler Air Force Base, home of the 326th Air Division.

Hangars and flight line at Wheeler Air Force Base.

Wheeler Field and Kolekole Pass.

Barracks at Wheeler Air Force Base.

D Quad at Schofield Barracks, home of the 25th Infantry Division.

Kaneohe NAS

A Seaplane Base up in Smoke

A PBY burning at Kaneohe Naval Air Station. NA

At the time of the Pearl Harbor attack, the Mokapu Peninsula on the northeast side of Oahu Island was the site of Kaneohe Naval Air Station.

The Army had established Fort Hase on the east shore of the peninsula in 1918, but the Navy did not build its base until 1939. A seaplane facility at the foot of Mokapu Point, the base was later expanded into a naval air station charged with coordinating the defense of the entire Kaneohe Bay area.

On the morning of Dec. 7, three of the station's twin-engine PBYs were out on patrol. The rest of the planes were in hangars, parked on the concrete tarmacs outside or moored in the bay.

At approximately 7:53, 11 fighters with red suns on their wings approached the naval air station from the northwest and attacked the seaplane facilities in long shallow dives. They strafed the area for 10 to 15 minutes, then flew off to the north. Despite the efforts of sailors to salvage burning aircraft, the damage was awesome.

At 8:55 a.m., 18* high-level bombers in the second attack continued the destruction. Hangar #3 received a direct bomb hit that destroyed four planes inside. Fires caused by the bombs and machine-gun fire set Hangar #1 ablaze, and the huge structure burned until only its steel skeleton was left. When the second attack was over, only 9 of the 36 planes based at Kaneohe were left; six of these were damaged. The only aircraft to escape harm were the three that were on patrol duty.

*Initially eight zeroes strafed then went to Bellows, then another nine strafed repeatedly losing one to ground fire.

Kaneohe Naval Air Station during its early years before the war. HA

Present-day Kaneohe Marine Corps Air Station and Mokapu Point. The Japanese came in from the sea to the left of the point, to attack the base which was then a naval station.

NAS Kaneohe, Aug. 11, 1941. NA 80-G-41187

The main hangar at Kaneohe was consumed by flames. NA 80-G-32565

Damage inflicted on Kaneohe Naval Air Station by the two Japanese attacks. NA

Rebuilt hangar today looks much as it did before the 1941 attack.

Burning PBYs at Kaneohe. USN

PBY of VP 12 destroyed at NAS Kaneohe. USN

Kaneohe Marine Corps Air Station as it appears today. The large hanger with the open door and the pier in the bay were heavily damaged during the attacks.

Modern-day view of the Kanėohe pier that came under attack.

Bellows Field

Wreckage of a Curtiss P-40 pursuit plane on the flight line at Bellows. AMC

The abandoned airstrip at Bellows on the east side of Oahu Island.

One of the Army's P-40s destroyed at Bellows Field. USAF

A disabled B-17 at Bellows Field. A flight of B-17s arrived at Oahu from California as the Japanese were beginning their attack. USAF

Ewa MCAS

Bloody Baptism for a New Base

Remains of an SBD Dauntless at Ewa. A C-33 is in the background. W.R. LUCIUS, HEALDSBURG, CALIF.

Just to the east of Barbers Point Naval Air Station on the southwestern tip of Oahu Island lies the abandoned runway of what was once the Ewa Marine Corps Air Station.

At the time of the Japanese attack, the Ewa base was not yet a year old. But the history of its use as a military facility dates to the 1930s, when the Navy leased a small piece of land from the Campbell Estate to build a mooring mast for the dirigible *Akron*. However, there is no record that the ship ever moored there.

In early 1940 the Navy acquired 3,500 additional acres from the estate and started construction of an air station for the Marine Corps. The airstrip was completed a year later, and plans were made to develop Barbers Point for naval aviation.

Two minutes before the Japanese attacked Pearl Harbor, one squadron of six Zeros came out of the northwest at an altitude of 500 meters feet and strafed the planes parked on the runway. Descending to within 20 feet of the ground, the enemy planes attacked single aircraft with short bursts of machine-gun fire, then pulled up over the treetops and reversed their course. Soon Vals were screaming in from the opposite direction strafing only.

In all, 33 of the 49 planes stationed at the base were destroyed and 16 damaged. Machinery was put out of commission, installations wrecked, and supplies destroyed.

During a momentary lull, Marines rushed out and dragged unburned planes off the runway. They attempted to mount machine guns on the aircraft to fire back at the attacking planes.

In the midst of the attack, a bright red base fire truck raced out onto the exposed runway toward the burning planes, and was attacked immediately by the enemy aircraft. The driver finally was forced to abandon the truck after machine-gun bullets had flattened his tires. When an officer complimented him afterward for having driven into a hail of bullets, the driver said, "Hell, Lieutenant, I saw a fire, and I'm supposed to put 'em out."

By 9:10 a.m. more Vals and Zeros worked over buildings and undamaged aircraft. As Ewa was near one of the post-attack rendezvous point for the Japanese planes, it presented a convenient target of opportunity for pilots departing the island after completing missions elsewhere.

Shortly after the first attack, six SBD dive bombers from the carrier *Enterprise* landed at Ewa, but were ordered back into the air to keep them from being caught on the ground.

Ewa casualties included four dead and 13 wounded.

Ewa Field, Oct. 27, 1941. NA 80-G451116

Mistaken Identity

On the morning of 7 December, 1941, I was a Marine supply sergeant living with my wife in a small cottage, specially built inside a water tower, overlooking Pearl Harbor We had just gotten up and were expecting guests for a picnic, on the grounds, later that day. Suddenly we saw an explosion over nearby Ford Island. My immediate reaction was a plane had hit the radio tower there during maneuvers; however, upon further examination I realized from the meatball insignia that the planes were Japanese. Both of us immediateiy jumped into our car and headed for our base—the Marine Corps Air Station at Ewa. The only road was repeatedly strafed by enemy aircraft during our journey. Upon reaching the town of Ewa, I dropped my wife off there, with civilian friends, and proceeded on to the base, a distance of approximately one-third of a mile.

Everything there was in a state of chaos. One specific incident: A Marine private by the name of "Lucas" had reportedly been found in the nearby cane fields starting fires in the shape of an arrow, obviously directed toward our base and which could be seen from the air. He was promptly shot by Marines. I proceeded on with the business involved and did not see my wife for several days. In the meantime, someone (and I am not sure of this—it could have been a civilian worker from the Ewa plantation) indicated Sergeant Lucius had been shot and killed as a spy, this being the only information my wife heard. This obviously was not correct, however, and upon being allowed by my commanding officer, Lt Col Claude A. Larkin to go see her, I assured her that I was alive and in no trouble.

My wife, May, after staying only briefly with our friends in Ewa, assumed a position as a civil service worker at Pearl Harbor. Upon my transfer to Midway Island in early May of 1942, she was evacuated to the United States via the *S.S. Lurline.*

Col. W. R. Lucius, USMC, Ret.
Healdsburg, California

Ewa Marine Corps Air Station was carved out of tropical brush in 1940-41 as the Corps' major base on Oahu.
USMC #145093, 145035, 145047

Ewa Mooring Mast derived its name when it was built in the 1930s for Navy dirigibles. The Navy, however, abandoned its dirigible program and the mast was eventually used as a control tower for the Marines' new air station built at the site in 1940-41. USMC 145094

This unfinished swimming pool provided a hiding place from the enemy planes. Ewa marines joked that it was the first time they dived into a dry swimming pool head first. USMC

Planes at Ewa Mooring Mast Field, near Barber's Point, alerted incoming *Enterprise* pilots to the fact that things were far from normal on the morning of Dec. 7. Here a Vought SB2U-3 "Vindicator" burns; wing fabric on the right wing has already burned off, and the plane has broken in half. LARKIN COLLECTION MCHC

Private automobile destroyed during the attack on Ewa Field. USMC #145135, 145133

Before the attack, Marines on a firing line practiced firing at low flying aircraft. In a short time these men would be engaged in the real thing. USMC #14517

Marines armed with Springfield model '03 rifles fire back at Japanese aircraft during the attack. This is one of the few action shots taken during the attack showing personnel fighting back. WALTER LORD

Ewa, today is abandoned.

Honolulu

The Falling Shells Were Ours

Damage at McCully and King streets in Honolulu, possibly caused by a small incendiary bomb. Most of the destruction in the city was caused by unexploded anti-aircraft shells falling back on the city.
CAMERA HAWAII/WERNER STOY

Though the Japanese plan of attack apparently did not include strikes on Honolulu or other civilian areas, it was almost inevitable that individual planes, either by mistake or design, damaged nonmilitary areas. A number of Oahu civilians were killed.

At Waipahu, just north of Pearl Harbor, two persons were killed and 7 wounded; at Ewa, next to the Marine Air Station, seven were wounded; and at Wahiawa, next to Wheeler Field and Schofield Barracks, three were killed and nine wounded.

The Waipahu sugar plantation's mill, hospital, company store and warehouse were hit and damaged badly. At Ewa, enemy planes shot up the sugar plantation's main street, mill, plant and workers' houses. At Wahiawa, stores and cars were attacked. When an enemy plane crashed in an adjacent pineapple field, local firemen and a Boy Scout bucket brigade put out the fire. At Wahiawa, a Japanese plane crashed into a house, setting the structure afire.

Waikiki Beach in 1938. The Royal Hawaiian Hotel (left) was taken over by the U.S. Navy as a rest and recreation center during the war. The Moana Hotel (right) is the oldest hotel in Honolulu (1901) and has recently been restored.

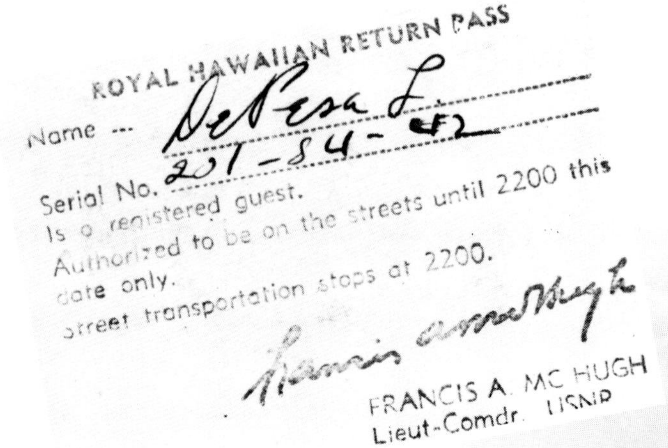

ROYAL HAWAIIAN RETURN PASS

Name ---

Serial No.

Is a registered guest.

Authorized to be on the streets until 2200 this date only.

Street transportation stops at 2200.

FRANCIS A. MC HUGH
Lieut-Comdr. USNR

Waikiki Beach in front of the Royal Hawaiian Hotel took on a wartime look after the attack but bathers still enjoyed its beautiful setting.

Honolulu residents, enjoying a peaceful Sunday morning, at first did not understand what was happening. Even when they heard the bombs and saw the smoke rising from Pearl Harbor and Hickam Field, many surmised the American military was engaged in training exercises.

But the reality of the attack became apparent when areas in the city itself were hit. Honolulu police received the first report of damage at 8:05 a.m. and more reports followed. At 9:30, explosions were reported near Gov. Poindexter's residence and on the grounds of the Iolani Palace.

The Honolulu fire department received 40 calls but most of the city's firemen already had been sent to battle blazes at Hickam Field. Major fires raged in the McCully district; the scattered explosions damaged buildings in virtually every section of the city. One shell struck the Lunalilo School on Pumehaua Street, fortunately unoccupied. Ironically, almost all of the damage was believed to have been caused by U.S. anti-aircraft shells falling back on the city. In the excitement of the moment, the armorers had forgotten to set the time fuses that would detonate the shells in the air. Errant projectiles thus exploded when they hit the ground in Honolulu.

At the present site of the Honolulu International Airport, then known as John Rogers Field, nine Zeros strafed the area, killing several people. Passengers on an inter-island flight to Maui that was just getting ready to take off were whisked off the plane and taken to safety. Five private pilots flying over Oahu at the time of the attack managed to land their planes safely, three were shot down.

The Dutch ocean freighter *Jagersfonteiu*, armed because the Netherlands was already at war, entered Honolulu harbor at 9 a.m. and fired at the enemy planes. Thus the Netherlands became the first country to fight alongside the United States during World War II.

There was some confusion in Honolulu and throughout the island, but Oahu residents quickly responded to the attack. Volunteers were everywhere. Members of the San Jose College and Willamette University football teams, on the island to play a post-season game, became volunteer policemen. Emergency medical and ambulance services went into action immediately as did all civilian defense organizations.

KGU and KGMB, the two Honolulu radio stations, were ordered off the air at 11:41 to prevent enemy planes from homing in on their beams.

Sixty-eight civilians were killed and 35 wounded in the two-hour attack.

DAMAGE IN HONOLULU AREA
DECEMBER 7, 1941

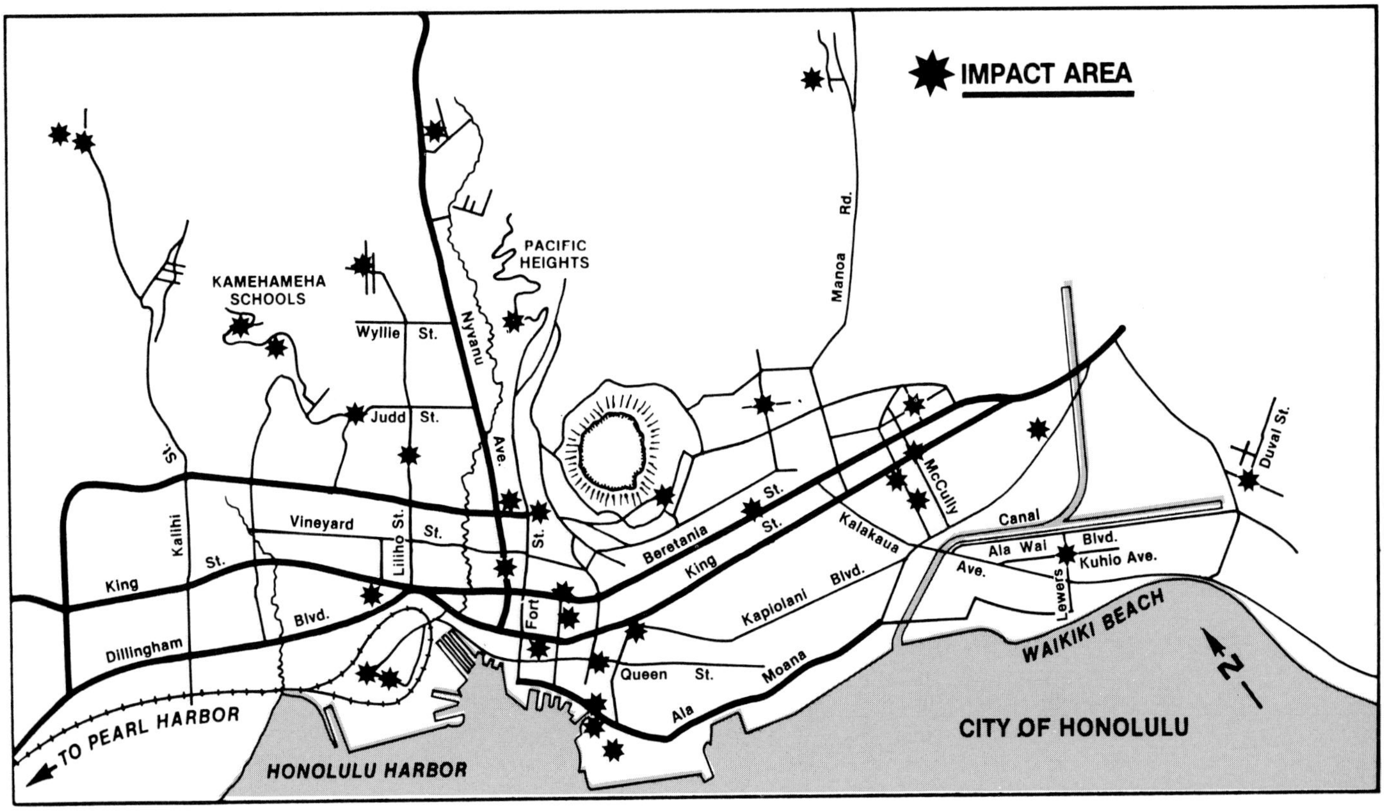

On Dec. 7, 1941, Capt. Gilbert Tefft and his co-pilot, Steve Rosetta, were in Hawaiian Airlines' DC-3 No. 9 with 24 passengers. They were preparing to taxi for a takeoff when the last Japanese plane to pass over the airport strafed No. 9 and the airlines' other planes. Passengers and crew members safely evacuated the plane. On the Japanese plane's first pass, No. 9's cockpit burst into flames. On the second pass, a stray bullet hit the cockpit fire extinguisher. The CO_2 escaped and put out the fire. The incident, one of dozens on that day, made the pages of Ripley's "Believe It Or Not." The plane eventually was patched up and put back into service.

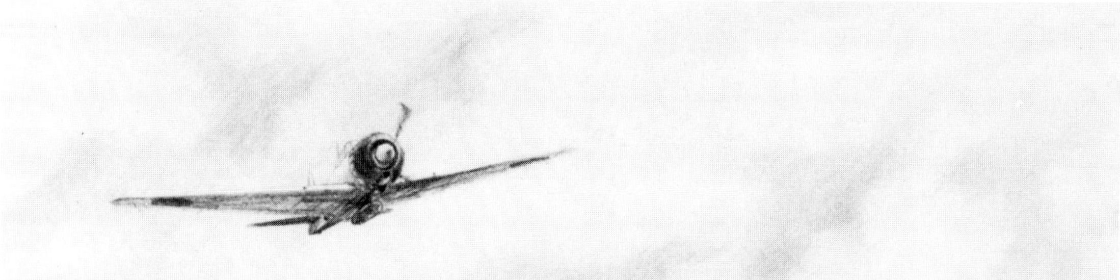

A lone Japanese fighter strafes a Hawaiian Airlines DC-3 at John Rodgers Airport. PAUL BENDER

Civilians move to temporary shelter after the attack. Concern about further Japanese air attacks or even an invasion was great for the next few days. USA

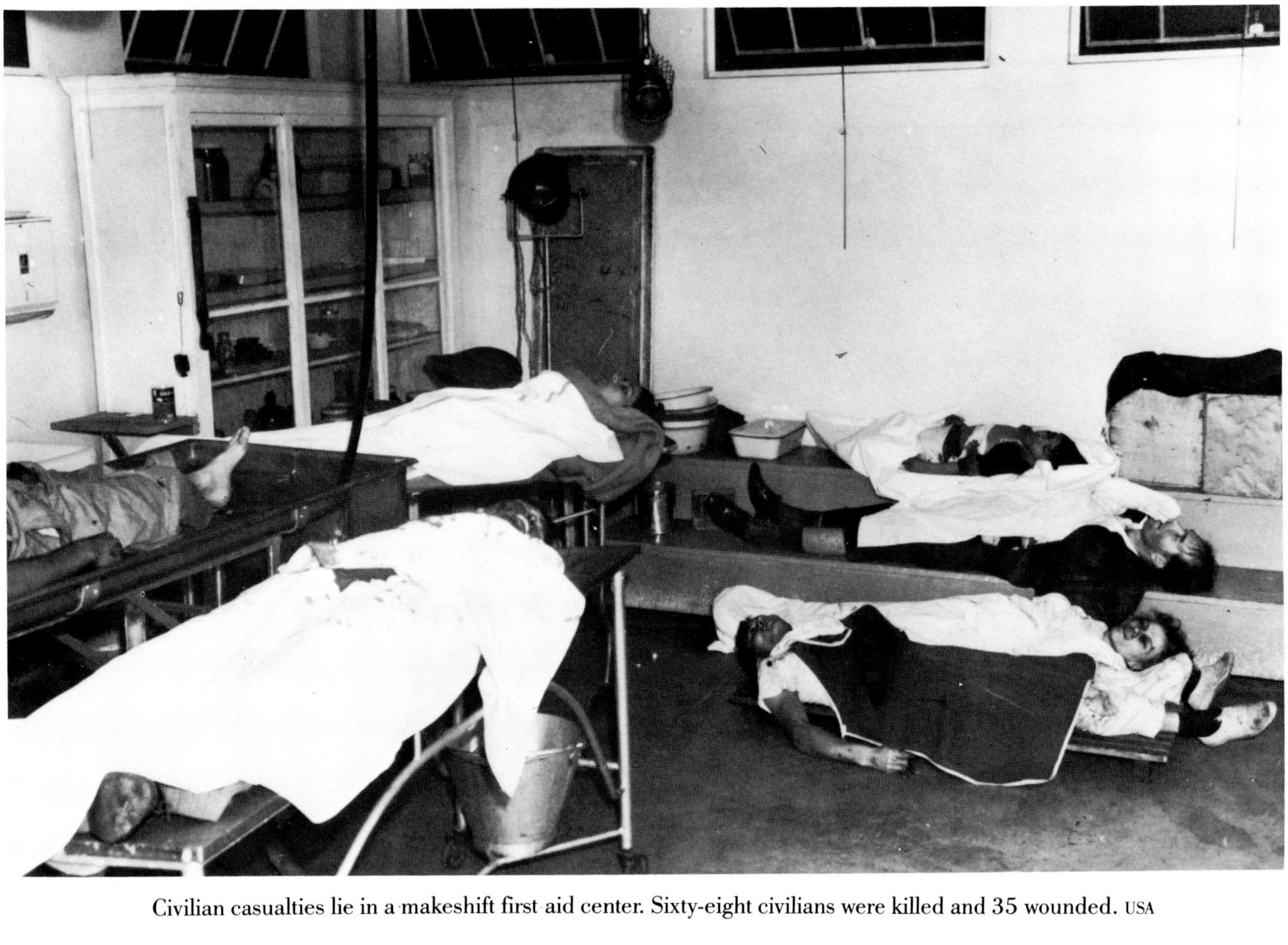

Civilian casualties lie in a makeshift first aid center. Sixty-eight civilians were killed and 35 wounded. USA

Anticipating another air attack, civilians dig bomb shelters at Kewalo Basin at 1 p.m. Concern about a renewed Japanese air attack was great all through the day. USA

A private car, the victim of a strafing Japanese plane. USA

Damage to structures in Honolulu. Antiaircraft fire from American guns falling back to earth actually started the fires rather than attacks from enemy aircraft. Top photo: U.S. ARMY MUSEUM. The middle photo shows a volunteer fireman aiding a man on the roof by handing him a fire hose. USA SC 242160. Bottom photo shows firemen fighting a fire with a store's showcases placed on the sidewalk. USA SC 242147

An unexploded bomb in a cane field after the attack. USA SC127870

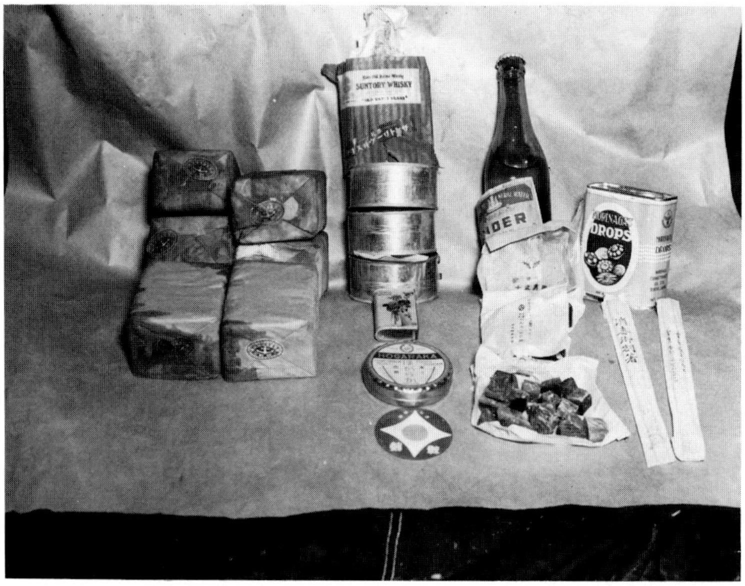

Japanese rations found in a downed plane. NA 80-G-32687

Artifacts recovered from a downed Val, included a portion of its instrument panel. NA 80-G-32780

Salvage

The Heroes Wore Hard Hats

Forward superstructure and bridge of the *Arizona* on Feb. 17, 1942. Her gun turrets were salvaged for use as coastal defenses on Oahu. USN

The Pearl Harbor attack devastated the Pacific Fleet and left U.S. Pacific defenses in shambles. Eighteen ships—300,000 tons' worth—were either sunk or damaged and most of the Oahu-based army and navy aircraft were destroyed or badly damaged.

The Japanese sunk or damaged five of eight Pacific Fleet battleships, thus wiping out the main striking force of the U.S. Navy. Only the aircraft carriers escaped unscathed.

Efforts to rescue trapped sailors from the sunken ships began while the attack was still under way. No one could be rescued from the battleship *Arizona*, which sank quickly, but one Navy man was brought out from the target ship *Utah* through a hole in her upturned hull. Six men were rescued from the capsized battleship *Oklahoma* the next morning after torch-wielding workers cut holes in her steel hull plates. Eleven more were found alive and recovered about noon and 13 more later in the day. In all 32 *Oklahoma* sailors were rescued, the last one on Dec. 9.

In June 1942, when the battleship *West Virginia* was placed in dry dock, the bodies of 20 sailors were found entombed in the ship. Three of them were found in a pump room; messages written on a bulkhead indicated the trapped men had lived until Dec. 23.

Because the Japanese had neglected to bomb the shipyards, yard workers were able to begin repairing the damaged ships almost immediately after the attack. The Navy decided to patch up the ships enough to make them seaworthy, then take them to the West Coast for complete repair, overhaul and refitting. Because the *Arizona*, with 1,102 men entombed in her, was too badly damaged to be refloated, salvage crews removed gun turrets and other components that could be reused. Due to dangerous gases trapped in her hull, the Navy decided not to try to remove the bodies. They were left there as a permanent memorial to the attack victims.

Hundreds of thousands of gallons of fuel oil had to be pumped out of the *West Virginia* before she could be refloated. Her hull patched with 650 tons of concrete, she was raised on May 17, 1942. After undergoing temporary repairs at Pearl, the battleship was sent to Puget Sound Navy Yard for rebuilding. She rejoined the fleet in July 1944 and participated in some of the remaining battles of the Pacific war. Having been patched and pumped out, the battleship *California* was refloated on March 24, 1942. She went to the Puget Sound Navy Yard in October 1942, was rebuilt and rejoined the fleet in late 1943. Salvaging the battleship *Oklahoma* proved to be a massive and time-consuming operation. She had not only sunk but rolled over. First, 350,000 gallons of fuel oil were removed from her hull and a huge air bubble was pumped in to lighten the ship. Twenty-one derrick-like towers were attached to her upturned bottom and connected by cables to 20-ton winches on Ford Island. Eventually the winch-cable system was able to pull the vessel upright. Owing to the delicate nature of the operation and the shortage of equipment and materials, more than two years had passed before the *Oklahoma* was finally drydocked in December 1943. After the Navy decided that she was not worth rebuilding, her superstructure was stripped and she was sold for scrap. In 1947, while being towed to the West Coast, she sank in a storm, never to be recovered.

Having gone aground at Hospital Point near the entrance to Pearl Harbor during the attack, the battleship *Nevada* had been pulled back off the beach by tugs and had backed across the channel to Waipio Peninsula, where she sank to the bottom in shallow water. She was raised on Feb. 12, 1942, received temporary repairs at Pearl and was restored and modernized on the West Coast. The *Nevada* returned to the Pacific Fleet in time for the Aleutian Campaign, then participated in battles in both the European and Pacific theaters.

The battleships *Maryland*, *Tennessee*, and *Pennsylvania*, whose damages were not severe, were repaired quickly and returned to service in late 1941 and early 1942. Also sent

Salvage Officer Capt. H.N. Wallin (left) and the Commander of the *West Virginia*, Lt. Comdr. W. White, during salvage operations in 1942. USN NH 64470

into action after quick repairs were three light cruisers, the *Helena, Raleigh* and *Honolulu.*

The destroyer *Shaw*, which blew up and sank along with her floating dry dock, was refloated, fitted with a makeshift bow and sailed back to the West Coast in February 1942. Rebuilt, she rejoined the fleet in late 1942.

Although the destroyers *Cassin* and *Downes* were beyond repair, their engines and other machinery were salvaged and shipped to the Mare Island Ship Yard near San Francisco, where new destroyers were built around them.

Considered a total loss, the rolled-over mine-layer *Oglala* was to be dynamited and used for scrap, but the Navy found that it would be just as easy to salvage her as to blow her apart. Refloated in April 1942 and temporarily repaired, she was rebuilt at Mare Island and rejoined the fleet in February 1944.

The *Vestal*, a repair ship, and the *Curtiss*, a seaplane tender, were repaired in 1942 and served in the remaining years of the war.

A stripped-down target vessel, the old battleship *Utah* was not worth the expense of refloating and repairing. Left in the water like the *Arizona*, she is today a memorial to the victims of the attack.

Both Army and Navy airfield were back in operation almost immediately. Repairs were made to bombed-out hangars and other installations within days.

Thanks to the quick action of salvage crews and repair teams, most of the ships damaged at Pearl Harbor eventually rejoined the fleet and took part in the war. On the other hand the Japanese warships that attacked Pearl Harbor would share a grimmer fate. Of the major vessels that participated in the attack, none survived the war. The Imperial Japanese Navy that had once ruled the Pacific was destroyed in the succeeding three and one-half years

The *West Virginia* was raised from her sunken grave in May 1942 and taken to drydock for temporary repairs.
WEST VIRGINIA STATE ARCHIVES

The port side of the *West Virginia* while in drydock at Pearl Harbor, June 1942. WEST VIRGINIA STATE ARCHIVES

Torpedo damage to the *West Virginia*. USN 83058

A sailor eyes an unexploded bomb inside the *West Virginia* during the salvage operation. USN NH 64305

A slightly abbreviated *West Virginia* being moved from drydock to a pier at the Pearl Harbor shipyard, September 1942. A *Mississippi*-class battleship is in the right background. USN NH 84005

Removing the "Basket" mainmast from the *California*, Feb. 13, 1942. USN NA 55038

Bow-on shot of the main deck of the *California* breaking water. USNI

The *California* in Drydock #2 just as it became dry, April 9, 1942. USN NA 64483

The *California* crossing the sill of Drydock #2 after being refloated from its sunken position on Battleship Row, April 9, 1942. USN

Two views of the *Nevada*'s ruptured deck, forward of No. 1 Turret, taken on Dec. 12, 1942. USN NA 64484, 50104

Temporary patch for the bow of the *Nevada* is floated toward the ship in Feb. 1942. USN NH 45464

The *Nevada* enters Drydock #2 on Feb. 18, 1942. She received temporary repairs there and was then refitted at the Puget Sound Navy Yard. She was ready for action again in the spring of 1943. USN

The gallant battleship *Nevada* leaves under her own power from Pearl Harbor for permanent repairs on the mainland, Dec. 2, 1942. USN

This 1953 view shows the memorial plaque placed on the *Utah*. NA 80-G-48454

A 1959 view of the capsized *Utah*, now a national memorial like the *Arizona*. USN 1056771

Charles Christensen from Clearfield, Utah, was on board the *Utah* Dec. 7. The bell he is ringing is now located in the Utah State Historical Society collection in Salt Lake City.
UTAH STATE HISTORICAL SOCIETY

Oklahoma, as she looked in February 1944 after being refloated. Not considered repairable, she was stripped of her superstructures and guns and finally, in 1946, sold for scrap. NA

The capsized *Oklahoma* lies at Battleship Row. Examination of battle damage photos indicates she may have been hit by as many as nine torpedoes. The torpedo hits, one after the other, quickly opened her sides to the sea. There was no time to counterflood to prevent the ship from capsizing. She rolled 145 degrees until her masts hit the soft mud of the harbor bottom.

Cable towers constructed over the capsized hull of the *Oklahoma* were part of the Navy's largest salvage job. Behind each of the 21 towers was an electric winch anchored in concrete on Ford Island. It took ten months to right the 35,000-ton ship and get her into a drydock. NA 80-G-300125

Winch-powered cables extend from Ford Island to the overturned *Oklahoma*. The towers were attached to the bottom of the ship. USN

One of the large winches placed on Ford Island, used to salvage the *Oklahoma*. USN SHIPYARD COLLECTION

Looking aft at the beginning of the righting operations on March 8, 1943. USN

Aerial view on March 19, 1943, showing the *Oklahoma* in its 90-degree position. NA 80-G-300131

View looking portside from the *Oklahoma* after the ship was righted. USN

Damage was extensive on the superstructure of the *Oklahoma*. USN

The *Oklahoma* in drydock, 1944. The damage was too severe to consider rebuilding her and she was sold for scrap in 1946. USN

More damage looking aft on the upper deck in the ship's 10-degree position on May 6, 1943. USN

Clinometer on the *Oklahoma* in about the 10-degree position. USN

Fourteen-inch shells being removed through the remains of Turret #4 on the *Arizona*. May 18, 1942. AMC

These views attest to the damage caused by the explosion on the *Arizona*, one of the greatest disasters in U.S. Naval history. USN

Removing the *Arizona*'s superstructure, May 1942. USN

Removal of *Arizona*'s ammunition aft. Working party equipped for work in first platform magazines (in face masks) and on topside (in respirators), July 1, 1942. USN

Divers emerge from water-filled compartments on the *Arizona* in May 1943. Some salvage work was done, but it was considered too dangerous to try to recover the bodies of the men who went down with the ship. USN NH 64303

Two of the *Arizona*'s 5-inch/51 guns that were recovered from the wreck. Tied up across the pier is the salvaged hulk of the destroyer *Cassin*.

Cassin (left) and *Downes* in Drydock #1, January 1942 while being salvaged.
USN NH 54562

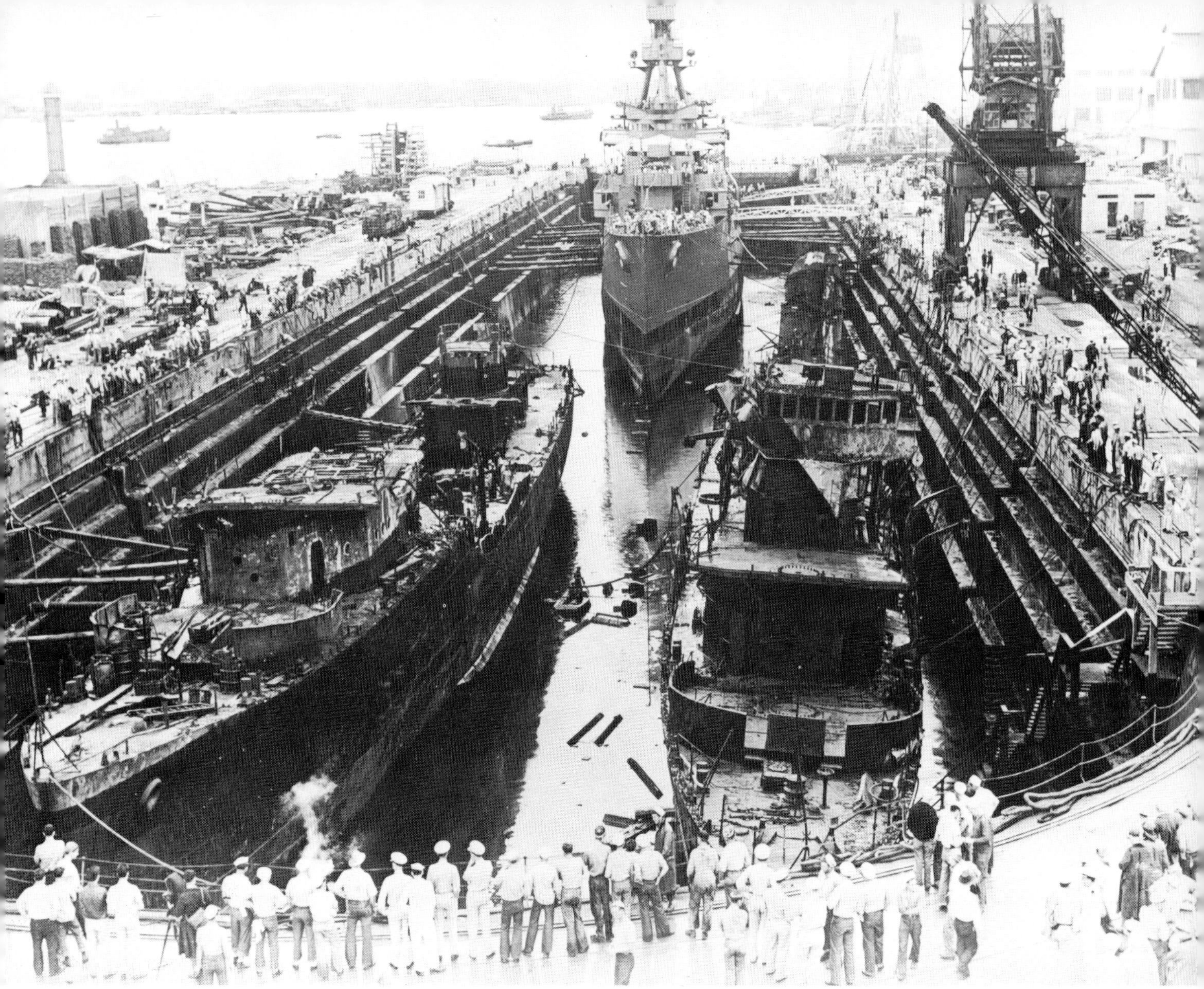

This February 1942 photo shows the *Cassin* (right) now righted, and both ships being readied for refloating. USN NH 54564

Massive damage inflicted on both destroyers in Drydock #1 is seen in this late December photo of the *Downes.* USN NH 54561

Two attempts to raise the *Oglala* in June 1942 ended when she re-sank each time. The third attempt on July 3, 1942, was successful and the ship was moved to a drydock for repairs. *Oglala* sailed under her own power in December 1942 for the West Coast, where she would be converted to an engine repair ship. The new *Oglala* (ARG-1) was recommissioned on Feb. 28, 1944.

The *Oglala* in 1943 after being raised and partially repaired. USN NH 64236

The *Shaw* was repaired with a temporary bow as shown in this February 1942 photo. She sailed back to California to undergo extensive repairs.
USN NH 50005

Adm. Chester Nimitz (center) with R. Adm. W. R. Furlong and Capt. H. N. Wallin at the raising of the *Oglala* in May 1942.
USN NH 50002

On April 23, 1942, the *Oglala* was turned next to her resting place at 1010 Dock.
USN SHIPYARD COLLECTION

Sunrise on the Fleet

0755 Hrs., December 7, 1941—The final moment of peace

Scale Miniature Diorama by Robert D. Bracci

This diorama is the culmination of nearly twenty thousands hours of labor and research. The three-dimensional replica encompasses a nine-square-mile area of the anchorage condensed within a four-foot-square display format. The piece is currently on loan to the U.S.S. *Arizona* Memorial Museum, where it it on exhibition at the visitors center, Pearl Harbor, Hawaii.

View north over fuel storage area and Marine Corps garrison grounds, with drydocks and navy yard/repair basin beyond. Ford Island is at upper left with "Battleship Row" at center; shoreline of Waiau, Waimalu and Aiea are at top of photo, with Kuahua at right.

Southeasterly view over northeastern tip of Ford Island, showing Battleship Row along mooring quays. Navy yard is visible at upper right with Hickam Field complex just beyond at top of photo. Kuahua Peninsula and Submarine Base come into view at upper left, with fuel storage area and naval residence complexes at top left.

Westerly view over Magazine Loch, the Submarine Base and the Ammunition and Supply Depot on Kuahua Peninsula. Beyond lay Ford Island with Battleship Row along shore. Navy yard is at center left with Waipio at top left and Pearl City at upper right. Hospital ship *Solace* (AH-5) is white vessel at right.

Oblique view, toward northeast, across Ford Island's Luke Field airstrip, with utility aircraft hangars along shoreline (left); large PBY seaplanes can be observed among larger hangars along shoreline at right. Waipio Peninsula's shoreline emerges at lower portion of photo; 1010 dock and navy yard are at extreme right.

Aftermath

Rebounding from Disaster

President Franklin D. Roosevelt delivers his war message to a joint session of Congress on Dec. 8, 1941, a day after the attack on Pearl Harbor. USN

By 9:45 a.m. the raid was over. The raiders rendezvoused 20 miles northwest of Kaena Point with their fighters and flew back to their carriers, which had moved away from Oahu.

Cmdr. Fuchida stayed behind to determine the damage they had inflicted. Flying to each attacked base, he snapped pictures through the smoke. Then he checked the rendezvous area for stragglers and—finding only one—flew to his carrier.

Most of the pilots got back to the carriers between 10:30 a.m. and 1:30 p.m. Twenty-eight of their comrades were shot down over Oahu or crashed into the sea, and one crash landed at Niihau. In the game of war, it was a small price to pay for the devastation inflicted on American ships and aircraft.

Flying officers on board wanted to go in for another attack and finish the job. But Adm. Nagumo, influenced by his chief of staff, Rear Adm. Ryunosuke Kusaku, vetoed those suggestions. He reasoned that the attack had inflicted most of the damage that was anticipated and they could not again achieve surprise. Their losses would be much greater now that American gunners would be poised and ready. Moreover, the whereabouts of the U.S. carriers was a question mark, and radio intercepts indicated that there were still some 50 operational aircraft on Oahu. The carrier-based Japanese planes, with their limited range, would be at a disadvantage if forced to tangle with fully alerted land-based aircraft.

The confident aviators proposing another attack also argued that a third raid would draw U.S. carrier aircraft, thus permitting the Japanese force to seek out the carriers and destroy them. But such a plan was risky, and meant radically changing the withdrawal route, and diverting tankers already headed for another rendezvous point. This Nagumo was unwilling to do.

So at 1630 hours (4:30 p.m.) the fleet set a northwesterly course for the Japanese port of Kure. On the way home, Nagumo detached Carrier Division 2 (*Soryu* and *Hiryu*), Cruiser Division 8 (*Tone*, *Chikuma*) and two destroyers to support the Wake Island invasion. Wake fell to the Japanese on Dec. 23, the same day the main Pearl Harbor force arrived home.

The I-Class submarines maintained their patrols in Hawaiian waters after the attack and one (I-7) launched its patrol plane to inspect the damage. The subs then positioned themselves between Hawaii and the American West Coast and one shelled the Oregon coast about Dec. 13. Months later, Japanese flying boats, refueled from I-Class submarines, dropped a few bombs on Oahu but cloud cover impeded their accuracy.

The Pearl Harbor attack was not, of course, an isolated raid. It was orchestrated with attacks on Hong Kong, Malaya, Guam, Wake and the Philippine islands on the evening of the 7th and Midway on the 8th.

Just before noon on Dec. 8, President Roosevelt addressed a joint session of Congress and made his famous "Day of Infamy" speech calling for a declaration of war. Within days, the United States had declared war on all the Axis powers—Japan, Germany and Italy. There was only one dissenter in Congress—Jeannette Rankin, congresswoman from Montana—who had also voted against America's entry into World War I.

At noon on the 7th, the Japanese consulate in Honolulu was placed under guard. That day and the next security agents arrested 370 Japanese, 98 Germans and 14 Italians in the islands. After the attack it was only natural that the Japanese population of Hawaii, at that time approximately 160,000, would come under suspicion; however, there was no sabotage or fifth column activity either during or after the attack. In early 1942 some Japanese were sent to internment camps in the United States. They were the first of

This fine German spyglass was confiscated from a Japanese alien in Honolulu just after the Pearl Harbor attack. The 50-power glass had a camera attachment for taking long-distance photos. NA

about 1,800 who would be sent from the islands. In early 1942, 20,000 Army and Navy dependents and 10,000 island women and children were sent to the mainland.

Soon after the attack, the 400 cadets of the University of Hawaii Reserve Officers Training Corps were called to active duty. Their ROTC unit was to be the only one in the United States or its territories to enter active war service. They were immediately converted into the Hawaiian Territorial Guard, and assigned to guard important public facilities against the expected enemy invasion.

All through the day and into the night, thousands of American gunners waited tensely for any sign of another attach. Tragically, they were too quick on the trigger, and mistakenly shot down five U.S. Navy carrier planes coming in for a landing at Ford Island. Several incoming B-17 bombers narrowly escaped being knocked from the sky by the over-anxious gunners.

The next day jittery American fliers strafed four fishing boats off Barbers Point, killing six civilians. Some were Japanese aliens who had put to sea before Dec. 7 and did not know of the attack.

Shortly after noon on Dec. 7, the commander of the Hawaiian Department, Lt. Gen. Walter C. Short, called at Governor Poindexter's office and requested an immediate declaration of martial law and suspension of the writ of habeas corpus in Hawaii. Although reluctant, the governor yielded to the military necessity of the day, and Hawaii became the first American territory to be ruled by a military government. Martial law was not lifted until Oct. 14, 1944, by proclamation of President Roosevelt.

On Dec. 17, the three major commanders in Hawaii were relieved of their commands pending an investigation of the surprise attack. Adm. Kimmel was succeeded by Rear Adm. Chester W. Nimitz; Lt. Gen. Short by Lt. Gen. Delos

RANKING NAVAL, ARMY OFFICERS HAWAII AREA LOSE COMMANDS

Japanese Pincer Attempt in Malaya

American Units Blast Japs Who Push Singapore

In Shakeup

Drastic Shakeup Comes as Board Launches Probe

Kimmel Replaced as Fleet Chief By Nimitz; Heads of Army's Land And Air Corps on Island Ousted

OFFICERS WHO TAKE OVER

'NOT ON ALERT,' KNOX SAYS

Mayor To Fight For Bond Vote

Bandits Get $90 Off Bus Driver

Two White Men Flee In Car After Holdup On Murfreesboro Road

Rebellious House Beats Efforts For Draft Limit Below 21 Years

Tire Rationing Begins Jan. 4

Will Prohibit Sales Except to Individuals Whose Need Approved

Emergency War Relief Drive For $200,000 Here Opens Today

The Traffic Toll

Deaths 61

Deathless Days

City 4 County 3

Gallant Hong Kong Defenders Hold; Spurn Surrender Orders

Today's Tennessean

Cost of Living Reported Higher

German Retreat From Moscow Too Fast To Bury Dead, Says Witness; Frozen Bodies Dot Roads

5 SHOPPING DAYS to Christmas Also GIVE U.S. Defense BONDS and STAMPS

C. Emmons; and Maj. Gen. Frederick L. Martin, commander of Army Air Force Hawaii, by Maj. Gen. Clarence L. Tinker.

The smoke of battle had scarcely cleared before the first investigative board from Washington arrived in Hawaii. The Roberts Commission, headed by Supreme Court Justice Owen J. Roberts, concluded its investigation in January 1942, but the analysis of the disaster was only beginning. In the succeeding five years, seven additional boards of inquiry were convened to study every aspect of the affair. Secretary of the Navy Frank Knox had gone to Pearl Harbor almost immediately after the attack for a first-hand inspection. Before he left Washington he sent a message to all naval ships and stations:

> The enemy has struck a savage, treacherous blow. We are at war, all of us! There is no time now for disputes or delay of any kind. We must have ships and more ships, guns and more guns, men and more men—faster and faster. There is no time to lose. The Navy must lead the way. Speed up—it is your Navy and your Nation!

Admiral Kimmel and General Short were never brought to trial to defend themselves against accusations that they were negligent in their duties. Perhaps this trial would have revealed more details about how and why the American forces had been caught so completely by surprise, but the final truths about this stunning moment in history will probably remain submerged in the past, their outlines obscured by the murky waters of time.

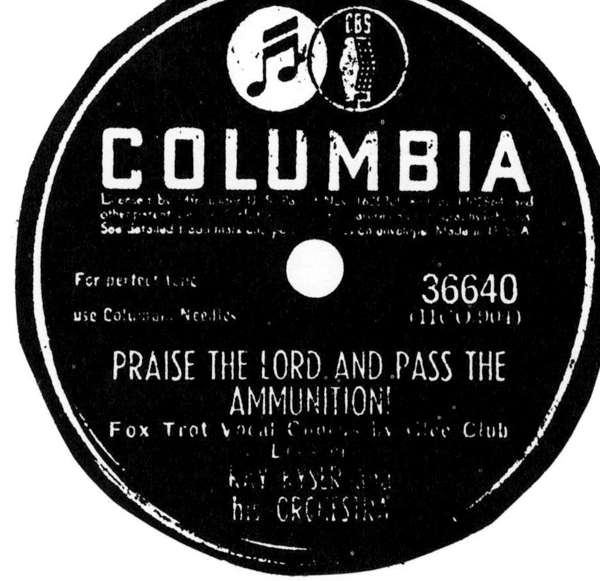

Chaplain Howell Forgy stationed on the U.S.S. *New Orleans* during the attack uttered the phrase that would become famous during the war, "Praise the Lord and Pass the Ammunition." The phrase was spoken while he and other sailors passed anti-aircraft shells to the ship's gun deck during the attack. This phrase was also made into a popular wartime song.

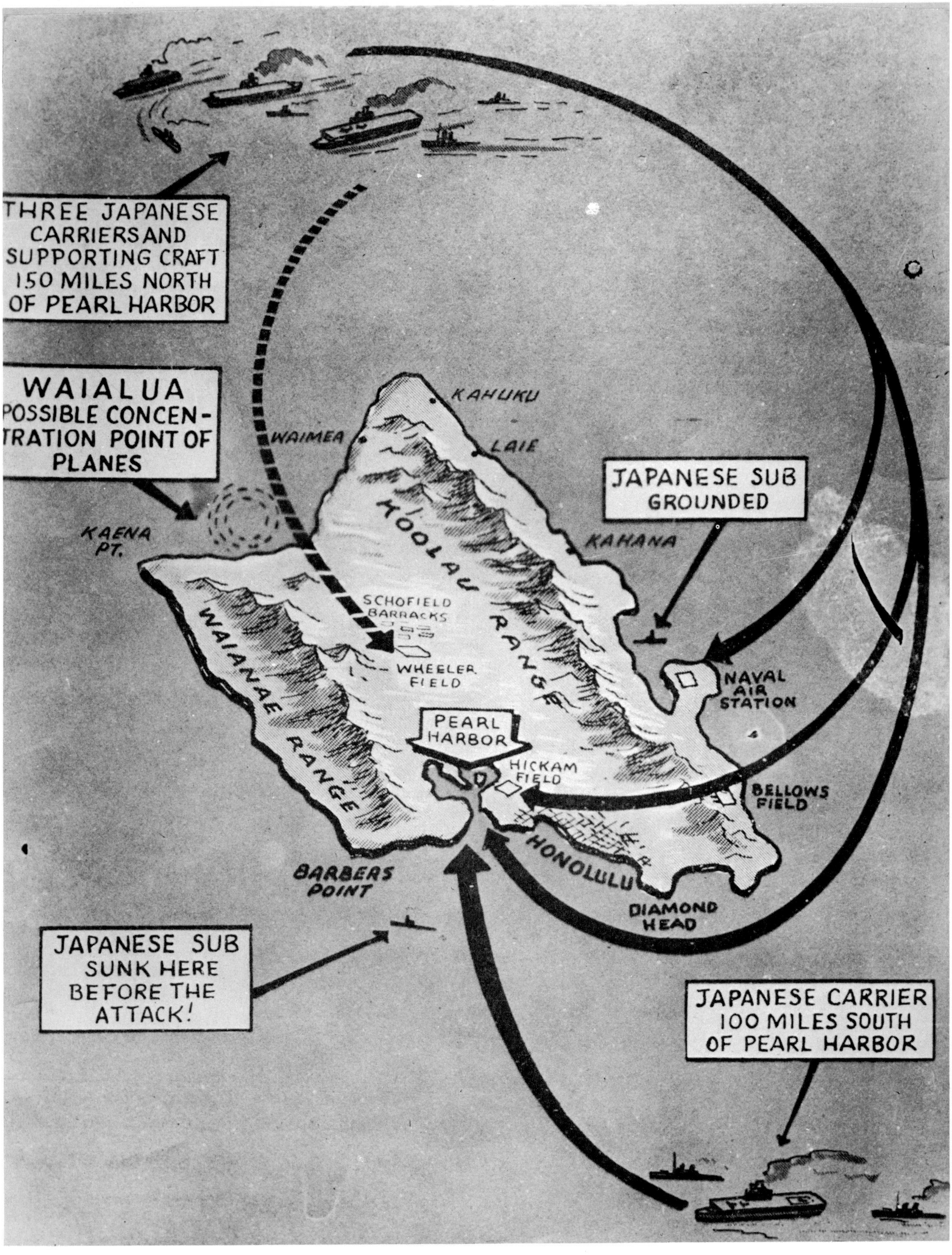

This map, published in the May 1942 tabloid *Hawaii at War* incorrectly places part of the attacking force to the south of Oahu, and errs on the route of the attacking planes. HA

Japanese internees in Hawaii are registered and fingerprinted by the military police following the attack. Although the Japanese-Hawaiians were watched closely and sometimes harassed, not one act of sabotage or violence was attributed to them during the war years. USA

At the Castle and Cooke Building in downtown Honolulu in early 1942, people crowd in to book passage for the mainland. Some were on their way to join the military or to take defense jobs; others were escaping the war threat. CAMERA HAWAII/WERNER STOY

Civilians at Kaneohe fill sandbags for defense after the base was attacked earlier in the day.

Fearing more Japanese air attacks, store owners in Honolulu taped their windows and took other precautions. USA

Downtown Honolulu in March 1942. Hawaii was now under military rule. USA

Fearing food shortages for their families, housewives rushed to grocery stores on Monday morning. UH

Gen. Delos Emmons, new military governor of Hawaii and commander of the Army's Hawaiian Department, leaves his headquarters just after assuming command from Gen. Walter Short on Dec. 17.
CAMERA HAWAII/WERNER STOY

Martial Law was declared in the Territory of Hawaii soon after the attack. It was not lifted until October 1944.

TERRITORY OF HAWAII

A PROCLAMATION

WHEREAS, it is provided by Section 67 of the Organic Act of the Territory of Hawaii, approved April 30, 1900, that, whenever it becomes necessary, the Governor of that territory may call upon the commander of the military forces of the United States in that territory to prevent invasion; and

WHEREAS, it is further provided by the said section that the governor may in case of invasion or imminent danger thereof, when the public safety requires it, suspend the privilege of the writ of habeas corpus and place the territory under martial law; and

WHEREAS, the armed forces of the Empire of Japan have this day attacked and invaded the shores of the Hawaiian Islands; and

WHEREAS, it has become necessary to repel such attack and invasion; and

WHEREAS, the public safety requires;

NOW, THEREFORE, I, J. B. POINDEXTER, Governor of the Territory of Hawaii, do hereby announce that, pursuant to said section, I have called upon the Commanding General, Hawaiian Department, to prevent such invasion;

And, pursuant to the same section, I do hereby suspend the privilege of the writ of habeas corpus until further notice;

And, pursuant to the same section, I do hereby place the said territory under martial law;

And I do hereby authorize and request the Commanding General, Hawaiian Department, during the present emergency and until the danger of invasion is removed, to exercise all the powers normally exercised by me as Governor;

And I do further authorize and request the said Commanding General, Hawaiian Department, and those subordinate military personnel to whom he may delegate such authority, during the present emergency and until the danger of invasion is removed, to exercise the powers normally exercised by judicial officers and employees of this territory and of the counties and cities therein, and such other and further powers as the emergency may require;

And I do require all good citizens of the United States and all other persons within the Territory of Hawaii to obey promptly and fully, in letter and in spirit, such proclamations, rules, regulations and orders, as the Commanding General, Hawaiian Department, or his subordinates, may issue during the present emergency.

IN WITNESS WHEREOF, I have hereunto set my hand and caused the seal of the Territory of Hawaii to be affixed.

DONE at Honolulu, Territory of Hawaii, this 7th day of December, 1941.

(SEAL OF THE TERRITORY OF HAWAII)

J. B. POINDEXTER,
Governor of the Territory of Hawaii.

Civilians dug air raid trenches all over Honolulu in case of further Japanese attacks. UH

Civilians, fearing another attack, built makeshift bomb shelters in their backyards. UH

Organized under fire and activated two hours after the attack, the Hawaii Territorial Guard was on duty at vital points by nightfall. UH

Sand-filled sugar sacks barricaded the telephone company entrance in downtown Honolulu. UH

Fallen sailors are honored by their comrades at Kaneohe Naval Air Station after the Pearl Harbor attack. KANEOHE MCAS

Tanks in the Honolulu streets were one sign of the military rule established after the attack. These were in front of Iolani Palace. USA

A memorial service for Pearl Harbor casualties, on Jan. 1, 1942, at Oahu Cemetery. Casualties totaled 2,403 killed and 1,178 wounded. USA

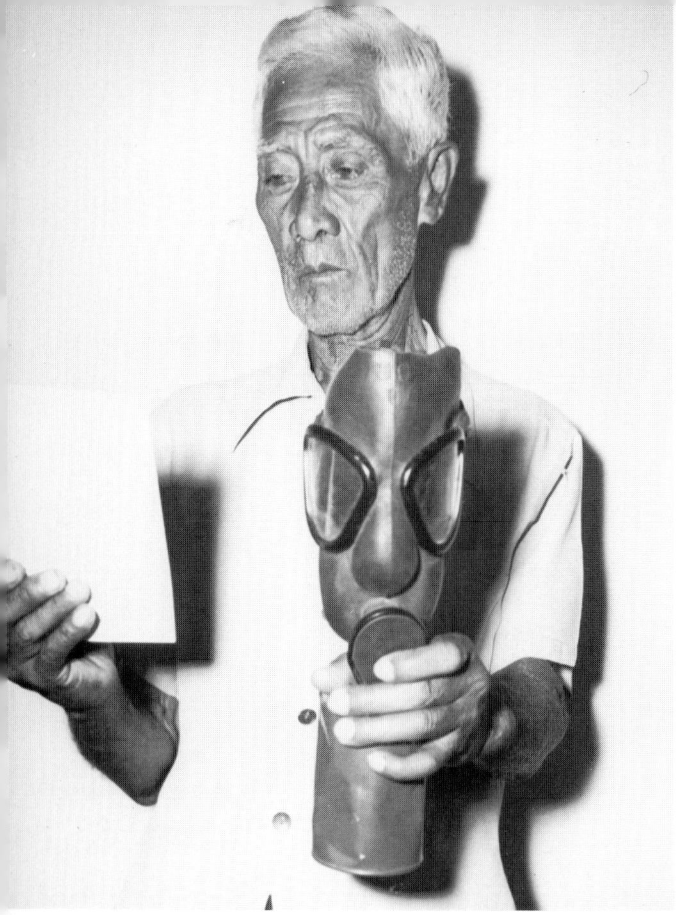

Frank Napookuvi Koho, an 84-year-old full-blooded Hawaiian, tries to figure out how to use his newly issued gas mask in January 1942. USA

A gas mask demonstration at the University of Hawaii on Feb. 15, 1942. Hawaiians were required to carry masks with them for many months after the attack. USA

Adm. Chester Nimitz awards the Navy Cross to SC2 Doris Miller for his futile attempt to move the dying Capt. Mervyn Bennion, the *West Virginia*'s captain, from an impending fire. Miller had attended Secondary Battery Gunnery School aboard the *Nevada* in 1940. Thus, with authority, he was able to man a machine gun while waiting for the stretcher's construction. He was the first black to be so honored. On Thanksgiving Day 1943 he was declared "presumed dead" in the sinking of the carrier *Liscome Bay*. FF-1091, U.S.S. *Miller*, commissioned in 1973 was named after Doris Miller.
· USN NH 62656

On April 1, 1942, survivors of the Pearl Harbor attack were decorated for bravery at Hickam Field. NA

The Pearl Harbor Investigations

■ **The Roberts Commission** convened on Dec. 18, 1941, concluded on Jan. 23, 1942. The record of proceedings and exhibits covered 2,173 printed pages.

■ **The Hart Inquiry** commenced on Feb. 12, 1944, and concluded on June 15, 1944. The record of proceedings and exhibits ran to 565 printed pages.

■ **The Army Pearl Harbor Board** began its sessions on July 20, 1944 and concluded on Oct. 20, 1944. The record covered 3,357 pages.

■ **The Navy Court of Inquiry** lasted from July 24, 1944 to Oct. 1944 and covered 1397 pages.

■ **The Clark Inquiry** was conducted from Sept. 14 to 16, 1944 and from July 13 to Aug. 14, 1945. The record of proceedings covered 225 pages.

■ **The Clausen Investigation** commenced Nov. 23, 1944 and concluded Sept. 12, 1945. The report covered 695 pages.

■ **The Hewitt Inquiry** commenced May 14, 1945 and concluded July 11, 1945. The record covered 1,342 pages.

■ **Joint Committee on the Investigation of the Pearl Harbor Attack.** First hearings were held on Nov. 15, 1945; the committee completed its work on May 31, 1946. The record covered 5,560 pages in 11 volumes. Pertinent exhibits and documents filled another 10 volumes. The additional exhibits and documents which were a part of previous investigations mentioned above filled still another nine volumes.

Members of the Roberts Commission pose in Honolulu with the mayor of Honolulu to the left, a Navy admiral and the bishop of the Episcopal Church in Hawaii, to the extreme right. CAMERA HAWAII/WERNER STOY

Pearl Harbor on Dec. 12, 1943, was the busiest naval base in the Pacific. A far cry from the devastation of two years previous. USN

A U.S. Army Honor Guard holds flags over the caskets of Ernie Pyle and four servicemen during internment service held at Punchbowl, National Cemetery of the Pacific, on July 19, 1949. An unknown serviceman, killed in the Pearl Harbor attack, was the first interned on Jan. 4, 1949. USMC

Battle of Niihau

Since their only link with the outside world was a weekly sampan from Kauai, the isolated inhabitants of the island of Niihau had no knowledge of the Pearl Harbor attack until a downed enemy pilot brought them the news.

About 2 p.m. on Dec. 7, a Japanese plane crashed-landed in a rocky field on the island. Hawila Kaleohano, a Hawaiian who lived nearby, took the pilot prisoner, confiscated his papers and sent for two Japanese island's residents, who acted as interpreters.

When the pilot told of the Oahu raid, his captors decided to keep him under guard until the sampan arrived from Kauai the next day, then turn him over to authorities on the larger island. But, because of the emergency, the boat did not make its weekly run. Finally, after several days of waiting, the islanders built a large fire as a prearranged signal of trouble.

On the same day, the pilot tried to bribe his captors into letting him go. Finally persuading one of his interpreters to help him, the pilot escaped. He and the interpreter searched Kaleohano's home in vain for the airman's papers, then salvaged the machine guns from the wrecked plane and threatened to kill everyone in the village of Puuwai if Kaleohano was not produced with the pilot's papers. Some of the villagers were ordered to find Kaleohano and bring him back. By dusk most of the natives had fled the village, but one, Benehakka Kanahele, tried unsuccessfully to sneak up behind the Japanese and steal their ammunition. He and his wife were captured but Kanahele's later attempts to persuade the interpreter to seize the enemy pilot's gun provoked a struggle in which the pilot shot Kanahele twice.

"This made him mad," the Hawaiian said later, and he grabbed the pilot by the leg and neck and flung him against a stone wall, killing him. The Japanese interpreter, who was struggling with Kanahele's wife, broke free, grabbed a gun and killed himself.

Meanwhile, Kaleohano and four other islanders were rowing through rough seas on a 16-hour voyage to seek help on Kauai. They returned with soldiers on Saturday, Dec. 13, only to learn that the "battle" was already over. The wounded Kanahele was taken to the hospital on Kauai where he recovered. During ceremonies at Fort Shafter in August 1945, he was presented the Medal of Merit and the Purple Heart, the last by virtue of a special authorization from Washington to permit its award to a civilian. His fellow islander, Kaleohano, was awarded the Medal of Freedom in May 1946.

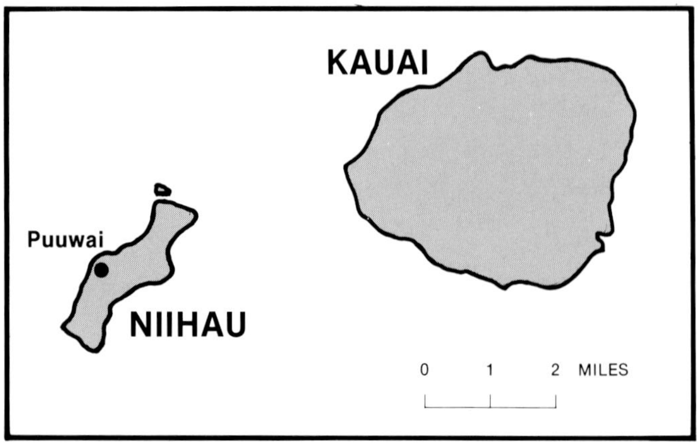

Benjamin Kanahele of the Niihau Island receives the Medal of Merit at ceremonies in August 1945. UH

Legacy of the Attack

From Tragedy to Triumph

The *Arizona* Memorial Visitor Center administered by the National Park Service. Construction funds were provided by Congress, the State of Hawaii and individual contributions. It was opened in October 1980. USN

Five decades have passed since the Japanese bombed Pearl Harbor, and many things have changed in Hawaii. It became the 50th state in 1959. Modern high-rise hotels, built to accommodate the postwar tourist boom, have transformed the skyline along Honolulu's Waikiki Beach.

Though they have remained a major presence, U.S. military forces on Oahu have fluctuated, in size through the years, depending on the amount of international tensions and the prevailing global strategies. The wars in Korea and Vietnam brought personnel and materiel increases, but the military presence never reached the levels it did in World War II.

Even with all the changes over the years, a serviceman going back to Oahu for the first time since 1941 will recognize most of the military installations.

Pearl Harbor Naval Base and Shipyard has changed considerably through the years to meet the needs of the modern Navy, but many of the prewar buildings are still in use.

Headquarters for 50 naval commands, Pearl Harbor is still the Navy's most important Pacific island base. More than 33,000 Navymen are stationed in Hawaii.

The airfields at Hickam and Wheeler have also changed dramatically, but many hangars, runways and other facilities are still recognizable.

Headquarters for the 15th Air Base Wing, Hickam Air Force Base supports 100 units in Hawaii and elsewhere in the Pacific, maintains aircraft repair facilities and operates the Wheeler, Bellows and Wake Island air bases. The Hickam population exceeds 11,500 active duty military and dependents, and 2,000 civilian workers.

Wheeler Air Force Base is home to the 326th Air Division, responsible for Hawaiian air defense. Fifteen other Air Force units are situated at the base, along with an Army aircraft unit.

Now an Air Force station, Bellows Field is the home of Detachment 1, 15th Air Base Wing. It serves as an antenna site for the Air Force's global radio network, a recreation area for all military services and a landing beach for Marine amphibious exercises. The old runways are still there, but are fenced off.

Haleiwa Field has been abandoned for years, its runway overgrown with weeds. As it has been since World War I, Schofield Barracks is a major base for the U.S. Army. Because many of its present facilities were built before World War II, the post looks today much as it did in 1941. It is now home of the 25th Infantry Division, including two active brigades, artillery, a support command and a reserve infantry brigade. The 45th Support Group and many of its units are also stationed there.

Abandoned for years, Ewa Marine Corps Air Station lies adjacent to the sprawling naval air station at Barbers Point. Some of its many acres of runways and parking aprons are used for a Go-kart track. More than 60 half-circle concrete revetments, built to house fighter planes, are scattered in the brush along with many delapidated Quonset huts. Some of the revetments are now used for horse stables.

Kaneohe Naval Air Station has been changed to a Marine Corps air station. It now is home of the Corps' only air-ground combat team, the First Marine Brigade.

The Marine Barracks, Hawaii—situated at Pearl Harbor—is still active and is the oldest Marine establishment in Hawaii. The second largest such facility in the Corps, it provides security for the naval installations on the island and performs ceremonial duties.

Still dotted with dozens of prewar and World War II installations, Oahu is a mecca for the military historian.

When the Arizona Memorial was dedicated in 1950, it was a temporary structure. Visitors stood on a small platform built over the sunken ship's main deck. The present memorial, rededicated in 1962 after money was authorized by Congress and raised by private subscription and donation, is a permanent monument to the more than 1,000 men entombed below.

A new visitors' center operated by the National Park Service was opened in October 1980.

Monument to the dead at Kaneohe Naval Air Station (now a Marine Corps Air Station).

This spot, located across from the Marine Corps Station, Kaneohe Bay Child Care Center, is believed to be the place where the first Japanese aircraft was shot down during the attack on Oahu military bases in 1941. The plaque at the site reads "Japanese Aircraft Impact Site, Pilot-Lieutenant Iida, I.J.N., CMDR, Third Air Control Group, Dec. 7, 1941.
KANEOHE MCAS

Monument at the headquarters of the Pacific Air Forces in the old Hale Makai barracks, Hickam Air Force Base.

Fort Shafter site.

Plaque marking the site of a bomb attack at Fort Shafter.

A mock-up of a P-40 used in the movie *Tora Tora Tora* is on display at the entrance of Wheeler Air Force Base.

The headquarters building at Schofield Barracks looks today much like it did in 1941.

Palm Circle at Fort Shafter, headquarters of the U.S. Army in Hawaii and Information Center for Radar at the time of the attack.

Dock area on the northeast of Ford Island where the *Detroit, Raleigh, Utah* and *Tangier* were docked.

The morgue at the Pearl Harbor Naval Hospital was unfortunately filled on Dec. 7. More than 2,000 wounded needed attention the morning of the attack.

Building 661 and submarine escape training tank at the sub base, Pearl Harbor. Admiral Kimmel's headquarters was in this building.

The Punchbowl National Memorial of the Pacific is located in an extinct volcanic crater near downtown Honolulu. More than 18,000 war veterans, including Pearl Harbor casualties, are buried here.

Entrance to Pearl Harbor taken from Hospital Point. The submarine nets were open the morning of Dec. 7 when a midget submarine entered the harbor.

Pearl Harbor with Ford Island in the background.

The U.S.C.G.C. *Taney* is the last surviving warship that was present during the attack on Pearl Harbor. It was commissioned in 1936 and berthed at Pier #6 in Honolulu Harbor at the time of the attack. She fired on attacking enemy planes. She spent the rest of the war patrolling and escorting in both the Pacific and Atlantic theatres of war. She also served during the Korean and Vietnam conflicts. She was decommissioned on Dec. 7, 1986, and is berthed in Baltimore, Md. NATIONAL PARK SERVICE

The U.S. Navy yard tug *Hoga*, built in 1940 and now called the fireboat *City of Oakland*, is typical of hundreds of World War II-era naval service craft. A well-preserved, largely unaltered example of this once-common type of craft, *City of Oakland*—ex-*Hoga*—is of exceptional significance in American history in that it is the only known surviving yard craft present at Pearl Harbor during the Japanese attack. These craft performed heroic service, extinguishing fires on burning battleships and other vessels in the harbor and rescuing wounded seamen from the oily waters of Battleship Row. *Hoga* particularly distinguished herself through her crew's actions in helping beach the burning and sinking battleship *Nevada* at Hospital Point. *Hoga* also fought fires on Battleship Row for 48 hours, particularly working on the blazing hulk of *Arizona*.
NATIONAL PARK SERVICE

World War II Japanese dive bomber leader Zenji Abe examines the remains of a "Val" dive bomber like the one he flew during his bomb run on USS *Raleigh*, Dec. 7, 1941. Photo was taken May 6, 1991, when Abe was in Fredericksburg, Texas, to participate in a Pearl Harbor 50th anniversary retrospective. This "Val" (Aichi D3A) is one of two in the United States. It was brought to the museum from Gasmata, a former Japanese airbase on New Britain Island. ADMIRAL NIMITZ MUSEUM

The *Utah* rests in the water on the west side of Ford Island. A memorial to the 58 lost sailors was dedicated in 1972.

Arizona and *Pennsylvania* Batteries

Sometime after the sinking of the *U.S.S. Arizona* on Dec. 7, work began to remove the huge after-turret 14-inch guns for use as coastal artillery.

Since permanent artillery emplacements were still considered to be a valuable part of coastal defense, the Army was authorized to install the Arizona's batteries on Oahu.

Battery *Pennsylvania* was to be placed on the tip of Mokapu Peninsula at Kaneohe Naval Air Station, to protect the eastern approaches to the island; Battery *Arizona* was to be installed on Kahe Point, to protect the southern and western approaches.

Salvaging these huge, heavy batteries and then moving them to their new sites was an enormous task, and reconstructing them was just as difficult. Large portions of the turrets had been cut away in the salvage operation. Many of the lost parts had to be built from scratch at a time when war materiel was at a premium, and many of the detailed drawings were missing.

After being placed at ground level atop large concrete casements, the turrets were to be connected to underground bunkers that would house the troops manning them.

The rebuilt turrets had to be floated on barges to beaches below the sites and hauled up specially built roads. It took more than two years to repair one of the big guns, then transport it to Mokapu Peninsula for installation as the *Pennsylvania* Battery. It was completed in August 1945 and, ironically, was test-fired on the day it became unnecessary—V-J Day. Still not completed by the end of the war in the Pacific, the Battery *Arizona* project was halted. A few years later when long-range jets and guided missiles had rendered such coastal fortifications obsolete, the massive turrets were cut up for scrap. Today the casements and underground bunkers are still intact, crumbling monuments to the old idea of fixed coastal defenses.

Remains of Penn Battery barbette on Mokapu Point. It was built to hold one of the gun turrets salvaged from the *Arizona*. The barbette is 70 feet deep with an external diameter of 50 feet and a wall thickness ranging from 9 to fifteen feet.

Above: Aerial view of *Arizona* on Sept. 25, 1942. USN *Inset:* Don Stratton of Yuma, Ariz., survivor of the *Arizona*. *Below:* A plaque was placed on the *Arizona* on Dec. 12, 1950, in memory of those who died on the ship. USN

The sunken battleship *Arizona* in 1950. A small platform on the main deck house was constructed in 1950. The present permanent memorial was dedicated in 1962. NA

The memorial to the *Arizona* and her entombed men was dedicated on Memorial Day, 1962. Construction began in 1958 after authorization by Congress and approval of President Eisenhower. The $500,000 project was designed by architect Alfres Preis.

The *Arizona* Memorial at Pearl Harbor.

Plaque on the *Arizona* Memorial.

The foundation for No. 3 gun turret on the *Arizona* as seen from the memorial.

Arizona remains were placed on Waipio Peninsula where they can still be found today.

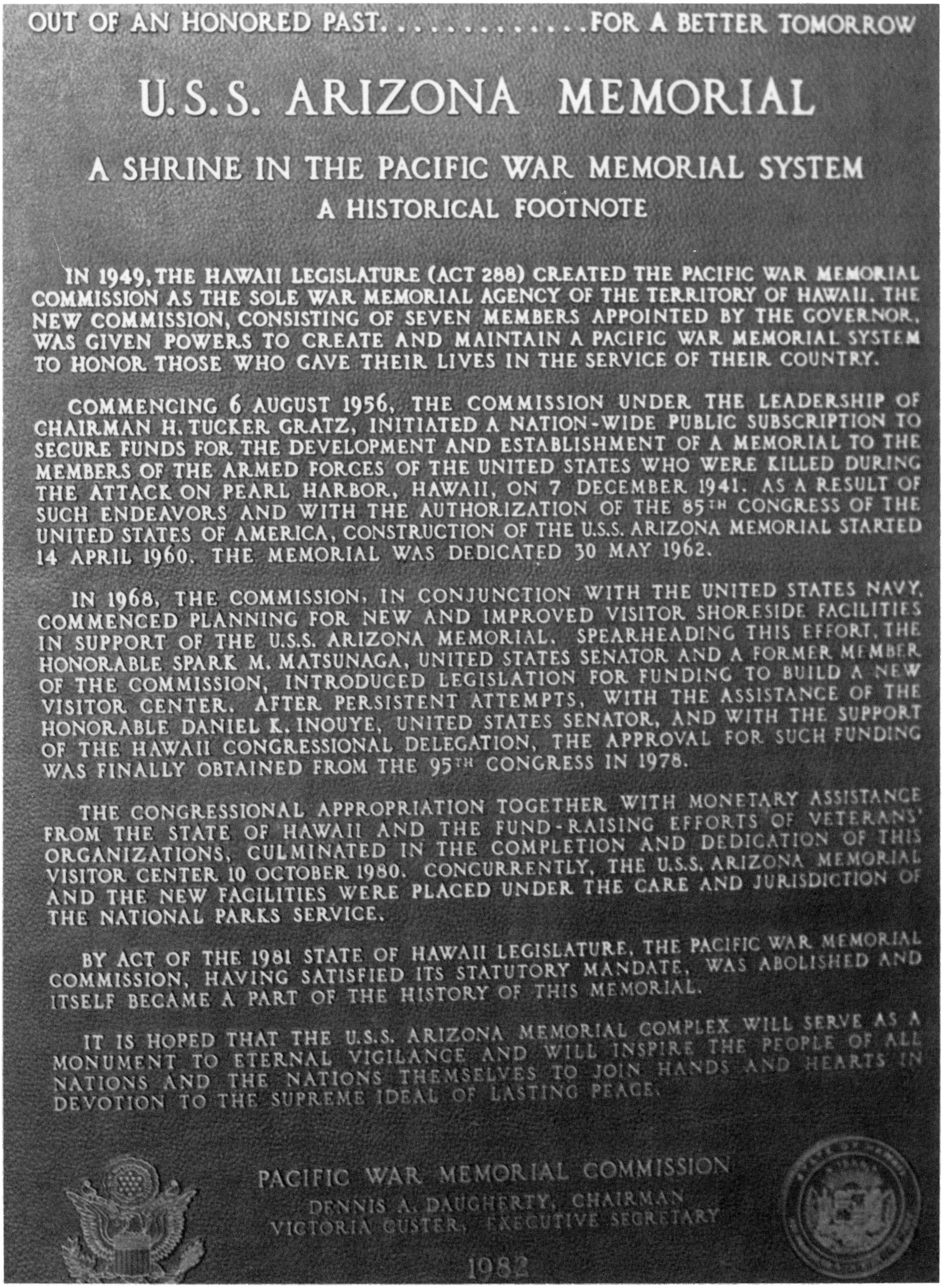
OUT OF AN HONORED PAST. . . . . .FOR A BETTER TOMORROW
U.S.S. ARIZONA MEMORIAL
A SHRINE IN THE PACIFIC WAR MEMORIAL SYSTEM
A HISTORICAL FOOTNOTE
IN 1949, THE HAWAII LEGISLATURE (ACT 288) CREATED THE PACIFIC WAR MEMORIAL COMMISSION AS THE SOLE WAR MEMORIAL AGENCY OF THE TERRITORY OF HAWAII. THE NEW COMMISSION, CONSISTING OF SEVEN MEMBERS APPOINTED BY THE GOVERNOR, WAS GIVEN POWERS TO CREATE AND MAINTAIN A PACIFIC WAR MEMORIAL SYSTEM TO HONOR THOSE WHO GAVE THEIR LIVES IN THE SERVICE OF THEIR COUNTRY.
COMMENCING 6 AUGUST 1956, THE COMMISSION UNDER THE LEADERSHIP OF CHAIRMAN H. TUCKER GRATZ, INITIATED A NATION-WIDE PUBLIC SUBSCRIPTION TO SECURE FUNDS FOR THE DEVELOPMENT AND ESTABLISHMENT OF A MEMORIAL TO THE MEMBERS OF THE ARMED FORCES OF THE UNITED STATES WHO WERE KILLED DURING THE ATTACK ON PEARL HARBOR, HAWAII, ON 7 DECEMBER 1941. AS A RESULT OF SUCH ENDEAVORS AND WITH THE AUTHORIZATION OF THE 85TH CONGRESS OF THE UNITED STATES OF AMERICA, CONSTRUCTION OF THE U.S.S. ARIZONA MEMORIAL STARTED 14 APRIL 1960. THE MEMORIAL WAS DEDICATED 30 MAY 1962.
IN 1968, THE COMMISSION, IN CONJUNCTION WITH THE UNITED STATES NAVY, COMMENCED PLANNING FOR NEW AND IMPROVED VISITOR SHORESIDE FACILITIES IN SUPPORT OF THE U.S.S. ARIZONA MEMORIAL. SPEARHEADING THIS EFFORT, THE HONORABLE SPARK M. MATSUNAGA, UNITED STATES SENATOR AND A FORMER MEMBER OF THE COMMISSION, INTRODUCED LEGISLATION FOR FUNDING TO BUILD A NEW VISITOR CENTER. AFTER PERSISTENT ATTEMPTS, WITH THE ASSISTANCE OF THE HONORABLE DANIEL K. INOUYE, UNITED STATES SENATOR, AND WITH THE SUPPORT OF THE HAWAII CONGRESSIONAL DELEGATION, THE APPROVAL FOR SUCH FUNDING WAS FINALLY OBTAINED FROM THE 95TH CONGRESS IN 1978.
THE CONGRESSIONAL APPROPRIATION TOGETHER WITH MONETARY ASSISTANCE FROM THE STATE OF HAWAII AND THE FUND-RAISING EFFORTS OF VETERANS' ORGANIZATIONS, CULMINATED IN THE COMPLETION AND DEDICATION OF THIS VISITOR CENTER 10 OCTOBER 1980. CONCURRENTLY, THE U.S.S. ARIZONA MEMORIAL AND THE NEW FACILITIES WERE PLACED UNDER THE CARE AND JURISDICTION OF THE NATIONAL PARKS SERVICE.
BY ACT OF THE 1981 STATE OF HAWAII LEGISLATURE, THE PACIFIC WAR MEMORIAL COMMISSION, HAVING SATISFIED ITS STATUTORY MANDATE, WAS ABOLISHED AND ITSELF BECAME A PART OF THE HISTORY OF THIS MEMORIAL.
IT IS HOPED THAT THE U.S.S. ARIZONA MEMORIAL COMPLEX WILL SERVE AS A MONUMENT TO ETERNAL VIGILANCE AND WILL INSPIRE THE PEOPLE OF ALL NATIONS AND THE NATIONS THEMSELVES TO JOIN HANDS AND HEARTS IN DEVOTION TO THE SUPREME IDEAL OF LASTING PEACE.
PACIFIC WAR MEMORIAL COMMISSION
DENNIS A. DAUGHERTY, CHAIRMAN
VICTORIA GUSTER, EXECUTIVE SECRETARY
1982

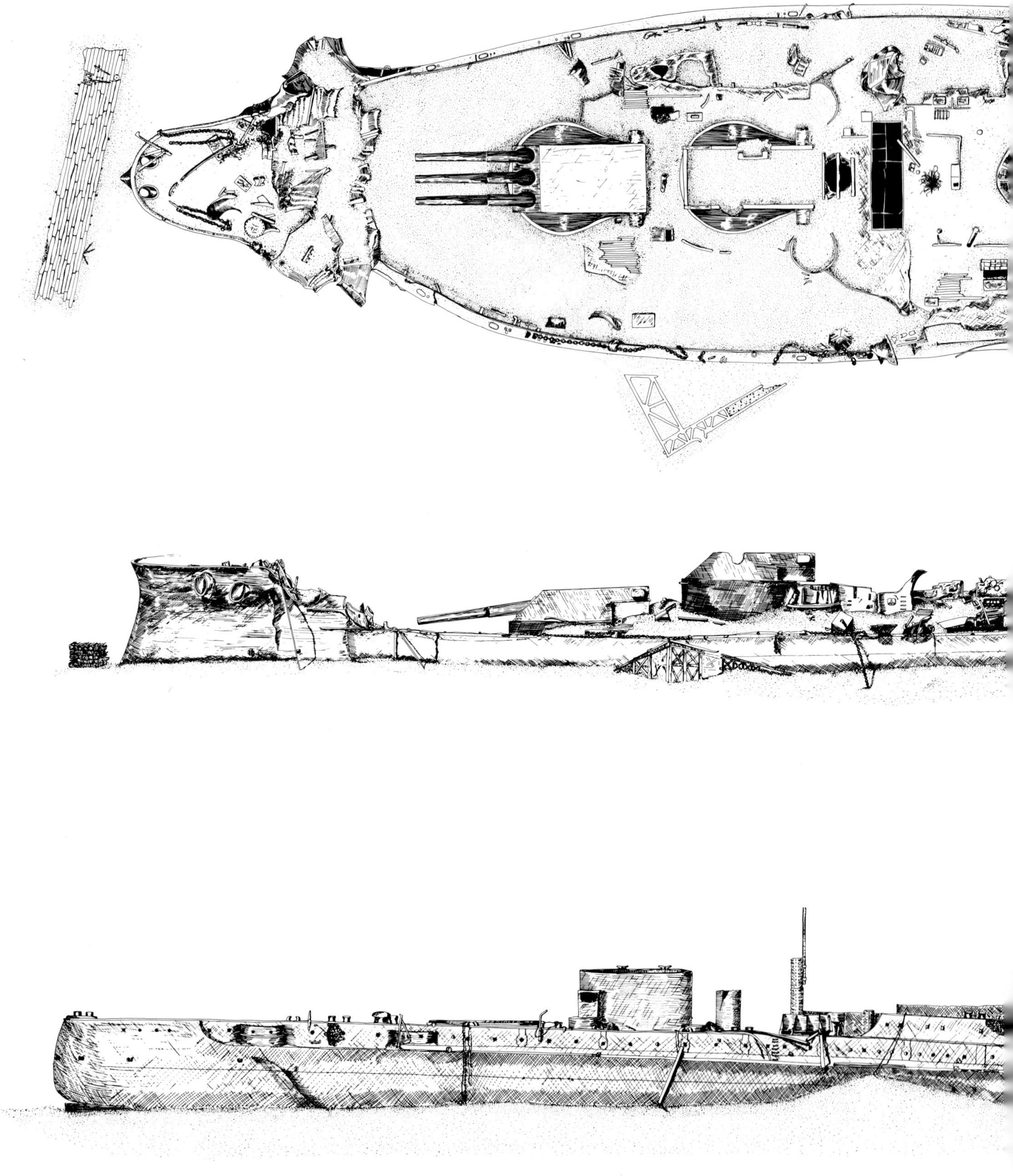

This set of drawings was developed from data obtained in the intense underwater mapping sessions that took place in 1984.

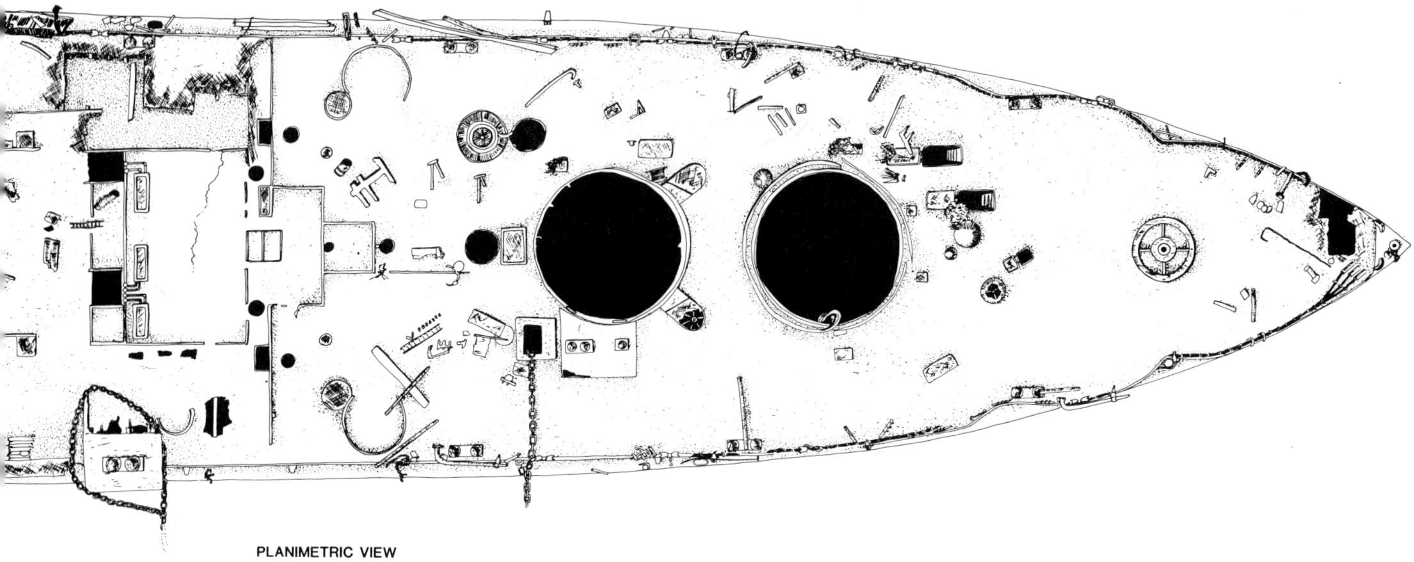

PLANIMETRIC VIEW

PORT ELEVATION

STARBOARD ELEVATION

U.S.S. ARIZONA

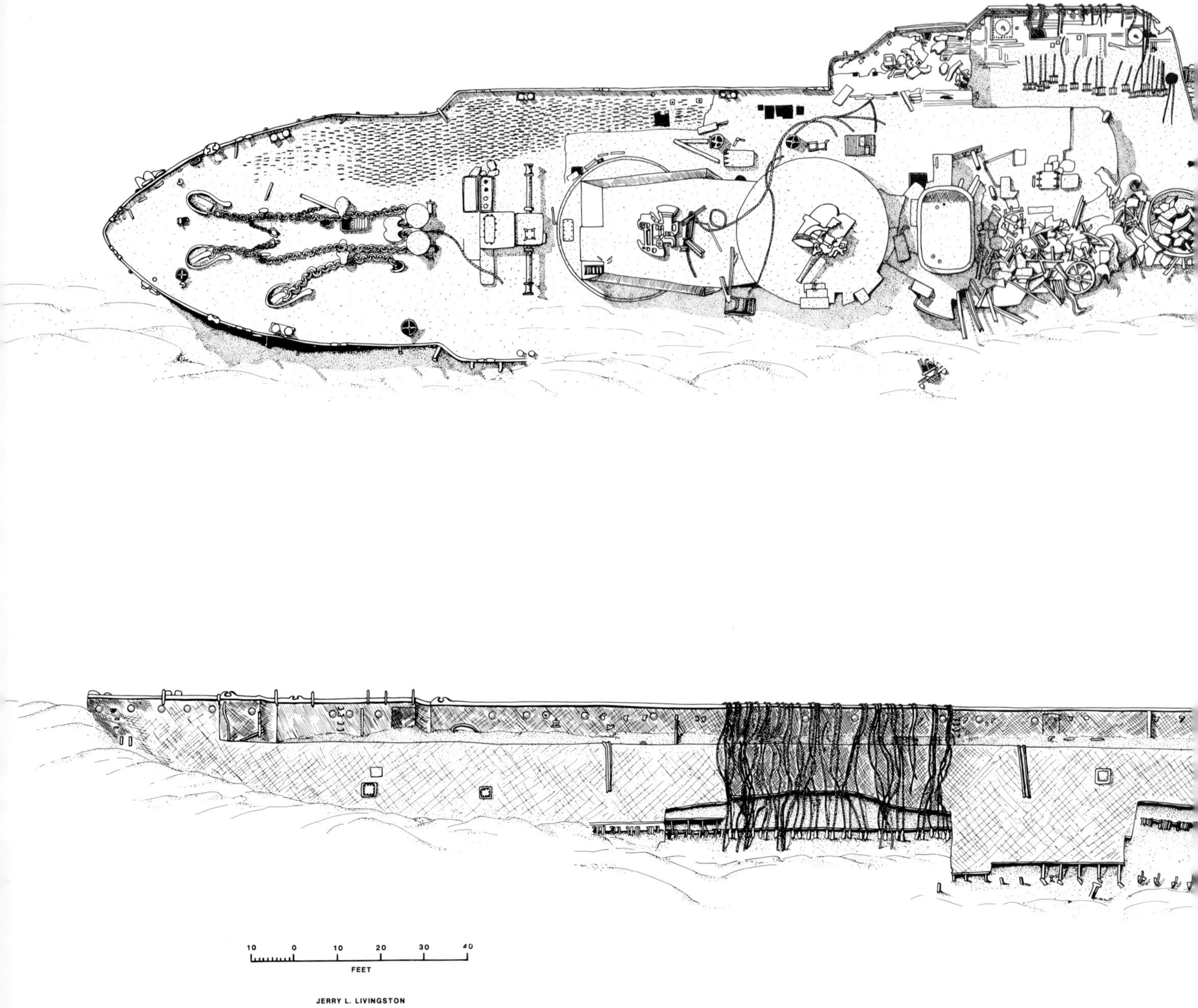

Two-part drawings of remains of USS UTAH. Drawn by Jerry Livingston from underwater operations conducted by SCRU and US Navy Reserve MDSU One (Det 319).

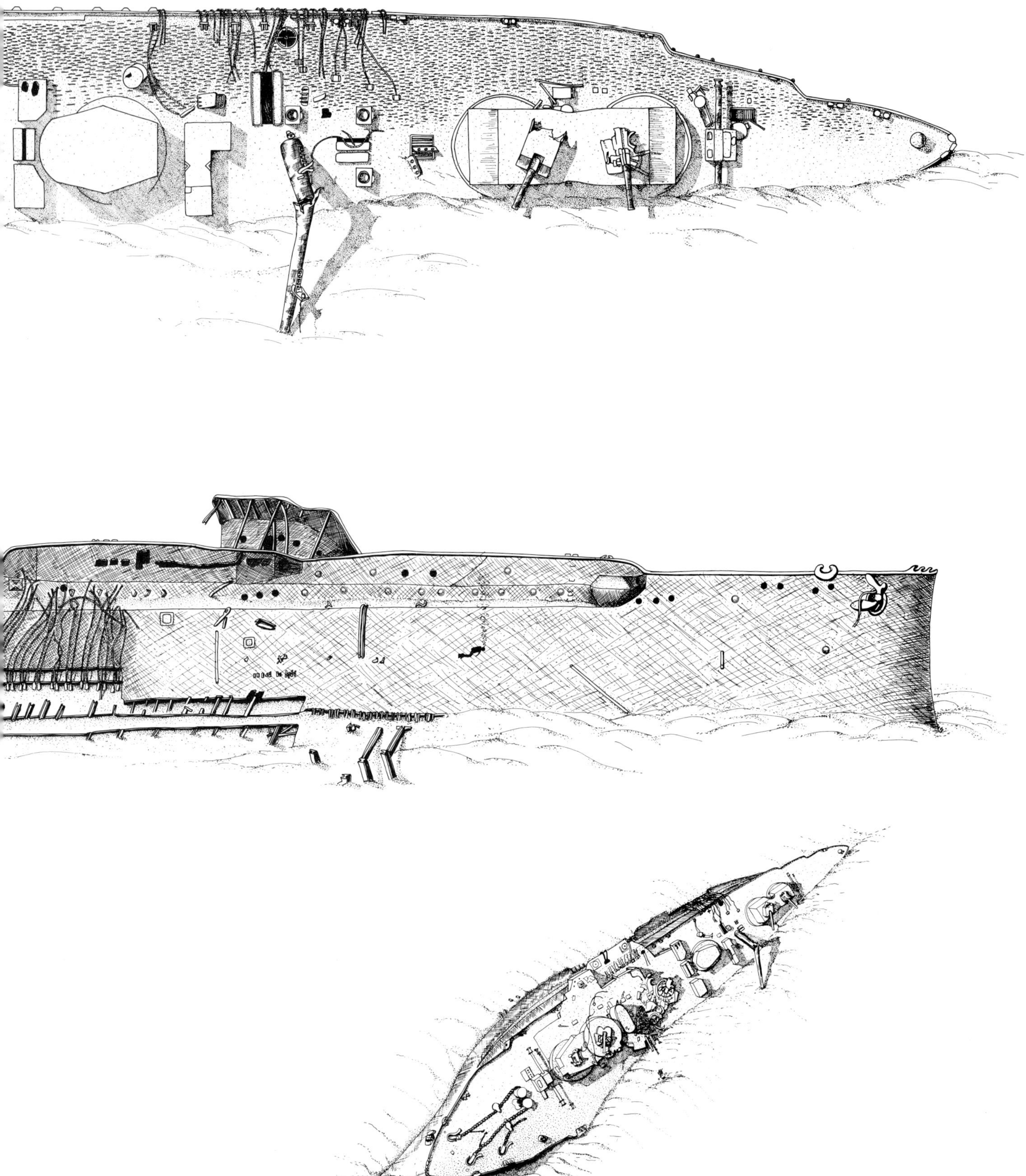

Oblique perspective of USS UTAH remains. Drawing by Jerry Livingston.

Underwater scenes of the *Arizona*.

The National Park Service's Submerged Cultural Resources Unit (SCRU) was given the task of mapping and photo-documenting both the *Arizona* and the *Utah* in 1984 and 1986. In 1988, underwater airplane crash sites were investigated using side-scan sonar with U.S. Navy cooperation.

Underwater measuring of the ship. After being drawn down, each feature is measured back to two points on a baseline. This allows accurate mapping through a simple geometric procedure called trilaturation.

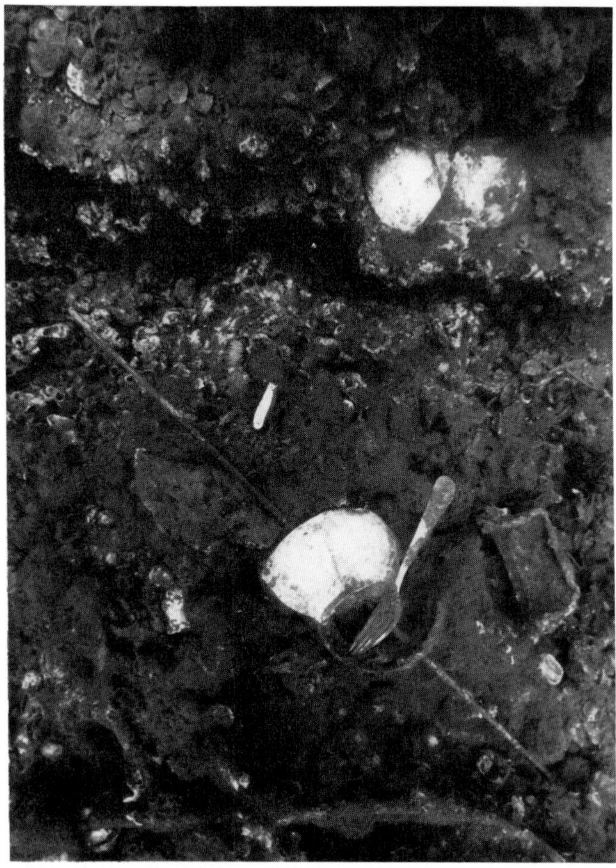

Artifacts in ship's galley area.

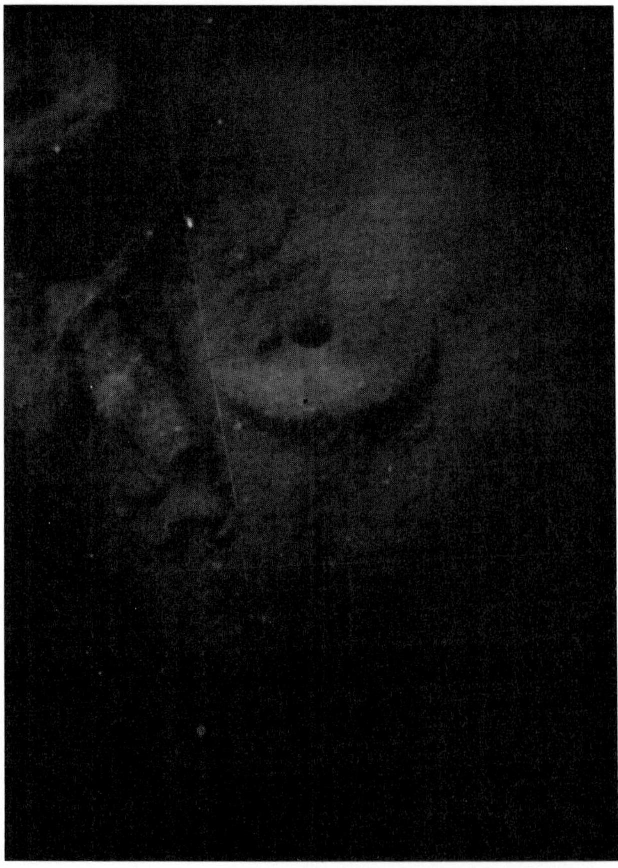

Jackstaff hole at stern, mooring bits visible to the left.

Ammunition.

Tile from galley area.

Teak decking.

An air cylinder protrudes from debris. U.S. Navy EOD divers were called in to rupture the bottle in case it was still under pressure.

Underwater scenes of the *Utah*.

Stairs lead down into the interior of the ship.

Chock on gunnel on starboard.

Pearl Harbor displays

Pearl Harbor display at the Admiral Nimitz Museum State Historical Park in Fredericksburg, Texas. The museum was established in the hometown of Adm. Chester Nimitz in 1970 by the Texas State Legislature. The museum is dedicated to everyone who served in the Pacific during World War II. ADMIRAL NIMITZ MUSEUM

A piece of the battleship *Arizona* on display at the Admiral Nimitz Museum.

Pearl Harbor display at the Intrepid Sea-Air-Space Museum on the Hudson River in New York City, N.Y. The battleship *Nevada* was used in the movie *Tora Tora Tora*.
INTREPID SEA-AIR-SPACE MUSEUM

Pearl Harbor display at Patriots Point Naval and Maritime Museum, Mount Pleasant, South Carolina.
PATRIOTS POINT NAVAL AND MARITIME MUSEUM

Cmd. Mitsuo Fuchida, commander of the Japanese air attack, is shown in this photo years after the war with former Doolittle Raider Jake DeShazer, who spent 40 months in a Japanese prison. Fuchida passed away in 1976 after suffering from old war wounds.

Japanese Torpedo Found at Pearl Harbor

by Burl Burlingame, *Honolulu Star-Bulletin*

A Japanese torpedo used in the attack 50 years ago came to the surface near Ford Island on May 2, 1991, in the jaws of a bottom-dredger clearing space for the battleship *Missouri*.

The location was off a pier built where the battleships *Maryland* and *Oklahoma* were damaged in the attack.

All ship operations in the harbor were halted when the torpedo was reported to port operations. The ferry ride to Ford Island, the path of which passes directly by the spot, was shut down, trapping people on either side.

Because of its unsafe condition, the Navy took the torpedo a mile and a half off Pearl Harbor and blew it up. A portion of it was recovered and is now in the hands of the National Park Service.

"There are very few intact artifacts from the attack," stated Bob Chenoweth, Arizona Memorial curator. "All that's usually left is bits and pieces. This one is particularly important because it is one of the two most important weapons used in the attack."

Appendix

Medal of Honor

Bennion, Mervyn, Capt., USN
Cannon, George H., First Lt., USMC
Finn, John W., Lt.(jg), USN
Flaherty, Francis C., Ens., USN
Fuqua, Samuel G., Capt., USN
Hill, Edwin J., Boatswain, USN
Jones, Herbert C., Ens., USN
Kidd, Isaac C., R. Adm., USN
Pharris, Jackson C., Gunner, USN
Reeves, Thomas J., Chief Radioman, USN
Ross, Donald K., Lt., USN
Scott, Robert R., Machinist's Mate first class, USN
Tomich, Peter, Chief Watertender, USN
Van Valkenburgh, Franklin, Capt., USN
Ward, James Richard, Seaman first class, USN
Young, Cassin, Capt., USN

Navy Cross

Austin, John A., Chief Carpenter, USN
Baker, Lionel H., Pharmacist's Mate second class, USN
Bolser, Gordon E. Lt.(jg), USN
Bothne, Adoloph M., Boatswain, USN
Burford, William P., Lt. Comdr., USN
Christopher, Harald J., Ens., USNR
Curtis, Ned B., Pharmacist's Mate second class, USN
Daly, Edward Carlyle, Coxwain, USN
Darling, Willard D., Cpl., USMC
Davis, Frederick C., Ens., USNR
Dickinson, Clarence E. Jr., Lt., USN
Douglas, C. E., Gunnery Sgt., USMC
Driskel, Joseph R., Corporal, USMC
Dunlap, Ernest H. Jr., Ens., USN
Edwards, John Perry, Ens., USNR
Etchell, George D., Shipfitter, USN
Fleming, W. D., Boatswain's Mate first class, USN
Gombasy, L. G., Seaman second class, USN
Graham, Donald A., Aviation Machinist's Mate first class, USN
Hailey, Thomas E., Sgt., USMC
Hansen, Alfred L., Chief Machinist's Mate, USN
Huttenberg, Allen J., Ens., USNR
Isquith, Solomon S., Lt. Cmdr. USN
Jewel, Jesse D., Comdr.(MC), USN
Kauffman, Draper L., Lt., USNR
Larson, Nils R., Ens., USN
Ley, F. C. Jr., Fireman second class, USNR
McMurtry, Paul J., Boatswain's Mate first class, USN
Mead, Harry R., Radioman second class, USN
Miller, Doris, Mess Attendant first class, USN
Miller, Jim D., Lt.(jg), USN
Moore, Fred K., Seaman first class, USN
Outerbridge, William W., Lt. Comdr., USN
Parker, William W., Seaman first class, USN
Peterson, Robert J., Radioman second class, USN
Pharris, Jackson C., Gunner, USN (upgraded to Medal of Honor)
Phillips, John S., Comdr. USN
Riggs, Cecil D., Lt. Comdr. (MC), USN
Robb, James W. Jr., Lt.(jg), USN
Roberts, William R., Radioman second class, USN
Ruth, Wesley H., Ens., USN
Singleton, Arnold, Ens., USN
Smith, Harold F., Boatswain's Mate second class, USN
Snyder, J. L., Yeoman first class USN
Taussig, Joseph K. Jr., Ens., USN
Taylor, Thomas H., Ens., USN
Teaff, Perry L., Ens., USN
Thatcher, Albert C., Aviation Machinists Mate second class, USN
Thomas, Francis J., Lt. Comdr., USN
Thomas, Robert E. Jr., Ens., USN
Vaeesen, John B., Fireman second class, USNR

Silver Star Medal

Kiefer, Edwin H., Lt.(jg), USNR
Marshall, Theodore W., Lt., USNR
Owen, George T., Comdr., USN
Shapley, Alan, Maj., USMC

Navy and Marine Corps Medal

Day, Francis D., Chief Watertender, USN
Schmitt, Aloysius H., Shipfitter first class, USN
Wright, Paul R., Chief Watertender, USNR

Army awards for heroism included five Distinguished Service Crosses and 65 Silver Stars.

CP 18TH PUR GP (INT)

2 JAN 42.

INTELL MEMO)
: INTERCEPTED BROADCAST FROM TOKYO ON BOMBING OF OAHU
No. 10)

The following intercepted broadcast from Tokyo, Japan, is furnished for the information and amusement of all Pilots and enlisted personnel of this Group:

RADIO TOKYO 1740 JANUARY 1ST 1942

FLIGHT COMMANDER'S REPORT ON THE GLORIOUS BOMBING OF OAHU, T.H.

EARLY THAT FATEFUL MORNING WE SIGHTED THE ISLAND OF OAHU AFTER LEAVING OUR CARRIER OUT TO SEA. CERTAIN UNITS HAD CERTAIN TASKS TO PERFORM AND IF SUCCESSFUL WE WOULD LEAVE OAHU A MASS OF SMOLDERING RUINS. OVER PEARL HARBOR WE PROCEEDED TO BOMB THE MUCH OVER-RATED AMERICAN PACIFIC FLEET. IN HARDLY NO TIME AT ALL RISING COLUMNS OF SMOKE BEGAN TO EMERGE FROM MANY SHIPS IN THE HARBOR INCLUDING A BATTLESHIP. OUR PILOTS HAD ALREADY MADE SHORT WORK OF WHEELER FIELD WHERE THE AMERICAN PURSUIT SHIPS WERE STATIONED. THEY BOMBED HANGERS AND AIRPLANES ON THE GROUND DESTROYING THEM IN GREAT NUMBERS. HANGERS WERE COMPLETELY SET AFIRE AND WERE DESTROYED DUE TO THEIR POOR CONSTRUCTION. AT NO TIME DID THE PESONNEL ATTEMPT TO FIGHT BACK DURING THE RAID. AFTER THE MAJOR OPERATIONS WERE COMPLETE, THE ANTI-AIRCRAFT BATTERIES BEGAN TO GO INTO ACTION. THEN - "I THOUGHT TO MYSELF" - "ALLRIGHT, IF YOU WANT SOME MORE I'LL GIVE IT TO YOU". WE RETURNED TO GET INTO THE FRAY ONCE MORE. THE GROUND TROOPS OBVIOUSLY BADLY FRIGHTENED DISPLAYED A POOR DEGREE OF MARKSMANSHIP AND WERE MERELY WASTING AMMUNITION. WE HAD NOTHING TO WORRY ABOUT FROM THEM. FROM AN ALTITUDE OF ABOUT 10,000 FEET WE REORGANIZED OUR DIVE BOMBERS AND WERE OFF AGAIN. "DOWN, DOWN AND DOWN WE WENT". AT 8,000 FEET WE RELEASED OUR DEADLY CARGO AND PRAYED TO OUR GUIDING FORCE THEY WOULD FIND THEIR MARK. THEN FAR BELOW US IT HAPPENED. THE HARBOR WAS A BLAZING INFERNO. WE MADE A DIRECT HIT ON A LARGE BATTLESHIP OF THE ARIZONA CLASS AND IT LITERALLY CRACKED IN HALF, SPROUTING INTO THE AIR AND DOWN AGAIN. ANOTHER LARGE WARSHIP WAS SEEN TO HAVE BEEN LISTING IN THE WATER AT A 42 DEGREE ANGLE. THE ANTI-AIRCRAFT WERE NOW BEGINNING TO GET THE RANGE AND ONE OF OUR SHIPS HAD A LARGE HOLE IN THE WING AND WE ALL PRAYED HE'D BE ABLE TO RETURN TO THE CARRIER. "BANZAI" WE ALL SHOUTED AS WE RETURNED. ANOTHER FLIGHT WAS TAKING OFF FROM THE DECK OF THE CARRIER TO COMPLETE MOPPING UP OPERATIONS. THERE WAS OAHU BEHIND US, OAHU IN FLAMES. A TASK WE THOUGHT SO GREAT THAT NONE OF US WOULD RETURN BUT ALL WE SUFFERED WAS A LARGE HOLE IN A WING TIP. THE HAND OF PROVIDENCE WAS WITH US . . . **END.**

Note: *It is obvious that there are several falsifications in this Flight Commander's Report, particularly the portion where the Flight Commander states the personnel made no attempt to fight back, but at the same time it must be remembered such falsifications are in keeping with established Japanese customs. They follow the German method of propaganda by "boasting and exaggerating". The record of the Pilots and ground pesonnel of this Group in fighting back on December 7th, 1941 speaks for itself, therefore it is not to be expected that an enemy such as the Japanese would admit that Pilots of our Group shot down any of their airplanes on Sunday, December 7th.*

By order of Major TYER:

FRANK E. STETSON,
1st Lieut., Air Corps,
S - 2

Yesterday, December 7, 1941--a date which will live in infamy--the United States of America was suddenly and deliberately attacked by naval and air forces of the Empire of Japan.

The United States was at peace with that Nation and, at the solicitation of Japan, was still in conversation with its Government and its Emperor looking toward the maintenance of peace in the Pacific. Indeed, one hour after Japanese squadrons had commenced bombing in Oahu, the Japanese Ambassador to the United States and his colleague delivered to the Secretary of State a formal reply to a recent American message. While this reply stated that it seemed useless to continue the existing diplomatic negotiations, it contained no threat or hint of war or armed attack.

It will be recorded that the distance of Hawaii from Japan makes it obvious that the attack was deliberately planned many days or even weeks ago. During the intervening time the Japanese Government has deliberately sought to deceive the United States by false statements and expressions of hope for continued peace.

The attack yesterday on the Hawaiian Islands has caused severe damage to American naval and military forces. Very many American lives have been lost. In addition, American ships have been reported torpedoed on the high seas between San Francisco and Honolulu.

Yesterday the Japanese Government also launched an attack against Malaya.

Last night Japanese forces attacked Hong Kong.

Last night Japanese forces attacked Guam.

Last night Japanese forces attacked the Philippine Islands.

Last night the Japanese attacked Wake Island.

This morning the Japanese attacked Midway Island.

Japan has, therefore, undertaken a surprise offensive extending throughout the Pacific area. The facts of yesterday speak for themselves. The people of the United States have already formed their opinions; and well understand the implications to the very life and safety of our Nation.

As Commander-in-Chief of the Army and Navy I have directed that all measures be taken for our defense.

Always will we remember the character of the onslaught against us.

No matter how long it may take us to overcome this premeditated invasion, the American people in their righteous might will win through to absolute victory.

I believe I interpret the will of the Congress and of the people when I assert that we will not only defend ourselves to the uttermost but will make very certain that this form of treachery shall never endanger us again.

Hostilities exist. There is no blinking at the fact that our people, our territory, and our interests are in grave danger.

With confidence in our armed forces--with the unbounded determination of our people--we will gain the inevitable triumph--so help us God.

I ask that the Congress declare that since the unprovoked and dastardly attack by Japan on Sunday, December seventh, a state of war has existed between the United States and the Japanese Empire.

Franklin Delano Roosevelt
President of the United States

The Ad Lib

BY DAVID AIKEN

Grace G. Tully, President Roosevelt's Personal secretary, was custodian of speeches. After the speeches, the reading original was always returned to Miss Tully. With few exceptions all original speeches are at Hyde Park in the Roosevelt Library.

The famous speech on Pearl Harbor never returned to Grace. She was furious. An investigation traced it from the Capitol to the White House foyer on the hat rack to the right of the front door. Alas, poor Grace, it actually never left the Senate Chamber.

With the records of the U.S. Senate, accessioned in the National Archives, is the reading copy of the "Day of Infamy" speech. For years researchers have utilized the "Draft No. 1" with all of its marked changes without knowing if THE ad lib given in the recording of the speech was truly typed on the reading copy or if it gave the deeper thrust into the mind of the President.

Few printed texts of the speech gave THE ad lib. They usually print the handout of the speech, "The attack yesterday on the Hawaiian Islands has caused severe damage to American naval and military forces. Very many American lives have been lost."

Now that the reading copy has been accessioned, we can now begin anew our thoughts. THE ad lib was not a last minute change. THE ad lib is truly an ad lib. The President gave his heart felt regrets regarding Pearl Harbor.

He had added, "I regret to tell you that . . ." before continuing with, "many American lives have been lost." Does this mean that he truly did NOT know about Pearl Harbor?

Series of Japanese post cards issued on Dec. 8, 1942, the first anniversary of the Pearl Harbor attack.

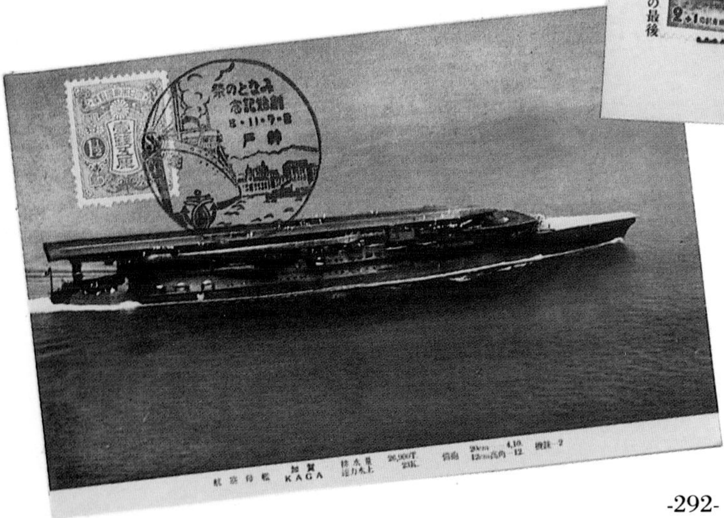

On Dec. 7, 1942, the Japanese government issued this commemorative stamp in honor of the Pearl Harbor attack.

A Japanese propaganda post card issued after the attack.

REMEMBER PEARL HARBOR!
WORK FOR VICTORY
FLORIDA CENTENNIAL
UNITED STATES POSTAGE
PUNTA GORDA, FLA. MAR 29 5-PM 1945

REMEMBER
PEARL HARBOR
BUY WAR BONDS
CLEVELAND, OHIO 1943
Rev. Victor Peterson
2763 Woodhill Rd.
Cleveland 4
Ohio

Remember
PEARL HARBOR
On Sunday morning, December 7, 1941, the Japanese, treacherously and without warning, while peaceful negotiations were in progress, attacked Pearl Harbor by sea and air.
WAR DEC 7 8 AM 1942 W. VA.
UNITED STATES POSTAGE
3 CENTS 3
Howard B. Simpson
P.O. Box 363
Mackinaw, Illinois

REMEMBERING PEARL HARBOR!
CORAL SEA
BISMARCK SEA
KULA GULF
MIDWAY
GUADAL
DEC. 7TH
1941-1943
U. S. DEC 7 1943 NAVY
PASSED BY NAVAL CENSOR
Mr. Earl F. Frank
2222 Burroughs Rd.
Toledo 9, Ohio

Facts & Figures

R.C. McClay was a navy ensign on lookout duty on the U.S.S. *Condor* the morning of Dec. 7. He spotted the conning tower of the midget sub that was sunk at the harbor's entrance by the U.S.S. *Ward*. McClay was thus the first American to sight the enemy the morning of the attack.

G.A. Myers was a Seaman 2nd Class on the submarine U.S.S. *Cachalot* berthed at 1010 Dock. He was the first submariner to die in the war.

Frank Knox (1874-1944) was Secretary of the Navy at the time of the attack. He was a "Rough Rider" during the Spanish-American War and served in World War One. His daughter Elyse was a movie actress and married football star Tom Harmon.

Joseph Grew (1877-1965) was the United States Ambassador to Japan at the time of the attack. He had previously served in Germany and the Austrio-Hungarian Empire during the early days of World War One. His wife was the granddaughter of Commodore Matthew C. Perry who opened Japan to the outside world in the 1850s. After he was repatriated in 1942. Grew became undersecretary of state.

Annie G. Fox was the first women to receive a Purple Heart when as a nurse she was wounded during the attack on Hickam Field.

Tadao Fuchikami was the RCA messenger who delivered a message from Gen. George C. Marshall to Gen. Walter Short advising him that after an ultimatum delivered to the United States government on Dec. 7, an attack was possible. Unfortunately the message was delivered while the "possible" attack was in progress.

George Cannon was a Marine Corps lieutenant stationed on Sand Island of the Midway Islands on Dec. 7. He was the first Marine to be awarded the Medal of Honor. He was a battery commander of a coastal battery when mortally wounded by a bomb from an attacking Japanese plane the night of Dec. 7. He refused to be evacuated until his men were cared for.

Edgar Rice Burroughs, the creator of the famous character "Tarzan" was a civilian in Hawaii at the time of the attack. He helped dig trenches on the beaches after the attack. He served as a news correspondent during the war.

Ship Losses:

Ninety-six ships were at Pearl Harbor on Dec. 7, 1941. Of these 19 were sunk or seriously damaged.

Battleships:

ARIZONA--sunk, total loss.
OKLAHOMA--sunk, total loss.
WEST VIRGINIA--sunk, later raised and repaired.
CALIFORNIA--sunk, later raised and repaired.
NEVADA--beached, heavily damaged, repaired.
PENNSYLVANIA--minor damage, repaired.
MARYLAND--minor damage, repaired.
TENNESSEE--minor damage, repaired.

Target Ship:

UTAH--sunk, total loss.

Light Cruisers:

HELENA--damaged, repaired.
HONOLULU--damaged, repaired.
RALEIGH--damaged, repaired.

Destroyers:

CASSIN--damaged beyond repair.
DOWNES--damaged beyond repair.
SHAW--severely damaged, repaired.

Other Ships:

OGLALA (minelayer)--sunk, salavaged and repaired.
CURTISS (seaplane tender)--severely damaged, repaired.
VESTAL (repair ship)--severely damaged, repaired.
SOTOYOMO (tug)--sunk.

Aircraft Losses:

US NAVY--92 lost, 31 damaged.
US ARMY--96 lost, 128 damaged.
JAPANESE--9 fighters, 15 dive bombers, 5 torpedo bombers.

Pearl Harbor Movies

The Japanese movie *I Bombed Pearl Harbor* was produced by Toho Ltd. and released in the United States in November 1961. It is a fictionalized account of a Japanese navigator who attacked Pearl Harbor and survived the Battle of Midway. It was produced by Tom Oyaki Tanaka and directed by Shue Matsubayashi.

From Here To Eternity, adapted from James Jones's novel, was released by Columbia Pictures in September 1953. It starred Burt Lancaster, Frank Sinatra, Montgomery Clift, Deborah Kerr, Donna Reed, Phil Ober, Mike Shaughnessy, Jack Warden and Ernest Borgnine. The movie was nominated for 13 Academy Awards and received eight. Sinatra received the best supporting actor award and Reed the best supporting actress award.

The *Final Countdown* was released by United Artists in 1980. It starred Kirk Douglas, Martin Sheen, Katherine Ross, James Farentino and Charles Durning. The movie concerns an American aircraft carrier in 1980 caught in a time-warp that takes it back to Dec. 7, 1941. It was filmed on the USS *Nimitz* in Norfolk, Va., and at Key West, Fla.

Tora! Tora! Tora!

For several years, there was great skepticism within both American and Japanese film circles about the making of *Tora! Tora! Tora!*. Yet, by the summer of 1968, both governments looked favorably on the re-telling of these dramatic events and moments in history. Bitter enemies no longer, but rather allies in an uncertain world, they agreed that the monumental story of both sides should be told—that it contained lessons for the future.

Perhaps Minoru Genda, the Japanese naval strategist who was given the assignment of planning the raid, summed it up best: "I would hope that we have all reached a level of intelligence, and understanding, where nations can treat history as it happened." So, after months of international negotiation, the Japanese motion picture industry joined with the American film establishment to launch what was to be a precedent-setting venture—one of the largest ever mounted, and certainly one of the most unusual.

There were two separate films to be made, one by the Japanese production unit, to be filmed in Japan with Japanese technicians and a Japanese cast, the other, by American technicians with an American cast. Once completed, these two films would be edited into a single three-hour roadshow motion picture.

Again, experienced production personnel on both sides of the Pacific viewed the project skeptically. Simultaneous filming by two separate and distinct companies on one story! Separated by thousands of miles! The great barrier of language! Different production methods! Different equipment!

Yet the importance of the film story would surpass any predicted difficulties. The one common denominator was the medium: film. The singular and overriding goal on both sides was to get the "film into the can." And not unexpectedly, the solution to creative communication between Japan and America in the making of *Tora! Tora! Tora!* turned out to be visuals—661 sketches representing scenes to be shot by each side.

For everyone involved, this was a pathfinder operation, a first in film history. It proved quite elegantly that the "impossible" was not impossible at all.

20th Century Fox

The battleship *Nagato*, 660 feet in length, was reconstructed of wood from the original plans. It was the largest film set ever built in Japan and was used for filming for seven weeks.
OTTO LANG

Another set was constructed of the *Akagi*'s hangar deck. Both sets were constructed at Ashuyu on the island of Kyushu.

The Pearl Harbor History Associates, Inc., is a non-profit corporation chartered by the Commonwealth of Virginia. Its purpose is to conduct research on the Pacific War and to provide educational information to all citizens. The organization has no interest in political activity or in furthering any cause, other than the records of the Pacific War, and Pearl Harbor in particular. The address is Box 205, Sperryville, Va., 22740-0205.

About the Author

Stan Cohen is a native of West Virginia and now resides in Missoula, Mont. He was only three years old at the time of the attack, yet has had an interest in Pearl Harbor and the Pacific War since he was old enough to read. After spending many years as a geologist, ski area manager and historical park director, he established Pictorial Histories Publishing Co. in 1976. Since that time, he has authored or co-authored 40 books and published another 100. He has traveled to many Pacific battlefields, and has interviewed many Pearl Harbor survivors at their reunions.

About the Contributors

Ernest Arroyo, a resident of Stratford, Conn., is a production manager for a printing firm. He has been a student of U.S. Naval history for over 35 years. He maintains a large collection of U.S. Navy ships and a reference library. He has contributed photos and data for over a dozen books on naval and maritime subjects. He is currently Vice-President of Pearl Harbor History Associates, Inc.

Robert D. Bracci, the creator of the highly detailed scale diorama of the Pearl Harbor naval base, has been researching the Japanese attack as well as the physical layout of the harbor and its surrounding land facilities as it existed in December of 1941 since he was a young high school student. He began actual construction on the project nearly 30 years ago after studying ships location charts of Pearl on December 7th. This appropriately titled piece, "Sunrise on the Fleet–0755 Hrs., December 7, 1941–The Final Moment of Peace" (copyright 1991), is the culmination of nearly 20,000 hours of labor and research. The three-dimensional geographical replica encompasses a scale nine-square-mile area of the tropical anchorage, condensed within a four-foot-square miniature display format. An award-winning model builder since his youth, his miniature vignettes and dioramas of 20th century military subjects have been displayed in schools, libraries and galleries as well as model conventions. He has been a member of the International Plastic Modelers Society since '74 as well as the Pearl Harbor History Associates, Inc., since '87. A native of Connecticut, he holds a degree in history (BA '69) as well as a degree in graduate studies (MPA '81). He served with the U.S. Army's 1st Air Cav Div. in Vietnam, 1969-71. Bob has worked in the field of law enforcement for the past 18 years.

David W. Aiken has been a contract illustrator for over 25 years. His work has been in color and industrial research, development, publications, photography and museology. His hobby is mineralogy.

Aiken has been a student of World War II for 35 years. In 1961, his study of Pearl Harbor began a deeper search of the Pacific War. Air Force duty at Hickam AFB, Hawaii, in 1966-67 guided his attention directly upon Pearl Harbor's American and Japanese missing in action airmen. He is a Pearl Harbor History Associates director.

His data base on Japanese aviation is utilized by many researchers, artists, authors, historians, museums and miniature builders. His personal interest is the Doolittle Raid, American aerial defense of New Guinea, the 49th and 475th Fighter Groups, the 100th Bomb Group (ETO) and MIA aircraft recovery.

Paul Bender is a marine artist with a strong interest in naval ships and aircraft of World War II. A member of the American Society of Marine Artists, Mr. Bender has supplied illustrations for other Pictorial Histories publications, as well as artwork for the Conway Maritime Press, United States Naval Institute Press and Newsweek magazine.

Dr. Martin Davis lives in Huntington, Long Island, N.Y., and he is the director of Historic Projects for the Destroyer Escort Sailors Association, the Intrepid Sea-Air-Space Museum of New York City and the North China Marine POWs of World War II.

Dr. Davis, who conducts WWII naval history seminars, was the superintendent of the Cold Spring Harbor (N.Y.) School District and is a professor at Hofstra University. During World War II he served in the Atlantic and Pacific aboard the destroyer escort, U.S.S. *Pettit* (DE-253).

About the Cover Artist

Mel Brown resides in Austin, Texas, with his wife and three children. He is a self-taught artist specializing in aviation and landscapes. Brown is a member of the American Society of Aviation Artists and a contributor to the prestigious USAF Art Collection. His lifelong fascination with aircraft is due in large part to being born and raised in San Antonio, Texas, home to four Air Force Bases and having a father in the USAF.

World War II is Brown's main area of interest and in this respect he considers his artwork to be of an historical nature rather than merely depictive. He has traveled in England and Germany to do research and also has an extensive personal library. Brown is an accomplished modeler and often builds highly detailed plastic models before beginning a painting of the subject. This attention to detail has brought him important commissions, including paintings now hanging in the U.S. Air Force Academy, the Air University at Maxwell Air Force Base and in private collections both here and abroad.